Beer in America

The Early Years—1587–1840

Beer in America

The Early Years—1587–1840

Beer's Role in the Settling of America
and the Birth of a Nation

Gregg Smith

An Imprint of Brewers Publications
Boulder, Colorado

Siris Books, an imprint of Brewers Publications
PO Box 1679, Boulder, CO 80306-1679
(303) 447-0816; Fax (303) 447-2825

Please direct all inquiries to the above address.

Printed in the United States of America

10 9 8 7 6 5 4 3 2 1

ISBN 0-937381-65-9

Siris Books. Who is Siris? She was the daughter of Ninkasi, the Sumerian
goddess of beer. Anthropologists personify Siris as the beer itself.

Library of Congress Cataloging-in-Publication Data
Smith, Gregg, 1952–
    Beer in America : the early years, 1587–1840 : beer's role in the settling of
America and the birth of a nation / Gregg Smith.
        p.   cm.
    Includes bibliographical references and index.
    ISBN 0-937381-65-9 (alk. paper)
    1. Beer—United States—Social aspects. 2. Brewing industry—United
States—History. I. Title.
TP577.S593   1998
394.1´3—dc21   98-17065
                                                                    CIP

To Darcy, Jessica, and Samantha

———⊰•⊱———

Jeffrey—Don't Give Up the Ship

Contents

INTRODUCTION • The Dawn of American Beer   1

PART ONE   *Beer Arrives in North America:*
            The Start of a Journey to Greatness   5

CHAPTER 1 • Building a Home and a Brewery, Too:
            The Early 1600s   7

CHAPTER 2 • Beer Settles in: The Late 1600s   25

CHAPTER 3 • Beer and the Birth of an American
            Culture: The Early 1700s   49

CHAPTER 4 • Independence: When Fermentation
            Aided Fomentation   73

CHAPTER 5 • Beer and the Revolutionary War   93

CHAPTER 6 • Life, Liberty, and the Pursuit of Porter:
            Postwar Beer   111

CHAPTER 7 • The Nation and Breweries Expand:
            The Early 1800s   129

CHAPTER 8 • Fame and Fortune: The Emergence of the
            Big Breweries of the 1800s   147

Contents

PART TWO   *Factors Influencing Beer Drinking and Brewing in the Colonial Period*   181

CHAPTER 9 • The Government Takes a Bite Out of Beer: Taxation   183

CHAPTER 10 • Beer's Home: The Tavern   193

CHAPTER 11 • Beer Drinks: The Colonial Cocktail   209

CHAPTER 12 • Homebrewing: America's Beer Heritage   225

CHAPTER 13 • Beer Under Fire: Temperance and Prohibition   237

CHAPTER 14 • Colonial Brewing Technology   251

APPENDIX • Colonial Beer Timeline   273

NOTES   289

BIBLIOGRAPHY   299

INDEX   305

Acknowledgments

Acknowledgments go to: Bob Brewer, whose use of his personal library and supportive friendship eased the task; Carrie Getty, whom I cannot thank enough for everything over the years; Daniel Bradford, for his support; Dave Heidrich, whose words, "Hey it's only beer," were constantly good reminders; and finally, Lisa Variano, for her contributions on the working text.

Introduction

THE DAWN OF AMERICAN BEER

Swinging gently on its anchor line, the ship was nearly silent in the predawn light. The low groaning of the rigging and the soft lapping of waves against the hull were the only sounds. Taking it in was a solitary figure, silhouetted in the light of an oil lamp. The shoreline, becoming more visible as the minutes passed, offered a strange combination of hope and fear.

The first one awake, the expedition's leader had finished breakfast before coming on deck, bringing with him only what remained of his morning drink. It was the drink that had him concerned, for on drawing his morning beer he had seen how perilously low the ship's supply of ale had dwindled.

At first light the small boats would be loaded and begin the process of shuttling the newcomers and landing their provisions. There was no thought of any delay, they needed to get ashore and begin brewing their own beer. On the previous evening, when the ship had arrived in the small harbor, the company of immigrants agreed on the priorities for construction of community buildings; a brewery was near the top of the list. The leader hoped the brewery would be functional before the meager supply they brought with them ran out. After all, beer was a necessity.

This scene was repeated many times from the late 1500s to the early 1700s in colonial North America. Small wooden ships crisscrossed the Atlantic, ferrying newcomers to an unspoiled land. They all had different reasons for making the trip. Some came for freedom of religion, speech, or philosophical beliefs. Others making the difficult passage were driven by political motives, and still more came for economic opportunities. A number were fleeing families, and a few were fleeing the law. Their reasons for leaving the relative security of Europe for an unknown land were certainly diverse, but most of them had one thing in common: they drank beer.

To comprehend the cultural importance of beer requires an understanding of its role in civilization. Beer and society have been inseparable companions for thousands of years. Literally, the two have gone hand in hand. When people first settled together they were motivated to do so by a common cause: the thirst for beer. All the thoughts, feelings, and beliefs the colonists brought with them to North America were the result of society's millennia-old marriage with beer. Indeed, drawing a fresh mug of ale was, at that time, as indispensable as drawing a breath.

More than a mere cultural habit, beer drinking evolved into a healthful practice. Brewers have to boil water to make beer, thus killing the microbes that imperil health. In Europe, fouled drinking water placed city dwellers in peril; those who used the fetid supply regularly developed serious health problems. In England, Parliament tried to enact laws against pollution, but it was too late to prevent widespread disease. Nearly every supply was horribly tainted.

True enough, the pristine streams running through the virgin forests of the new land were pure and clean, but still, the settlers simply wouldn't

An ancient brew house.

drink the water, because they brought with them frightening memories of their homelands' deteriorating water supplies. There, rivers and streams were becoming the equivalents of flowing dumps.

By the mid-1400s the bias against drinking water in Europe was deeply ingrained. Sir John Fortescue wrote of the English peasants: "They drink no water unless it be . . . for devotion."

Settlers in the Americas lost sight of the fact that European beer drinking, and avoidance of water, was driven by fear of pollution; they simply didn't trust it. No amount of reasoning about the safe supply running in the rivers of the New World could make them drink it. Luckily they knew of a safe alternative: beer.

For settlers, one of the most precious cargoes their tiny ships held was beer. It was more than a comforting reminder of the

3

homeland, more than a bottle of liquid bread. Beer was healthy nourishment. Each new ship would anchor off the coast and passengers would spend their last night aboard going over the plans for a new community. At dawn they would venture ashore and start to hack an existence from the wilderness. Obtaining food and shelter was high on the priority list, and in virtually every North American settlement one of the first buildings constructed was a brew house.[1]

Part One

Beer Arrives in North America: The Start of a Journey to Greatness

---

One

BUILDING A HOME AND A BREWERY, TOO

The Early 1600s

At first light the settlers left the safe confines of the ship's quarters and began assembling on deck. Sky and sea slowly brightened, the heavy woods along the shore formed a dark barrier. Looking toward shore, the settlers were filled with confused emotions that ran the gamut from apprehension to excitement, fear to joy. Only a short boat ride away their new home beckoned them, and though it promised hope and opportunity, it was totally devoid of both essentials and comforts—especially beer.

It had been a long journey. Too much of it was spent confined in cramped, dark quarters below deck. Sickness was common, food was poor at best, privacy was nonexistent, and the accommodations offered scant physical comfort. Despite all the unknowns ashore, they were eager to leave the ship.

One by one they went over the side, dropping to the small, open launch that would ferry them ashore. Slowly the sun climbed along its daily arc and the ship's crew brought in more of their supplies. On the voyage across the Atlantic the store of food and beer had looked large and comforting, but once stacked on land it seemed much smaller and insubstantial. For this reason they set priorities for their first days. No matter where they landed, or from which country they hailed, all newcomers developed a similar list. Ranking highest was constructing shelter, finding food, and building a brewery. Their beer supply from the Old World wouldn't last long.

On September 9, 1620, the Pilgrims set sail from England. Although they had planned to leave earlier in the summer, when the crossing would have been smoother, delays in procuring a seaworthy ship had pushed their departure perilously close to the bad weather of winter. Originally they intended to land in the northern regions of the Virginia colony, in what is now New York State, on a tract of land William Brewster had acquired.

When they first saw the North American coast, the Pilgrims had every reason to believe they had found northern Virginia. Shortly thereafter they knew better. After crossing with the trade winds the ship had turned north too soon. It was a critical error, one that pushed them farther up the coast than they had planned. Overshooting their intended landfall, they first spotted the shoreline well into New England.

Despite the mistake the passengers were filled with wonder. As far as the eye could see stretched a long horizon of unspoiled land. Nothing ashore resembled the small plots of land they had left behind in England. Before them was an unbelievable expanse of virgin forest. Trees dominated the landscape. By the time the Pilgrims came to the New World, Europe's old growth timber was close to extinction. Long before it had been logged for building and heating the homes of England, France, Spain, and Germany. What remained was vigorously protected by the government and far removed from the common man. This fact alone underscored the contrast between what they had left behind and what awaited them.

Before long their navigation error became apparent. Traveling up the coast, they began searching desperately for a suitable anchorage. They needed a sheltered harbor for the ship. Equally important, they worried about how settling on a tract other than the one assigned would be viewed back in England; their leaders realized that settling on the wrong parcel could ruffle feathers an ocean away. Survival depended upon maintaining a friendly relationship with the Crown. Amicable relations were the key to trade and a necessity for economic survival, not to mention a supply of beer.

Sailing past present-day Boston, the settlers curtailed their search and set course back to the most favorable spot they had seen, near what would become Plymouth. According to William Bradford, the leader of the party that landed at Plymouth, rations were running low. He recorded in his firsthand account, *History of Plimouth* [sic] *Plantation,* that "We had yet some beer, butter, flesh and other victuals left, which would quickly be all gone; and then we should have nothing to comfort us."[1]

It was no accident that Bradford listed beer first. Beer occupied a prominent place in daily life. Indeed, it was the thought of

9

beer that caused the Pilgrims finally to make up their minds. They decided to put ashore:

> So in the morning, after we had called on God for direction, we came to this resolution—to go presently ashore again and to take a better view of two places which we thought most fitting for us; for we could not now take much time for further search or consideration, our victuals being much spent, especially our beer, and it now being the 19th of December.[2]

That first fall and winter were especially cold. Legend tells of settlers leaping from an overloaded boat to steady it. Knee deep in the breaking surf, their clothes, drenched in saltwater, froze stiff as boards. Fortunately they found a large rock to tie up their skiff, then set foot on their new home.

Immediately feeling the effects of a beerless state, the Pilgrims thought their situation most trying. Fortunately, the *Mayflower's* late crossing forced the sailors to winter over in New England. The savvy captain, Captain Christopher Jones, had no stomach for tempting fate. He knew that fierce storms made a winter crossing of the North Atlantic perilous. The settlers occasionally sought refuge back aboard the ship. Bradford noted the lack of beer: "Monday, the 25th, 1620, being Christmas day, we began to drink water aboard. But, at night, the master caused us to have some beer; and so on board we had, divers times now and then, some beer, but on shore none at all."[3]

Water was never the drink of choice, especially aboard the ship. Stored in the hold, it spoiled quickly, and there was no efficient method to replenish the supply. Even if they could have maintained a fresh supply, it is doubtful they would have embraced it.

The newcomers considered beer essential to the infant colony's social, cultural, and physical health. Beer was more than a necessity, it was as indispensable as breathing. With a vigilant eye, they sought any opportunity to obtain beer.

In each of the new settlements the need for breweries was immediate. No matter how small the colony, the population expanded faster than imports of ale from Europe could provision. Of all the hardships endured, the lack of beer was the one that caused the most displeasure. Bradford, the governor of Plymouth Colony, was known to complain long and bitterly about this deprivation, and with good cause. Drinking water was considered a dangerous practice. Roger Clap of the Massachusetts Bay company recounted that it was "accounted a strange thing in those days to drink water."[4]

In his *New England Prospects,* William Wood, an early settler from the *Mayflower,* complained of drinking water. He had no fondness, taste, or patience for it. Wood summed up his feelings about drinking water with the understandable statement, "I dare not prefere it before good beere."[5]

Anchored out in the harbor, sailors on board the *Mayflower* knew their stock of brew was running low. To continue issuing rations to those who moved ashore would leave an insufficient supply for their return trip to England. Thus the crew had no recourse but to cut off their former passengers. The reaction on land was panic, anger, and increased grumbling, followed by desperation. Bradford noted how the settlers "were hastened ashore and made to drink water, that the seamen might have the more beer."[6]

Bradford did his best to plead for a ration of beer, but the sailors responded they would give none, "not even if he were their own father."[7]

The settlers were facing a situation of poor shelter, low food supply, a hard winter, and, to make matters worse, no beer. Finally, Captain Jones, though he knew it put the ship's crew at risk, was overwhelmed by the hardship of those on land and declared there would be beer for all who had need, especially the sick.

This decision brought those on land temporary relief, but the lesson was hard, frightening, and effective. The realization of this critical shortage motivated them to include a brew house among the first structures erected in the winter of 1620–21 at Plymouth.

The situation faced by those at Plymouth was not unique in the New World. Passengers on the increasingly frequent voyages from Europe had no trust for water. When compared with the palpability and longer shelf life of hopped beer, water would not be chosen by thirsty travelers. Even the strict Puritans, sailing on the *Arabella* to what is now Boston in 1630, took along

Interior of a seventeenth-century brew house.

12

over three times as much beer as water. On arrival, these settlers also hit the beach brewing.

South of Plymouth, Rhode Island was established in 1637 by Roger Williams. As did others in New England, the colony placed beer high on their priority list. Within two years the settlement could boast of its own public house. Located in Providence, it was typical of other colonial taverns and included a beer, wine, and grocery store.

Though it would be centuries until science cracked the mysteries of microbiology, settlers did try to counteract the effects of bad water on the beer. Boiling it during brewing easily killed the deadly microbes. The settlers knew from experience that beer produced none of the deleterious consequences of water, but it would be years before they realized that boiling alone would make the water safe for drinking. They were not particularly interested in water when they had beer, anyway. Beer was nourishment, was like both a refreshing drink and a bottle of bread. The custom of the day proclaimed that beer was good for your health, while water might be the end of it. In the New World the key to survival, and beer, came from an unexpected source.

At Plymouth, the Pilgrims' arrival hadn't gone unnoticed. From the cover of the surrounding forest, the natives studied their every move. After determining that the visitors were harmless and inept at survival, they emerged from hiding to welcome the strangers to the New World. The first meeting between the Indians and the Pilgrims is a scene that has achieved legendary symbolism in America.

The colony suffered terribly that first winter, with half the settlers perishing. Were it not for the assistance of the natives, the

13

entire group might have suffered a fate similar to that of the "lost colony"* of Virginia. During the first winter they were taught to hunt and fish, and learned of the various foods indigenous to the region that eventually would be called New England.

Barely surviving the first winter, the Pilgrims recognized the debt they owed their neighbors. In celebration of the first harvest, in fall 1621, they invited their new friends to a communal feast. School children today know the legend, and in fact, though embellished, it is not far from the truth.

Samoset, a lesser chief in the Wampanoag tribe, joined in the celebration with enthusiasm.[8] First, the combined party of settlers and Indians went on a hunt to augment their feast. They returned to the settlement with fresh venison and fowl.

After preparing their bounty, the celebrants tapped a keg. All were happy, including Samoset, who was described by writers of the era as both a lover of ale and a responsible drinker. This alliance with the Wampanoag tribe proved critical to the birth of American brewing, for it was the Indians who introduced the colonists to corn, which they learned to mash and ferment.

Plymouth was not the only colony introduced to the use of corn in brewing. English attempts to settle near the border of what are now South Carolina and Virginia in 1584, though unsuccessful, included one of the first recorded experiences of using corn as a supplement in brewing.[9] It wasn't what the settlers were accustomed to, but it served its purpose.

Captain George Thorpe described attempts to find a substitute for beer in the Virginia Colony in 1620:

* The "lost colony" of Virginia was a group of English settlers who were put ashore to establish an outpost and village in 1585. When ships from England returned with provisions in 1587, no survivors, or traces of them, were found.

Mr. Russell, the chemist, tried to introduce sassafras tea into Virginia as an artificial wine in July, 1620. . . . There is in Virginia, or is likely to be shortly, three thousand people. And the greatest want they complayne of is a good drinke—wine being too dear, and barley charge-able, which though it should there be sowen, it were hard in that country, being so hot, to make malt of it, if they had malt, to make good beer.[10]

Thorpe continued to observe the state of beer and later noted that his fellow colonists had "found a way to make a good drink from Indian corn, which he preferred to good English beer."[11]

(Apparently, "beer deprivation" has often resulted in accept-ing lesser substitutes. This situation has often been repeated in American history, most noticeably upon the end of Prohibition in 1933, when Americans readily embraced a new style of beer that used liberal amounts of corn and other grains. The difference between this situation and that of the colonies was that post-Prohibition beer benefited from the science and technology of the three intervening centuries, knowledge that helped produce a cleaner beer in both taste and appearance.)

Beer in the 1600s was dark and cloudy, was flavored with hops, and in the popular version, it carried an alcohol level approaching 6 percent. With the exception of the addition of hops, it was very much like the beer brewed for hundreds of years. Modern beer drinkers would hesitate at its appearance. Beer was not an attractive beverage, but despite its foul appearance, people knew beer was good for them; indeed, it was a major part of their diet and continued to be so throughout America's early years.

In New Amsterdam, colonists from the Netherlands set foot on their own beerless patch of land. Dutch claims to North American colonies were based on the explorations of Henry Hudson, who was seeking the Northwest Passage to the Far East. In 1609 he sailed his ship, the *Half Moon,* up the river that now bears his name. Although he never found the Northwest Passage, Hudson did discover a kind of treasure.

At first Hudson's hopes swelled as the river widened near Tappan Zee, but they rapidly evaporated by the time he reached present-day Albany, where he discovered the river was no longer tidal. These early trips were looked upon as a calculated risk; the Dutch were a leading trading and banking power of the world and they intended to stay in that position. If the New World had treasures to yield, the Dutch wanted in on it.

Encouraged by reports of abundant, unspoiled lands, the Dutch moved ahead. Their biggest obstacle was to settle the land inexpensively. Seeking a solution that required little investment on their part, the government developed what was known as the "Patroon" system. With a payment of the equivalent of $50 and the promise to settle and work the land at their own expense, government-issued rights to huge tracts of land were chartered to any settlers over 15 years of age. As a bonus, each tract was awarded considerable river frontage, no small offer in those days, when rivers were the highways of America, and tributaries supplied inexpensive power for mills. When at least 50 people agreed to a plan, the colony was chartered and approval granted for settlement.

The Dutch settlers also brought beer to New Amsterdam. More sophisticated than English brewers, they had been among

16

A sixteenth-century tavern.

the first to use hops in beer. Though better supplied and less desperate for beer than the Pilgrims, they too set about building a brew house immediately upon arrival. Some accounts tell of brewing as early as 1612, but the most accepted date is in 1613. In that year Adrian Block and Hans Christiansen converted a log house they had erected on the southern tip of Manhattan into a brewery.

In 1614 their brewery was host to the first birth in the colony: within its sheltering walls was born Jean Vigne. Such a place of birth must have been an omen, because when setting out to make a living on his own, Vigne chose brewing, eventually operating his own brewery on the bustling thoroughfare named Brouwer Street.

As the Dutch solidified their position they erected satellite villages to expand control over the region. In 1623 a group settled at

Fort Nassau, present-day Camden, New Jersey. That same year another group established Fort Orange at Albany. As these outposts were erected, beer traveled along. A witty Dutch visitor to Albany wrote of the habits of the early settlers: "They all drink their beer here from the time they can hold a spoon."[12]

It was about 1626 when Peter Minuit of the colony closed the all-time craftiest real estate deal by purchasing the island of Manhattan. Minuit thought he'd pulled a fast one, but in reality it was the Indians who had the last laugh. Minuit made payment to a passing tribe, not to those who lived on the island.

William Penn.

Looking at present-day New York, it is hard to believe it was once a pristine wilderness. In colonial times, reports abounded of six-foot lobsters and oysters a foot across netted from the harbor, while the forests of the mid-island teemed with deer and other game. Sturgeon swam the Hudson River and salmon were so plentiful they were considered food for the impoverished. All that was lacking was beer. Dutch administrators solved that problem by including a brewery among the colony's first structures. Before long this wise move resulted in New York's emergence as a major trading post.

In what is now Philadelphia, conditions were considerably easier than those encountered by settlers in New York and Plymouth. One historian has written: "Native Americans lived here and

William Penn's brew house.

enjoyed the bounty of the land, and in the water the mighty Delaware provided additional sustenance. It was open fields, woods and sparkling waters. But when [William] Penn's colonists arrived this was already changed."[13]

Far from the silent greeting the Dutch and the Pilgrim colonists had received, William Penn's arrival in 1681 found a small village spreading along the shore. Arriving ahead of him, a group of Swedish and Finnish settlers from the failed outpost of New Sweden had relocated to the more favorable location that later became Philadelphia. Fortunately for the newer arrivals, crops were already growing. Philadelphia's establishment was easier than that of Plymouth.

As the organizer of the expedition, William Penn had big plans for his venture in the Americas, and he intended to do it right. Like the patrons, he intended to use the resources of the settlers to finance his dream of an American empire. But Penn went even further, distributing pamphlets in 1682 that advertised the colony throughout Europe. Written in Dutch, French, and German, these pamphlets shamelessly hawked the real estate. Penn also provided instructions on how to arrange passage and what to bring.

Appealing to Europeans excluded from the land-owning class was the promise Penn extended of rent for a 200-acre tenant farm. His price was only a penny an acre. Better yet, for 100 British pounds, the new settler could own a 5,000-acre estate. With this enticement, settlers flocked to the new colony. Within two years the town had 357 new houses, and by 1685 the population had grown to more than 9,000.

What made Penn's offer so attractive was not only the opportunity to own land, but complete religious freedom, something essentially thwarted in Europe. Colonists from a variety of nationalities flowed in in ever greater numbers, and the town attained a cosmopolitan flavor unique on the young continent. Each of these cultures brought with it a thirst for beer. One settler, Thomas Paschall, wrote in 1683: "Here is very good Rye . . . also Barly of 2 sorts, as Winter and Summer . . . also Oats, and 3 sorts of Indian Corne (two of which sorts they can Malt and make good beer as Barley)."[14]

With large sales of land and a rushing tide of immigrants, the colony prospered and grew into the largest town in the New World. Returning home to England, Penn boasted, "I have led the greatest colony into America that ever any man did upon a private credit, and the most prosperous beginnings that were ever in it are to be found among us."[15]

Penn gave William Frampton, a settler in his colony, the honor of being first brewer, and Thomas Paschall credited brewer/baker Frampton's talents with producing "as good bread and . . . as good drink as ever I [had] in England."[16]

Frampton's beer must have impressed the Paschall family, because Thomas Paschall's son eventually forsook the family's pewter trade and became a leading maltster of Pennsylvania.

Many of the nation's formative events and much of its brewing went on in the north, but colonies spanning large territories in the Middle Atlantic and southern areas also had an impact on brewing. The first colonies actually were established along the southern coastline.

Thirteen years before the Pilgrims made their famous landfall, the vanguard of English settlers had arrived. In 1607, the English had established the first permanent settlement in America at Jamestown, Virginia. Unlike the New England colonists, the Jamestown party lacked the foresight to include brewers among their number. Within two years this oversight had become a major problem. Faced with the growing frustration of the colonists, the governor, Sir Francis Wyatt, approved an advertisement in England for two brewers to make the crossing. So eagerly was the arrival of brewers anticipated that one of the first crops planted in the settlement was barley.

These inhabitants of Virginia were no more partial to water than their New England counterparts, and for the same reasons. If water could be avoided, it was. It was beer they desired, and desire it they did. Along with the two brewers they imported beer, closely followed by malt to extend their home-grown supply. When no malt was available, they resorted to the same methods as their colonial neighbors: a record of 1620 indicates that makeshift ale was produced from maize.[17]

Similar situations existed up and down the eastern seaboard. In Salem, New Jersey, John Fenwick reported that the settlement on the Delaware River had its priorities correct. He noted, "they straight away busied themselves in erecting breweries for manufacturing beer for common drink."[18]

People were quick to take matters into their own hands. As in New England, brewing was concentrated on homesteads and farms. Newspaper accounts, particularly in advertisements of real estate sales, give the best indication of how much homebrewing was taking place. One ad placed in a New Brunswick, New Jersey, paper extolled the virtues of a farm that was on the market: "There is also a large new Brewhouse . . . containing 22 barrells . . . the water is exceedingly good, soft and washes well. "[19]

Southernmost of the original colonies, Georgia was settled relatively late. One reason was the method by which the land was occupied. Original settlement occurred along the coast, where harbors and shipping meant access to England. Coastal communities enjoyed both ease in exporting the harvest of the new lands and access to luxuries imported from the homeland. It wasn't until these areas became more populated and real estate prices rose that interior areas were settled. Most of Georgia's area is inland.

When Governor James Ogelthorpe established the colony of Georgia in 1733, he knew the task of building a competitive colony was daunting. He wanted the people to work hard from their very first day ashore. Concerned over lost productivity from drunkenness, he plotted to please colonists' palates while avoiding the slothfulness of over-indulgence. Ogelthorpe, and the London trustees of Georgia, banned hard liquor in the colony in the year 1735.

To look after his colonists' health and the general well-being of the settlements was Ogelthorpe's motivation. He wanted them to drink, and avoid water, but he thought healthy "English Beer" the best alternative. To that end he formulated what he thought a sure-fire plan to encourage temperance.

James Oglethorpe.

Generously, Ogelthorpe offered each new settler 44 gallons of beer. He had high hopes they would heed the message that they should never drink anything stronger. However, his generosity also proved his undoing. Unwittingly, he included, among other supplies provided, 65 gallons of molasses. The settlers fermented and then distilled the molasses into a beverage that kept better in the hot Georgia climate: "demon rum." Members of the Georgia colony developed a firm taste for spirits. It would be centuries until beer was able to challenge the hold spirits had on its inhabitants.

Georgia notwithstanding, beer was the dominant drink of the new American colonies. Wherever settlements sprang up, beer was loaded ashore. It was always considered a necessary food source, but it was more. Beer was often the one comfort. More important, it was the one connection with a distant home, an element of constant routine as the settlers adjusted to life in a strange and often frightening land.

Part One

As settlements, towns, and villages were established, brew-eries followed, and when colonial economies first blossomed, taverns appeared. Colonial North America and beer were insepa-rable. Although the number and size of brewing operations in the 1600s remained small, the relationship of beer and the continent was forged from the moment settlers arrived. In the years that followed that relationship strengthened and beer crept inland as the country expanded westward.

Two

Beer Settles in

The Late 1600s

Laying in a provision of food, clearing land, surveying town sites, constructing shelter, erecting meeting houses, and brewing beer were all top priorities for the new arrivals to North America. After establishing themselves with the building of villages, they were able to direct attention to other aspects of life. Sufficient food, clothing, and shelter allows a society to address other considerations, such as business, economics, the arts, and science. As the early settlers shifted their attention to more advanced concerns, maintaining a beer supply remained a focus of interest.

Brewing was never far from colonial thoughts. The ability to keep beer over extended periods of time was more than two centuries away, and transportation systems were virtually nonexistent. Replenishing the beer supply was a local task that required continual repetition. To ensure they had a constant supply, they turned to the past.

The women came to the rescue. Under their direction, most early American kitchens were designed with the job of home-brewing in mind. Once the kitchen had been built, the colonial housewife directed her attention to another brewing-related job, locating beer supplies.

In Massachusetts the first attempts to cultivate barley were unsuccessful. To the settlers' dismay, they had to continue to import malt and hops. Deliveries from England were infrequent at best and unreliable at worst. Ship owners and captains had other priorities and often as not the brewing supplies ran short. Brewers, though discouraged, never gave up. They merely turned to other methods. Creating variations on traditional brewing was common practice.

Both in town and on the frontier the women brewers impro-vised, substituted, and fabricated alternative ingredients for brew-ing. Well-to-do families also corrupted beer formulations. In part, they used grains such as corn to make up for the lack of malt.

In 1622, John Winthrop Jr., governor of Connecticut and son of John Winthrop, the governor of Massachusetts, produced an ersatz beer from Indian corn. In England the Royal Society was sufficiently impressed with Winthrop's feat to extend an invitation to educate brewers in London on the details of his process.

Substitutions didn't end with Winthrop's use of Indian corn. Many a "Pious Pilgrim" stretched recipes with liberal replace-ments. Repeated with a frequency that made it the norm, the technique of substitution was accurately reflected in a poem of the 1630s:

If barley be wanting to make into malt,
we must be content and think it no fault,
For we can make liquor to sweeten our lips,
Of pumpkins, and parsnips, and walnut-tree chips.[1]

In the face of shortages several brewers and their taverns became well known for various concoctions of spruce, birch, and sassafras beer. By the mid-1650s these substitutions and other corruptions reminded colonial leaders of similar problems that had occurred centuries earlier in Europe. In that era the English authorities in North America responded by enacting purity laws. Laden with strict penalties for failure to comply, these regulations were basically the first form of consumer protection laws. North Americans, brewing with questionable raw materials, drove the governors to dictate similar measures.

Administrators reacted with new statutes that regulated the brewing process. Consumers who relied on a short reservoir of commercial beer and were desperate for any beer were caught between feelings of gratitude for the purity codes and fear that they would put an end to an already precarious supply. To their relief, they found the great American institution of the "loop-hole." New laws had no effect at all on homebrewing, and non-tavern-owning brewers, who also sold significant quantities, were exempt. The laws were without teeth and further corruption of beer continued.

By 1667 the issue of quality prompted Massachusetts to legislate beer regulations stipulating that beer had to be made from good quality malt and could not be diluted with molasses or coarse sugar.

Authorities along the Delaware River also worried about the quality of their locally produced beer, and were forced at times to purchase imports from the brew houses of New Amsterdam (Manhattan) at inflated prices. Vice-director of the colony, Jacob Alrichs, reported to the commissioners from Fort New Amstel that the price and quality of beer were completely out of balance:

> And whereas, considerable provisions and liquors are being forced here at excessive prices by private individuals, as well retailers as tavern-keepers and tapsters, and as there is neither baker nor brewer here, and their drink makes hungry bellies, which recoil on the shore, and as working people must sometimes take a drink of beer . . . to comfort their hearts, I resolved with the advice of the municipal government and on the representation of those authorized by commonalty, that the tapsters and tavern-keepers should not retail the can of Manhattan beer for any more than nine stivers . . . may be regulated for the good, relief and advantage of all the inhabitants and settlers.[2]

Governor Jonathan Printz of New Sareden, a colony that included parts of what now are Delaware, Pennsylvania, and New Jersey, observed that part of the problem sprang from the high price of imported malt. In 1644 he wrote of its cost: "Everything is fearfully dear here. One barrel of malt, Swedish measure, is worth seven, yes even eight, six-dollars, a pound of hops, half a rix-dollar."[3]

Southern colonies, too, felt the pinch created by a lack of malt. In 1623 the Virginia Assembly had written to England with a recommendation that new emigrants provision themselves with "a proportion of mault to make . . . beer, that the sudden drinking of water cause not too great alteration in their bodyes."[4]

Among the colonists, the New York Dutch were first to realize that the climate and soil were well suited for producing all of beer's ingredients. Vast fields of grain were sown along the banks of the Hudson River. Both shores of the Tappan Zee, a section of the Hudson River that widens above what is present-day Manhattan, were so productive that the major village in the region was named Tarrytown, after the Dutch word for wheat. With grain on hand, brewing began in earnest. Nicasius de Sille, a councilor for the West India Company who would eventually become sheriff of New Amsterdam, reported, "This country suits me exceedingly well . . . Beer is brewed here as good as in Holland, of barley and wheat."[5] Another early visitor praised the beer, writing home that the settlers "brew as good beer here as in our Fatherland, for good hops grow in the woods."[6]

Others made similar positive observations. However, poor beer surfaced time and again. Reports of inferior beer finally promoted a decree, issued in 1664 by the Duke of York. Referred to as the "Duke's Laws," it specified

> That no person whatsoever shall henceforth undertake the calling or work of brewing beer for sale, but only such as are known to have sufficient skill and knowledge in the art and mystery of brewing.
>
> That if any undertaker for victualling of ships or other vessels or master or owner of any such vessels or any other person shall make it appear that any beer bought of

any person within the government do prove unfit, unwholesome and useless for their supply, either through the insufficiency of the mault or brewing or unwholesome cask, the person wronged thereby shall be and is hereby enabled to recover equal and sufficient damage by action against the person that put the beer to sale.[7]

Further ordinances stated that the smallest amount of malt used in brewing a hogshead (54 gallons) of beer must be four bushels of malt.

Despite the craftiness of various individuals, the General Court remained aware of large-scale substitution of ingredients, and in the late 1600s continued to pass laws for assuring the quality of beer brewed and sold in Massachusetts.

Upriver in Albany, matters progressed at a similar pace. On December 26, 1646, the courts recorded a decision against a local man named Cornelis Segersz, who defied the local authorities by operating an unlicensed facility.

Whereas, their Honors of the court of this colonie find that Cornelis Segersz, notwithstanding former placards and prohibitions, has still presumed to meddle with what is not his business—with beer brewing—directly contrary to the grant and authorization given to the brewery of this colonie;

Therefore, their Honors expressly forbid the said Cornelis Segersz to brew, or cause to be brewed, or otherwise to manufacture any beer, except so much as shall be required by him for his own housekeeping, on pain of

forfeiting twenty-five Carolus guilders, besides the
brewed beer. The said Cornelis Segersz is further warned
that no cloak, or idle excuse, shall hereafter avail, but
that this ordinance shall be maintained and executed on
the spot without court process, if he shall make any mistake. Let him therefore, prevent his loss.[8]

Significant in the passage was that the court considered
homebrewing vital to the welfare of his family, and although agi-
tated by his opening an unauthorized brewery, they made no
attempt to prevent him from producing his own supply of beer.

Behind the regulations and the court decision against Segersz
was the patroon of Fort Orange, Kiliaen van Rensselaer. Writing
about his lands, Rensselaer repeatedly mentioned the importance
of beer: "[With] a supply of grain on hand, I intend to erect a
brewery to provide all New Netherlands with beer, for which
purpose there is already a brew kettle there."[9]

Rensselaer's brewery was probably opened sometime around
1633, although records of the exact date have vanished. Local
ordinances instituted by Rensselaer allowed homebrewing but
prohibited commercial breweries. His intention was not to elimi-
nate competition, but to set up the process of formally licensing,
and collecting operating fees from, the brewers he expected the
colony to attract.

On June 15, 1647, Rensselaer licensed the first of the offi-
cially recognized brewers:

Whereas, Joan La Battie, the carpenter, solicited that he
might be permitted to build a house at Fort Orange and

use it as a brewery without injury to the interests of the Company . . . so it is that this boon has been granted to him, viz: that he may make use of the house which he builds in the fort as a brewery and remain in possession of said soil so long as the Company shall retain the property possession of Fort Orange—and the Company's affairs and interests are not neglected by La Battie. [10]

In return for his charter La Battie was assessed an annual licensing fee at a rate of six merchantable beavers. Strange as the contract may seem, the payment underscores a problem that plagued the colonies, and later the infant United States, for nearly two centuries: lack of hard currency.

When money was available, it was the preferred method of payment. One brewery of early Albany, licensed in 1649, required a payment of 450 guilders per year plus one guilder for each tun of beer brewed. Among the partners of this establishment was the first of many brewers from the famous Rutgers family, who would dominate New Netherlands brewing for decades.

What made some of the early settlements prosper and grow while others faded? In many cases the answer was a tavern. Taverns were the focal point of the community. They served as a place to hear the latest news, conduct business, and socialize with neighbors. Nearly everybody of note passed through the taverns' doors. Because they provided drink, food, shelter, and space to conduct business, the taverns of the New World were the hotels of that day. Would-be towns clamored for a tavern because they knew traveling merchants were more likely to conduct business

A colonial ale house.

in a place that could provide creature comforts. So it was that in any area, the opening of the first tavern was greeted as a sign that business would soon be good.

Increased business activity translated into more travelers, who of course placed money directly in the pocket of the tavern owner. Not surprisingly, colonial tavern keepers usually ranked among the area's wealthier citizens. That was all the motivation needed for frontier entrepreneurs to line the paths leading west with taverns.

As taverns moved west, breweries naturally followed in their wake. Local breweries were an absolute necessity. The tavern owner and the brewer formed a happy partnership in the world of supply and demand. But what if no brewery followed? How did the tavern get its beer?

Constructing a tavern with no brewery nearby, or with no prospects for one in the near future, made new tavern owners more than a little uncomfortable. Under those conditions, many inn keepers resorted to a common practice: they brewed their own. Think of those taverns as the first brewpubs, dispensing fresh beer from barrels filled only a few feet away.

Within the original colonies, brewing in New Amsterdam proper (Manhattan, New York) proceeded in much the same manner as in other colonies. At first the "company" brewery was located within the safe confines of the settlement's fort. Later, as the town grew, breweries were licensed outside the post. Director-General Peter Minuit authorized the first of New York's public breweries in 1632. Located on what was called Market Field (now Whitehall Street near Stone Street), it opened for business in March 1633. For the next five years it served the small citizenry of New Amsterdam, until other commercial enterprises rendered it redundant.

Water supplying the early New Amsterdam breweries came from a small stream called the Heere Gracht, which ran along a tiny valley known as Beaver Path, in later times the site of Manhattan's Beaver Street. Over time it was artificially widened into a canal named De Heere Gracht, and still later it was filled in

Early New York City.

to form Broad Street. As Broad Street it became home to the wealthiest brewers and merchants of the young city.

Philadelphia's celebrated brewing heritage was begun by none other than the colony's founder, William Penn. Twenty miles upriver from Philadelphia, in Buck's County, Pennsbury manor was the location he selected for his brew house. Outfitted with copper kettles and a wooden mash tun, it immediately began turning out beer. Penn wrote of its workings in 1685: "Our beer was mostly made from molasses which well boyld, with Sassafras or Pine infused into it, makes tolerable drink; but now they make mault . . . "[11]

Others promptly followed in Penn's wake, and although they represented competition, Penn must have known there was plenty of business for all. In a rather unconcerned observation he remarked, "In our great town there is an able man, that has set up a large Brew house, in order to furnish the people with good Drink, both there and up and down the river."[12]

Slowly the number of towns in the colonies increased and the population expanded. This occurred as commerce was established and farming expanded beyond growing what was needed for local consumption. The changes that accompanied this growth had a long-lasting impact, especially on New England brewing.

Restricted monetary distribution and an agricultural-based society were the major factors that conspired to inhibit the construction of commercial breweries, but geography and transportation also played a role. Wealth was concentrated in the new merchant and trade classes and focused on the coast, where there was easy access to British markets and imports. Meanwhile, inland areas remained devoted to the production of agricultural goods. Even then farmers were on the short end of the commodities stick. The fruits of their labor were shipped to the coast, where merchants reaped the profits to be made from their sale and export.

Determined inland farmers hacked out a tough existence by opening up the thick virgin forest and removing the seemingly inexhaustible supply of rocks from the fields. A day of this type of work was surely enough to drive a person to the comfort of an ale, but settlers without home breweries had no way to slake their thirst.

The general lack of currency in this period further compounded the difficulty of acquiring beer. But where there's a will, there's a way, and supplies were acquired through trading. In his history of the United States, Page Smith described a typical scene: "Grain was taken to a mill to be ground, and some of it was swapped for Rum or Gin or Beer at the tavern adjacent to the mill."[13]

As hard currency became available, beer remained relatively inexpensive. The common price for a quart was just a penny, and the price was regulated. By 1634, sixpence was the legal fixed price for a meal and an ale-quart of beer cost one cent. Increased demand of taverns desperate for a steady beer supply finally led to the start of commercial brewing. As early as 1635, Captain Robert Sedgwick was licensed as a common brewer in the Massachusetts Bay Colony.

Almost as soon as taverns were established, the government became involved and formal licensing started. There were but a few registered taverns in Boston during the 1630s; by the 1680s, there were dozens. Taking a lesson from the economic history of

England, government leaders recognized the importance of the tavern in trade and marketing. The position of the tavern as a community focal point was considered so important to the growth of New England that the Royal Governors began enacting laws to encourage their proliferation. The government could, and did, direct local areas to open one in each village. The idea was to make the Puritan businessman's travel and business activity more comfortable and therefore more frequent. The system worked and the small inland towns began to grow.

The difference between an inn and a tavern was even less distinct than back in England. Both were names for houses where lodging was available along with stabling, meals, and beverages that included beer, cider, and wine. Beer sales outdoors were unrestricted, but taverns were subject to regulation. The license of each establishment defined the restrictions on sales.

Despite the disadvantage of needing a license for sales conducted indoors, the taverns flourished. No one wanted to stand outside drinking beer on a wintry New England evening. Thus, as Puritans roamed the streets of 1677 Boston, they had a choice of 27 places to quench their thirst. In only seven of those was wine available, but beer was stocked in all.[14] This was, in part, because beer was considered a victual. (Of course this number represents only legitimate taverns; many others quietly conducted business on the sly, and continued to as long as there was no trouble.)

One of the best ways to locate colonial taverns is through records of the courts. In colonial times people didn't go to trial, the trial came to them. Traveling judges "rode the circuit," and one of them, Judge Samuel Sewall (best remembered as writing the first American protest to slavery, "The Selling of Joseph"), kept an extensive diary of his travels on the circuit from 1674 to 1725.

Sewall was the original responsible drinker: once he checked into a tavern, his horse stayed for the night. His journal contained thousands of entries, but curiously his mention of taverns when at home was restricted to rare occasions, such as a 1697 dinner with a "company of Young Merchants" who entertained the Governor and council at a favorite Boston watering hole, Monck's Blue Anchor Tavern. It was one of the few times he entered a tavern in the city. Sewall was an exception—generally, members of the local population welcomed and provided enthusiastic support for their community tavern.

In all probability Sewall never made a leisurely visit to a Boston tavern, even to his neighborhood establishment, the Wallis Tavern, on the south side of Boston. When he was on the road, he had no choice. His diary records over 300 stays at taverns in Lynn, Scituate, and Roxbury.

The first well-known American writer, Cotton Mather, a teacher, clergyman, and recorder of early New England life, observed that ale and beer were commonplace in Massachusetts by 1675, and every other building in Boston was an ale house.[15] Governor Pownall made a similar estimate of the number of Boston taverns more than 100 years later. The taverns flourished despite government pressure to restrict new licenses.

Boston's Green Dragon Tavern, on Union Street, provided a typical example of opportunities within the tavern business. It first tapped a keg in 1680, and remained popular until the end of the 1700s, over 120 years of serving up tankards of fresh Boston ale!

Typical of port cities, Boston's taverns were usually situated in the commercial districts that grew along the waterfront. They were erected there intentionally as a convenience to sailors, most of whom were known to tip a few pints on occasion. A typical example was Thomas Bailey's Blue Anchor near Haver's Dock, which promised "Refreshment & Entertainment of Boatmen and others." But the location on the docks made it clear that there was another competitor with taverns for the precious supply of ale.

As the seventeenth century progressed, the belief that the simple act of drinking water was taking your life into your own hands persisted, and this was especially true among sailors. Little, if any, progress had occurred in the technology of effectively storing water aboard ship from the time the Pilgrims made their thirsty transit of the Atlantic. Water was thought of with scorn and there was little hope of convincing a sailor that water was a substitute for beer. The persistence of these attitudes prompted an agreement in 1638 between ship owners and crews that set the beer ration for each member of a New England sailing ship at one quart of beer per day, a rule sailors in our present-day navy no doubt wish were still in effect. Thus, the stores loaded on any vessel included a substantial amount of beer.

With a convenient demand present, entrepreneurs stepped forward. John Hull was one of these. He owned a general store along Boston's docks. Hull was a chandler who specialized in outfitting ships. His ledger recorded frequent purchases of beer from a brewer named Seth Perry. During the years 1685–89, the accounts credit Perry with supplying the ketch *Endeavor* with seven barrels and the brigantine *Robert* with six.[16]

39

These orders were fairly ordinary in quantity, but they appear large when considering that these vessels were closer in size to harbor boats. Certainly they must have had very happy crews. Mr. Perry, like many entrepreneurs of his time, was also a supplier of malt and his records reveal sales to "Mr. Nathaniel Clark—20 bushells" and "Mr. Abell Plats with yet another 20." These two customers were among the many citizens who continued to brew their own beer. Homebrewing of that sort throughout New England makes it difficult to determine an accurate number for colonial production and consumption.

While commercial brewing was gaining a toehold in Massachusetts, New York City witnessed brewing history. In 1660, the citizens of that small town experienced something never before seen. In that year, in lower Manhattan (previously New Amsterdam), a brewery was first identified by a brand name. The Red Lion Brewery was thus a departure from the practice of simply using the owner's name. From these simple origins the colony would eventually become a major brewing center, first in Albany, as a premier ale center of America, and later downstate, with renowned lager brewers.

Despite setting a new trend in brewery names, brewing activity in Manhattan didn't get off to as quick a start as it did in Boston, but it caught up in short order. New Amsterdam's first tavern appeared 30 years before the establishment of the Red Lion. It was known as the Stadt Harberg (City Tavern) and was constructed at the direction of Director-General William Krieft. As the first inn opened in the city, Krieft correctly reasoned that it would aid trade with Virginia and Massachusetts by providing accommodations for visiting merchants. Built of stone, it was a well-known landmark in

Stadt Huys.

the town, and in 1643 was leased to Philip Girritsen, who in the process was granted rights to operate a brewery on the premises.

By 1653 the tavern had reverted back to the government and was renamed Stadt Huys (City Hall). New Yorkers may not know it, but their first city hall was once a brewery that served what one visitor of the 1640s called "[beer] as good as that brewed in the Fatherland."[17]

New Amsterdam's second tavern was opened by councilman Crefier on a building site that became 9-11 Broadway. It was followed shortly thereafter by the ale house of Peter Koch at number 1 Broadway, facing Bowling Green.

Growing slowly, the colony had just 350 residents in 1629, but in 1632 it saw fit to construct its own brewery. This brew house was located on one of the first streets laid outside of the fort, aptly named Brouwers Street. As was the custom of the day,

41

influenced by the Old World practice of guilds, similar businesses were all located in one area.

For a couple of decades the central location of Brouwers Street was well suited to New York; however, over the years a problem developed. Breweries were naturally wet, and as was the custom in pre-industrial times, waste water was thrown into the only collection area available, the street. Compounding this problem was the constant traffic of heavily laden beer wagons.

Over the years business increased in proportion to the rapidly growing population of the town; Brouwers Street became a larger and larger quagmire. By the year 1657 the condition of the thoroughfare was intolerable. Implementing the easiest solution, the city fathers simply laid down stone paving and in the process created the first paved street in America. Proud of their accomplishment, they changed the name from Brouwers to Stone Street. To this day it exists under that name and runs between Broad and Whitehall.

In her *Historic New York,* that great documenter of colonial life, Alice Morse Earle, wrote of both Brouwers Street and Stadt Huys:

> Brouwer straat began at the rear of the city hall. It could be reached directly by persons going from the Stadt Huys by walking through a flower-bordered path in a trim garden, which was bright with hollyhocks and tulips, and later, when it became known as the Stadt Huys garden, was filled with waving grain raised by the burgomaster's secretary. At the end of the path an entrance opened into the street.[18]

Soon the number of breweries crowding Stone Street forced construction in other areas as well. One was the brewery of

Dutch brewer Jacobus on the corners of Pearl and Old Slip Streets. Not long after, in 1645, Oloff Stevenson van Courtland established another brewery on Market Street. New Amsterdam residents were opening several breweries a year. Government officials were brewing alongside tavern keepers, and many common citizens brewed at home. Houses that advertised a home-brewery were most sought after in the local real estate market. It seemed everyone was brewing.

Regardless of the amount of beer they brewed, New Yorkers couldn't keep up with demand. They continued to import beer from Holland and Great Britain. Even after the breweries became able to keep up with demand, in the late 1640s they continued to import vast amounts of beer. Traders turned over the beer and redirected it to southern colonies such as Virginia at a profit. Despite the amounts shipped out of the harbor, New Amsterdamers weren't abstaining, anything but. One government official reported that residents were regularly "occasioned by immoderate drinking."[19]

Other colonies witnessed the birth of local breweries as well. Commercial ventures were established as soon as the population and economy expanded enough to support the business. Philadelphia's first commercial brewer was Anthony Morris, who constructed a brew house during 1687. Located on Front Street, it was near the small bakery/homebrewery operated by William Frampton.

Succeeding as a brewer, Morris went on to become one of Philadelphia's leading citizens. He amassed great personal wealth and was honored as its second mayor.

Recognized as the city's first tavern was the Blue Anchor, occupying the corner of Front and Dock Streets. According to local legend it was the first house built in the city and was host to William Penn on his initial visit to the region. For years the Blue Anchor was the center of the town's commerce and social activity.

Across the harbor in New Jersey, brewing was first established along the Delaware, but on the arrival of John Fenwick in 1675, the interior of the colony welcomed beer. When Fenwick's followers arrived, they "straightaway busied themselves in erecting breweries for manufacturing beer for common drink. There were four of them in the small township of Elsinborough, John Thompson's, Nicholson's, Morris's, and George Abbott's. There were several more throughout the county."[20]

Throughout the colonial period there were so many people tied to brewing that it is hard to identify anyone who wasn't. Not even the clergy abstained from the pleasure of a beer. When Reverend Thomas Shepard of Newtowne, Massachusetts, was ordained head of the church, the parishioners ensured that a special "ordination beer" was on hand for the festivities. In its aftermath the celebration left many of the attendees glad they were relying on their horse's legs rather than their own.[21]

Still more beer drinkers were found on campus. Before arriving in the New World, John Harvard, founder of the university and namesake of a modern Boston brewpub, allegedly learned the art of brewing from William Shakespeare. On founding his college in 1636, Harvard made the beer supply one of his earliest priorities. He developed plans to construct a brew house to supply the needs of both faculty and students. Beer was an inescapable part of Harvard life.

Beer was considered critical among Harvard's staples and was one of the president's most important responsibilities.

Unfortunately, the institution's first president, Nathaniel Eaton, ignored this all-important duty.

President Eaton was responsible for a variety of functions considered essential to the smooth running of Harvard's college, but in a monumental blunder he turned over control of beer production to his wife, who paid scant attention to maintaining the beer supply. Rations were often extremely limited or nonexistent.

By 1639 the students were nearly revolting. Turning more and more bitter, they considered the lack of beer intolerable and complained loudly that "they often had to go without their beer and bread." When Eaton was brought up on charges of mistreating the assistant master, it was the shortage of beer that contributed to his dismissal.[22]

Beer continued to play a central role at Harvard. In a tradition borrowed from the great universities of England, it was a common staple of the school. Within the college rules of 1667 were instructions on the operation of the college brewery to furnish both small and strong beer. Furthermore, it directed the college butler in his beer-related duties: "[The butler] receiving his Beer from the steward, single beer at 2 shill. & double at 4s the barrell shall advance four pence upon the shilling."[23]

By 1686 the beer situation at Harvard was greatly eased, when Increase Mather, father of Cotton Mather, a student of history and no fool, was appointed to run the college. He knew what to emphasize and drafted a Code of College Laws that addressed the beer supply. In the process Mather shrewdly dictated the minimum volume of a beer barrel: "The steward shall deliver in unto the Butler his bread at 5 shillings per bushell, and his beer at 4 per barrel, each barrel consisting of sixteen gallons of Beer measure allowing thereto two pecks of Barley Malt."[24]

At least three different brew houses occupied the campus, the last of which was described as a wooden structure approximately 25 feet square. Times changed, and by the late 1700s the provision demanding a steady beer supply was withdrawn. The brewery was relegated to the unglamorous role of storehouse.

Mather's encounters with brewing continued beyond his Harvard experience. Bringing a legal matter of the town before a court, he petitioned the jurists to encourage "Sister Bradish" that she might be "countenanced" in her baking bread and brewing of beer: "such is her art, way, and skill that shee doth vend such comfortable penniworths for the relief of all that send unto her as elsewhere they can seldom meet with."[25] This was actually a self-serving action related to the position Increase Mather held at

Harvard, ca. 1726.

Harvard. It was from Sister Bradish that many of Mather's students secured their beer ration.

People like Sister Bradish were following a trend that England had seen earlier in its history, when common citizens learned the trade of brewing as a means of supplementing their income. Government again involved itself in the production of brewing, and under the guise of protecting quality the authorities mandated that a brew permit was required. In 1633, when William Whyte of the Massachusetts colony was accused of selling ale without a permit, his defense was that he only wanted "to brew a little beere, for ye Collyers and other workmen."[26]

Officials passed judgment against Mr. Whyte. This was one of the cyclical periods in America's history when concerns arose about drinking. Whyte suffered because the colonial leaders were becoming preoccupied with the practice of drinking at work.

It was customary for the workers of that period to consume tremendous quantities of beer throughout the workday. In a tradition brought over from Europe, employees received drink as part of their wages. In fact, most could not get through their day without refreshment to "comfortably proceede in their works." With growing concern over abuse, laws were passed to prevent such activity. The first in a series of statutes was recorded in 1633 in Massachusetts. These were widely disregarded, and a ration of ale as part of the work contract would continue well into the 1700s.

Authorities were alarmed about society outside the workplace as well; they worried about a general trend of excessive consumption. By 1648 the colony had "hoalsome laws provided and published" for the encouragement of temperance, but these too were largely ineffective. On a visit in 1682, Edward Ward commented that the general disregard of any statute to curb the public's ale consumption made "all their laws look like scare-crows" and the public was wise to ignore the unwise restrictions. America's worry over the enjoyment of alcohol neither began nor ended in the 1600s, and local attempts to curb it provided no lessons for the future. Beer played much too important a role in daily life to pry it away from the settlers, farmers, and merchants in the growing colonies.

At the approach of a new century, beer was solidly rooted in the culture of the populace. Although commercial brewing was a small industry, people's taste for beer was driving it toward a large-scale business.

Natural laws of supply and demand would dictate beer's future. Despite the large number of imports from England, colonial breweries had shown they were profitable enterprises. As the 1600s waned, the coming century would bring about far-reaching changes that would affect the people and politics of the new land. In that process, beer would play an important role in shaking the very foundations of the world's greatest power.

Three

BEER AND THE BIRTH
OF AN AMERICAN CULTURE

The Early 1700s

When the new century began in 1700, the position of beer in North America was secure. Demand for beer and other alcoholic beverages remained high as the towns and villages along the coast evolved from settlements to population centers. Of all these, the relatively new center of Philadelphia was poised to seize recognition as America's brewing capital.

Only 18 years after the colony's founding, Philadelphians enjoyed a well-established, and highly regarded, brewing industry. In part, William Penn deserves a measure of credit for the industry's success, because Penn built the city that attracted the greatest ethnic diversity on the continent.

Philadelphia's diversity sprang from the effective advertising Penn conducted throughout Europe. Immigrants flocked to Pennsylvania for two reasons. First was the opportunity to obtain inexpensive land. Second, but of equal importance, was the fact that Penn's charter promoted self-government and religious tolerance. Freedom was what attracted a large German population, among other groups.

Naturally the new arrivals carried the culture and traditions of their old country, as did others before them. For the Germans and other northern Europeans that meant beer. Breweries prospered and the population expanded rapidly. Surrounding areas and once outlying villages were soon absorbed by the ever-growing city. By 1700 the city had surpassed New York, and was challenging Boston, as the cultural center of North America.

To the north, New York was thought of as the second brewing city of the New World. A city roster of the early 1700s contains the names of at least 17 brewers. Foremost among early New York brewing families were the Rutgers.

From the original brewery established in Albany in 1649, Anthony Rutgers moved back down the Hudson River to Manhattan. By 1717 Rutgers was operating an admired brew house located on the north side of Stone Street near Nassau. Among his customers was the secretary of the province, George Clarke, who commented on the quality of Rutgers's product. With a reputation for excellent beer, the family gradually opened other breweries throughout the region. One of the first mini-brewing dynasties of the New World was formed when Anthony Rutgers's daughter married into another of New York's leading beer families, that of Leonard Lispenard.

Up and down the eastern seaboard merchants placed orders for New York beer. From Boston in 1737, tavern keeper Peter

Faneuil regularly ordered beer for his better customers. He wrote to his supplier, Gulian Verplank, to ship "Six barrels of your very best Strong beer," and later reported that "On the whole the bread & flour proves well in kind as well as beer."[1]

Breweries thrived, but New Yorkers, then as now, weren't satisfied with a selection limited to local products. As did other towns on the coast, New York had unfettered access to English shipping. Combined with its advantage as a trade center, which brought in money to spend, this made it possible for New Yorkers to purchase large quantities of English ale. But unlike Boston, which continued to rely heavily on imports to augment local production, New York breweries flourished. Virginia's climate was too warm for brewing, and New York beer was shipped down the coast with increasing frequency.

Although New York's brewing future looked bright, one factor started to inhibit production by the latter half of the 1700s: a limited supply of water in Manhattan, a problem that haunted inhabitants well into the 1840s. Part of the response to a lack of potable water was increased dependence on beer as well as "cider, punch and madeira."[2] However, down the eastern seaboard in Philadelphia, unhindered by the water problem New York brewers faced, breweries continued to thrive.

Thirsty new arrivals to eastern Pennsylvania were greeted with a large selection of beer. One of Philadelphia's newcomers arrived not by boat from Europe, but on foot. He traveled down the long, dusty Old York Road past many a tavern, such as the White Oak in Branchburg, New Jersey. Fleeing a domineering brother in Boston, the young man was destined to become a

Benjamin Franklin.

legend in Philadelphia, but he arrived with only three cents in his pocket. Overcoming the formidable obstacle of no money, little schooling, and only a rudimentary apprenticeship in his trade, he eventually won the respect of the colony, and was known as its most eminent citizen. In his spare time, he invented the library, fire department, bifocals, and a stove that bears his name. More than that, he was regarded as America's first internationally distinguished figure.

Benjamin Franklin started his life avoiding beer and ale. In his early days he was incredulous that fellow print shop workers would even sacrifice wages for a beer. However, as Franklin matured his views changed. As business brought in fame, and a modestly prosperous income, Ben became a man of comfort. With some time on his hands after a busy day of philosophy and invention, he turned to the friendly confines of a tavern for a little relaxation.

It was a pleasant experience, of which he became especially fond. There was nothing quite as satisfying as sitting around the tavern room with friends. Philosophical discussions resumed along with his new favorite pastime, lifting a few pints of ale. On a typical late evening all took to singing a few songs and Franklin penned some of his own. One verse in particular illustrated his acquired love of beer:

The antediluvians were all very sober
For they had no wine and brewed no October;
All wicked, bad livers, on mischief still thinking,
For there can't be good living
where there is not good drinking.[3]

Franklin wasn't completely correct. Noah did have beer with him on the ark, but the Oktoberfest style hadn't been invented. What he was most likely writing about was the type of strong, harvest-time ale, or October ale, long popular in the farming areas of England. He further revealed his taste for beer when confiding to a friend in 1745: "I like . . . the concluding sentiment in the old song called 'The Old Man's Wish' where in, . . . wishing for a warm house, in a country town, an easy horse, some good authors, ingenious and cheerful companions, a pudding on Sundays, with stout ale."[4]

Franklin was yet another member of the ranks who looked upon beer as a healthful tonic. He lived to witness the birth of a new nation, and when he died in 1790 he had reached the extremely advanced, but beer-enhanced, age of 84.

Though no record exists of Franklin's favorite brand, it might have been that made by Philadelphia's leading brewer of the century, Anthony Morris. From the time Morris opened in 1687, his Front Street brew house was considered the best of Philadelphia breweries. Thomas Paschall, who commented on the quality of Philadelphia's beer in the late 1600s, was a regular customer of the Morris brewery. His son, Thomas Paschall Jr., became a leading maltster of the colony and counted Morris among his customers. By 1705, Morris was purchasing 50 bushels of malt at a time. Paschall's business continued to prosper, and by the mid-1700s he was a leading merchant in the city, his fortune built on the beer trade.

Massachusetts beer drinkers began the eighteenth century with a feeling of optimism. They were living with an expanding economy, permanent settlements, and the beginnings of unique American customs. Most important, their healthy thirst for beer was being satisfied by one means or another. Beer was secure in its role in New England society. Colonial pantries reserved a special spot for ale, because it was considered an essential item in all households. As much as farming, running a store, or any other job was part of life, so was a supply of beer. No one in New England escaped the touch of beer. Everyone drank it, from the lowly farmhand to the affluent merchant.

Boston's leading brewer in the early part of the century was Sampson Salter. A native of Boston, Salter was born in 1692 and by the 1730s had found a rewarding clientele beyond the local market. Salter teamed up with merchant Peter Faneuil in supplying ships with beer from his brew house on Leveretts Lane. Ledgers show numerous sales all along the wharves of Boston.

Another of Boston's famous pre-revolution brewers was Robert Whately. Using the same strategy employed by Slater, Whately also sold directly to ships and their crews. It was Whately's brewery that sold beer to the brigantine *Lydia*. Outfitted by John Hancock's uncle Thomas, the *Lydia* later played an important role in events that fired the revolutionary flame. Yet another noted brewer was John Carey who, on April 6, 1710, was granted permission to operate a brew house on Cambridge Street. Before long some shipmasters started brewing their own supplies, as in the case of Captain Nathaniel Oliver on Water Street. From the time of the Pilgrims up through the Revolution, setting sail without an outfitting of beer was unthinkable, and the brewers of Boston wisely profited from the custom.

Other breweries were constructed throughout Boston's formative years, but they never kept up with the demand from the taverns. Entrenched in its position as a colonial trade center, and with the increased shipping that came with this status, it was easy for Boston to buy imported beer. During the first part of the 1700s beer supplies were plentiful. There was practically an ocean of beer waiting to be tapped, and Boston was content with what appeared a permanent solution.

Down the coast from Boston, the city of Newport was the financial center of the Rhode Island colony. Its first notable brewer was Daniel Sabree, who brewed from the start of the century until his death in 1745. George Rome, representing a group of English businessmen, took title to a brew house in exchange for forgiveness on a debt. Rome capably operated the brewery on Spring Street, south of the First Baptist Church, until the start of the Revolution, upon which he returned to England. Other brewers also took up business in the city, including Anthony Young, John Wright, John Lance, Joseph Belcher, and Giles Hosier. Enjoying popular approval of his beer, Hosier had the distinction of renting lagering space for his brew in the basement of the Statehouse.

Beer sold briskly in the southern colonies as well, but brewing never caught on as it did in New York and Philadelphia. There were several good reasons for this. First, for all but a few months of the year the climate was much too warm. Beer ferments best at temperatures of 70 degrees Fahrenheit or lower. Above that temperature yeast produces fusel oils, which impart an undesirable taste similar to a strong solvent. Yet another factor restraining southern brewing was storage. Beer spoils easily if not kept cool. Until artificial refrigeration was introduced, the beer production of the South always lagged well behind the northern colonies.

Producing less beer was one story, consumption was another. Southerners loved beer. James Ogelthorpe, founder of the Georgia colony, mentioned this fact often, and the secretary of the province wrote of a shipment received from New York on October 7, 1738: "Having good Plenty of well brewed Beer aboard, which at this season of the Year was much wished for by most People; more went without any than those few who could find Money to buy and the publick Stores had none."[5]

Four years later the citizenry were continuing to welcome the arrival of beer shipments. An account written in the year 1742 describes exactly how much beer the colonists in the Georgia settlement of Frederica were capable of consuming: "The New York Sloop having sold most part of her dry provisions, began to Set out for Frederica with what she had else, which being about 150 barrels of Beer, twas Supposed might Serve there for 3 or 4 days Draught."[6]

In Virginia, a college was operated following the fashion initiated at Harvard. William and Mary College established a brewery on its grounds in 1693. When it was destroyed by a fire that ravaged the campus in the early 1700s, officials immediately undertook a complete reconstruction. Considered essential, the brewery was one of the first buildings rebuilt. Describing it in 1705, Robert Beverly detailed a layout consisting of "a Quadrangle, two sides of which, are yet only carried up. In this part are already finished all conveniences for Cooking, Brewing, Baking."[7]

Virginia's neighbor to the north, Maryland, was also considered a southern colony, and like others below the Mason-Dixon line, it was short of breweries. Traveling through the colony in the 1730s, a British observer noted the lack of commercial brewing, and bemoaned the shortage.[8]

In the mid-1740s, Maryland witnessed the opening of the Globe, its first significant commercial brewery. Constructed by a ship's captain, Daniel Barentz, in 1744, it was located on the corner of Baltimore's Conway and Hanover Streets. Built of brick, its aging cellars were expanded over the years and reached over 200 feet in length. Improvements and additions were made throughout the years and operation of the brewery continued in various hands until 1963.

Considering the importance of beer, living without breweries might seem a trial, but the situation was greatly relieved by the South's relationship with England. Exporting crops of tobacco and cotton set up an agreeable barter system that brought back English beer. Tobacco, a crop impossible to grow in England, soon dominated southern farms. Southern farmers looked at the profits from tobacco and quickly dismissed any desire to grow barley. Instead, they forged an agreement that supplied everyone with their favorite vice. By the early 1700s the trading partners had established an informal exchange rate of 40 pounds of tobacco for one gallon of brew.

Supplementing the British shipments were recurring deliveries from the northern colonies. George Campion, a Philadelphia brewer, regularly shipped beer to Georgia, and nearly all the brewers of that city sold beer to merchants and plantation owners in Virginia. Reports on the arrival of Philadelphia beer shipments appeared frequently in the *Virginia Gazette*. Francis Louis Michel, seeking passage from Virginia to Philadelphia, wrote of finding "a sloop, in accordance with my desire, which had brought beer from Philadelphia."[9]

Shipping, sailors, and beer provided a foundation for another fruitful profession, the dockside tavern keeper. Ship-related taverns congregated around the ports in New York, Boston, and Philadelphia. Known variously as slop shops, tippling houses, and grog shops, they paid close attention to both the sailors' needs and their wallets. A typical evening in one of the wharfside taverns was described by seaman William Fredenburgh as he related his experience of drinking and gaming in 1720: "Stayed there playing at cards & Truck till two a Clock in the Morning. That the Depont and the rest of the Company which was with him Drank four tankards of Flipp for which the aforesaid Richard Woodman paid to the Said Jacob Swan three Shillings."[10]

Until war broke out the areas around ports were an important market for the early colonial breweries. Carrying over the custom of the previous centuries, ships continued to provision for voyages with large stores of beer. Shipboard storage of fresh water had improved little over the 100 years since colonization of North America began, and beer was the beverage of choice. Not surprisingly, a fair number of tavern owners were ex-sailors. But beer wasn't limited to the seafarers.

On land, newspapers reflected an importance placed on beer proportional to that of the mariners. Newspapers of that era frequently ran stories with a focus on household management that helped readers cope with the hardships faced in a developing country. They offered advice on any number of topics. Beer- and brewing-related articles were as routine as columns with hints on how to keep bears out of the garden and which moss was best to seal cabin walls. In the *Boston Newsletter* of November 28, 1728, a writer described his model budget for a typical family of eight. His "Scheme of Expense" was designed to assist the planning of "Families of Middling Figure who bear the Character of being Genteel." He rightly devoted the most time and space to what was typically a family's greatest daily expense—beer: "4 [sic] Small Beer for the Whole Day Winter and Summer. In this article of the Beer I would likewise include all the molasses used in the Family, not only in Brewing but on other occasions."[11]

More than just interesting anecdotal information, this article provides a glimpse of what colonists were using as beer's raw material. Malt and hop inventories continued to remain at low levels in the early part of the 1700s, and brewers struggled with the lack of brewing ingredients just as their predecessors in the 1600s had done.

Understandably, beer's prominent cultural role was what prompted recurring references in colonial correspondence. Beer shortages were of more than passing interest, they were a disruption of daily routine. Boston experienced a shortage of barley in 1711 that captured the attention of the entire city. Within days word spread of the low stock, turning the situation into a crisis. Rather than accept their uncomfortable predicament, the town sprang into action. Bostonians gathered in a large crowd when Andrew Belcher, a Boston merchant, attempted to ship barley out of the port, blocking the shipment. They had no intention of allowing barley to leave Boston if the citizens were going to face a beer shortage.

The blocking of the Belcher shipment illustrates another change that was taking place in the society of the early 1700s. Economic conditions had improved and grown healthy enough to allow people to worry about buying, instead of making, beer. Prior to the 1700s brewing was a mandatory household chore. People had to have beer, and they had to make their own. Vigorous economic growth encouraged them to indulge in the luxury of buying commercially brewed beer. Greater turnover of currency placed more luxuries, including relief from household work, within reach of the growing populace.

While purchasing professionally brewed beer was laying the foundation for a commercial brewing industry, the bulk of colonials, especially those residing outside a population center, continued to brew their own. With shortages of brewing ingredients common, their attention was often fixed on the success of the farmers. As harvests directly affected the beer supply for the coming year, homebrewers anxiously watched the crops and prayed for good yields.

Citizens following the barley crop came from virtually every walk of life. John Adams was one. Though deeply enmeshed in deliberations during the Continental Congress, he managed to make time for inquiry about the barley crop back in Massachusetts. Throughout his travels Adams exchanged a devoted correspondence with his wife, Abigail. Letters between them are now a treasured window on colonial life.

With an unusual attitude for the time, John considered Abigail more than a spouse; she was his partner in life. More than once Adams's letters expressed how he was "a little anxious" about their fields of barley. Adams did not question his wife's ability to run the farm, he thought her "so valorous and noble" a farmer. Yet even while helping set the framework for a new country, he couldn't help offering advice about how to manure the barley field.

John Adams.

Adams was joined in his concern over the barley crop by every other North American colonist. Usually the settlers expected, and could rely upon, favorable results, because barley grew well in the Maritimes. Though consumption continued to outpace production in that era, city dwellers usually had sufficient imports to augment the local yield. Crop failures came more infrequently and eventually the barley harvest met colonial demand.

Citizens gradually shifted to locally brewed beer, and grateful brewers enjoyed unprecedented demand. However, even while barley farms succeeded, and shortfalls declined, another ingredient continued to be in short supply: hops.

Hop inventories for the local brew industry were dependent upon a harvest of native, wild hops found growing on vines in the forests. Late each summer groups would scour the forest picking

61

the flowers, but as breweries grew in number, there weren't enough hops for them to meet the needs of local production.

In 1747, the collector of New York described the hops problem in a commerce report he filed with the English Board of Trade. Attached as a summary, he included a tally of all imports. Hops was prominently listed. Two years later the report again listed hops as an import item of substantial quantity. Hops continued near the top of the report's list for more than two decades, well into the administration of Governor William Tryon in 1774. Tryon again listed hops, but also included barley among the colony's "Natural produce & Staple Commodities." Tryon also placed malting and brewing among the significant "manufactures" of the New York region. Hops shortages continued to plague the brewers until the 1800s, when cultivation of hops thrust New York into the lead as a major hop producer of the United States.[12]

Shortages continued to disrupt both brewing and daily life, but colonists refused to accept life without beer. On running out of ingredients, they used a little Yankee ingenuity to find an acceptable, if not satisfying, substitute. As with the earliest settlers, this sometimes meant tolerating a less-than-acceptable version of beer. Brave (or desperate) settlers went on with making beer out of almost everything imaginable.

Home wasn't the only place where a colonist's attention was focused on beer. In the workplace beer was considered every bit as critical to daily routine as in the home. Drinking was considered a fundamental part of the colonial employee benefit package. Offices, shops, and job sites were nearly swimming in beer. On-the-job drinking was so strongly ingrained in the work routine that it defied repeated attempts to abolish it. Like their English counterparts, colonial laborers and craftsmen expected to take part of their compensation in beer. Ben Franklin, reflecting on his early career in Boston, remembered the custom in his brother's print shop:

> We had an alehouse boy who attended always in the house to supply the workmen. My companion at the press drank everyday a pint before breakfast, a pint at breakfast with his bread and cheese, a pint between breakfast and dinner, a pint at dinner, a pint in the afternoon about six o'clock, and another when he had done his day's work.[13]

Legislation attempted to stop this practice again and again, but workers ignored the ordinances and continued enjoying periodic "beer breaks." Ineffective laws designed to curb job-related drinking were instituted from 1645 to the mid-1700s.

In Boston, cook Richard Briggs was certain beer was an invaluable job aid. He wrote not only of its benefits, but of what type to drink. Shunning small (or light) beers, he was convinced strong beer was required to get a person through the day. He observed that consumption of low-alcohol beer "is not good, the drinkers of it will be feeble in summer time, incapable of strong work, and will be subject to distempers."[14]

For health, vigor, stamina, and endurance, Briggs and thousands like him believed beer was a necessity. The healthful benefits of beer reached far outside the workplace. Beer was considered medicinal, as illustrated by this beer-based formula for medicine:

four gallons of strong Ale, five ounces of Aniseeds, Liqourish scraped half a pound, Sweet Mints, Angelica, Eccony, Cowslip flowers, sweet marjoram, of each of these handfuls, Palitoy of the Vval one handful. After it fermented two or three dayes, distill it in a Limbech and add Cinnamon, Fennel, Juniper, rose buds, Apple, dates, distil again, add sugar candy.[15]

More than just a cure, beer was also a considered preventative medicine. People from all walks of life thought it synonymous with wellness, and its daily use was second nature. At both the breakfast and dining table beer or cider was common, and children also partook. Life without it was unthinkable. Social events from barn raisings to harvest, and field clearings to church gatherings, always featured a keg. Constantly ready to serve the demand were the taverns. As a social center of an area, the inn or tavern struggled to maintain a supply of the patrons' most social drink.

Beer was secure in its position, but it forced the Massachusetts legislature into a corner created by two conflicting issues: maintaining the health, well-being, and economic benefits of drinking, while ensuring productivity remained high. What leaders saw was troubling. Workplace, home, and social consumption of beer increased in locked step with greater production. Though the colonies' existence appeared stable, colonial leaders knew their continued success relied heavily on productivity, and they worried that over-consumption would bring serious consequences. They harbored fears about the growing problem of conspicuous consumption (or more correctly, what they deemed as overindulgence). Beer was everywhere. By 1756 the number of licensed taverns in Boston had grown to 156, with many more operating on the fringe of legality.

Most of the apprehension stemmed from chronic displays of public drunkenness. This was a real problem, not a whimsical concern of pious teetotalers. Lawmakers weren't prudes, most of them drank beer, but they felt compelled to push for regulations governing drinking. They were accurate in their assessment: records indicate that the colonial period suffered from some of the highest alcohol consumption rates in American history. High consumption stemmed, in part, from the colonists' resistance to water. However, even after allowing for the role beer played in their diet, alcohol abuse was all too common an occurrence. Problems with drink were not confined to the lower classes, prominent families were equally susceptible. The clergy, too, was not immune. In the mid-1600s Virginia reprimanded several ministers for "Drunken and riotous conduct."

Correct as legislators were in identifying the problem, their focus was inaccurate. In nearly all instances, hard liquor was the problem, not beer. Young John Adams, riding the circuit as a judge, and recording everything (as all the Adamses seemed prone to do) complained frequently about the excesses of drinking. His objections were almost exclusively limited to spirituous liquor. Medical knowledge of the day counseled for moderate beer or wine drinking, and who, thought Adams, was he to argue with the professionals? Of course he was partial to beer, cider, and wine, so he, like most of his peers, condemned excessive consumption of other liquors while continuing to partake themselves.

Part One

Although continually wrestling with the drinking problem, colonial administrators recognized that ale houses and taverns functioned as a focal point for commerce. Following the trend originally observed in the late 1600s, the tavern continued to encourage the growth of business, and in turn benefited from its associated travel. Taverns functioned in the same fashion here as in old England, by providing a comfortable meeting place for merchants to conduct trade. Sparsely settled interior lands made distances between homes and neighbors considerable, limiting the opportunity to socialize. Taverns offered both a reason and a place to assemble. Chronicles by William Black of Massachusetts reported the appearance and atmosphere of the typical tavern. Black wrote of the "Pleasures of Conversation and a Cheerful Glass," in a room with few tables, many chairs, and a happy, talkative clientele.

In the South, too, as the population increased, suppliers established a lucrative tavern trade. Demand for beer was as natural, and regular, as the changing seasons. Tavern owners knew settlers longed for the security of old English habits, and were dedicated to providing it. Transplanting the venerable institution of taverns was the logical way to satisfy their needs. Exactly as in the North, southern ale houses provided the function of social, religious, and trading centers. Maryland was typical—it passed laws to stimulate tavern keeping for "all persons as well as strangers as others."[16] Merchants would surely call on an area with a tavern.

Motivation for the establishment of taverns reached well beyond the initial impact of encouraging commerce; self-interest was at work. Locations for conducting judicial proceedings were

66

needed, and if the government could avoid a capital project like building a courthouse, so much the better. Thus, the South employed the methods New Englanders had used so effectively. Maryland authorities passed a bill encouraging tavern keeping for these dual ends. The courts needed a place to convene because of the "distance of our habitacons [while] being many tymes Constrayned to appeare for the Administration of Justice for the houlding and attending Courts and upon other occasions."[17]

In southern districts there was a rush equal to that in the North for building inns, taverns, and ale houses. At first it was satisfying to watch the area mature, but again, with the sudden swell in numbers southern officials grew alarmed. With no more originality than had been exhibited in the North, they simply enacted laws to restrict licensing. Feeling horribly left out, newer settlements, and those that had outgrown the established taverns, desperately petitioned the authorities for relief from the constraints. In Londonbritain, Pennsylvanian Thomas Lunn was granted permission to build because he pleaded that "There is no Tavern in all the town and the Town's business being Entirely Done in Y$_r$ Humb. Pett's house."[18]

Edward Thomas, who lived in Radner, Pennsylvania, next to Saint David's church, similarly petitioned for, and was awarded, relief because he was "Obliged to Entertain many People y^e came to worship."[19]

Some individuals entered the business as a primary occupation, while others looked at it as a way to supplement their regular income. Such was the case with William Faris of Annapolis, Maryland. Although an accomplished silversmith, he opened a tavern adjacent to his shop in August 1764. In an attempt to combine both businesses, he designed a tankard that remains the only known example of its type in a 1700s silversmith's pattern book.

Southern colonies also used taverns as centers of politics. This circumstance was most likely the actual cause of governments' shift from support to limitation. Drunkenness was a convenient excuse to control public activity. It should be noted that most accounts of this problem refer to rum ("Rhum") or whiskey as the culprit.

Tavern owners grew wealthy with the combination of regular local customers and the accommodations provided to business travelers. With prosperity, owners of the more popular establishments were often influential businessmen such as John Marston, who bought the Golden Ball Tavern on Boston's Merchants Row. Marston also operated the Bunch of Grapes on King and State Streets.

Consumption of beer throughout the day was as common in Philadelphia as in New England. A standard breakfast of the period included "cold meat with a pint of good ale or cider."[20] Accounts of the city's drinking habits appear often in the period's press and in correspondence of the inhabitants.

Naturally, as problems arose, the citizens remained determined to sustain the flow of beer, even as they looked for alternatives. Among them, the American Philosophical Society, founded by Franklin, offered its assistance in the form of a recipe for a pumpkin ale.

Let the Pompion be beaten in a Trough an pressed as Apples. The expressed juice is to be boiled in a copper a considerable time and carefully skimmed that there may be no remains of the fibrous part of the pulp. After that intention is answered let the liquor be hopped culled fermented & c as malt beer.[21]

North of Philadelphia, in New York, great attention was also paid to the beer supply. Tavern owners sought a more local supply chain and the brewers reaped the benefits. Repeal of the Stamp Act in 1766 eased the situation temporarily and the city celebrated with "a roast ox, a hogshead of rum, and twenty-five barrels of ale, which were dispensed freely as long as they lasted."[22]

It was a well-savored victory, one of the first times the colonials stood up for and protected their rights as "Englishmen," but it also demonstrated the vulnerability of an imported beer supply. Before long the crown countered with the Townsend Acts, which led to the first united act of the colonies. Again taxes and restrictions were protested in New York by the colonial legislature. Despite a threat of retaliation, they voted to oppose the acts with the greatest weapon they had: refusal to furnish the King's garrison with beer.

Shifting the emphasis from imports to local beer was more complicated than simply placing an order with a colonial brewery. In the mid-1700s everyone, including brewers, had to contend with other disruptive factors, chief among them transportation. As the Revolutionary War approached, the colonies were burdened with a system of roads best described as poor. The most common type was dirt. A slightly improved version was made by felling trees and laying the trunks side by side, which were then covered with a layer of dirt. Known as "corduroy roads," they were only slightly better than no roads at all. To make matters worse, roads didn't follow direct paths.

The difficulties of shipping by land forced brewers to rely on transportation by water. This alternative was no better. Securing shipping was at times difficult and the taxes involved made it prohibitive. Transportation was one of the factors that continually drove the colonials back to English imports after each new supply crisis was averted.

Obstacles aside, trade in beer expanded with the ever-rising demand. Breweries, hampered by poor roads, required the support of a sizable local population to ensure financial feasibility. Success hinged upon the ability to deliver beer to people in the surrounding areas, but two things made that nearly impossible. First, of course, was the rough condition of the roads. Second, and of greater difficulty, was the relationship between colonies. None completely trusted the others and all ran their affairs as unrelated, sovereign governments. Conduct of trade between them was bogged down in 13 different sets of requirements. Both these obstacles limited breweries to confined sales territories. In many areas the towns remained too small in the mid-1700s to justify the expense associated with brewery construction and operation. Yet, slowly, circumstances were changing.

Imported beer was subjected to ever-increasing shipping costs, and unsettling conditions with the homeland of England made a steady supply uncertain. No other factors had more impact on the development of colonial brewing. As brewers watched the population expand, they knew it was only a matter of time before the dream of opening a local brewery reached the point of financial reality. Yet it would still take almost a hundred years, and some revolutionary events, to gain independence in beer production. As the midpoint of the century faded into history, beer's future, and that of the country, was placed in the hands of delegates heading to Philadelphia. Throughout the countryside people waited and watched.

Four

INDEPENDENCE: WHEN FERMENTATION AIDED FOMENTATION

Through the birth and youth of American brewing, Philadelphia moved along a path with an even greater destiny, one with a much more pronounced effect on the colonies. Philadelphia was about to answer a call from Boston.

Wars never produce winners; one side just loses more than the other. After decades of constant conflict and periods of open warfare with the French, in 1763 England secured its grip on the North American continent. It didn't hold all the territory, but it certainly had seized what seemed the most attractive lands. Little did the authorities in London imagine that their victory also ensured its eventual loss.

Every shot fired in conquest of America rippled through the British treasury like a tornado on a mill pond. The consequences were devastating. England's back was up against the wall, and there was no recourse other than to rely on the colonies to assume a disproportionate share of their domestic problems. Over and again the Crown bled as much from the Americas as possible, and then reached for more. Year upon year colonists felt their work amounted to nothing more than servitude to the throne's coffers. Imports from the motherland were burdened with one tax, tariff, and duty hike after another. The colonists' patience was wearing thin.

At first the smoldering resentment spread slowly, but merchants, tradesmen, and craftsmen became increasingly irritated with the treatment they received. Isolated signs of protest began to appear. One brewer in Virginia voiced what was becoming a popular sentiment, by advertising:

> The severe treatment we have lately received from our Mother Country, would, I should think, be sufficient to recommend my undertaking (tho I should not be able to come up to the English standard, which I do not question constantly to do) yet, as I am satisfied that the goodness of every commodity is the best recommendation, I principally rely upon that for my success.[1]

Time passed and the situation grew more tense. Increasing political action, a need for more control, and a huge British debt from waging war with rival France led to imposition of the Revenue Act in 1764. The financial impact of this act was a direct tax on liquor and among the first to respond were students. At Yale College, students turned to beer, and they announced in the *New York Gazette* of November 22, 1764, that "The Gentlemen of the College cannot be too much commended for setting so laudable an Example . . . All Gentlemen of taste who visit the College will think themselves better entertained with a good glass of Beer or Cider."[2] It was a tax revolt and a sign of things to come.

The next British misstep was the Stamp Act of 1765. Histories of the period always carefully cite the pernicious effects of the Stamp Act. Another of England's attempts to pay for the debt it had accumulated in its many wars with France, the act was intended to generate cash by mandating the purchase of special stamps as a premium for the right to conduct trade. Affixed to the goods, the stamps indicated that the business or merchant had paid the necessary fee.

Stamp Act tax.

North Americans objected to the stamps because the Crown once again had failed to consult with the colonists. Their first news of the new levy came after was it was enacted. Colonials weren't looking for independence. They acknowledged Britain's government and in fact believed they were Englishmen, yet they felt isolated from every aspect of Parliament's lawmaking. Reaction to the Stamp Act was particularly bitter because it touched some of the most fundamental aspects of life, and worst of all, beer.

Its effect on beer was to impose, on top of local assessments, a fee for taverns in the form of special stamps that had to be purchased and fixed to the license. Imported kegs of beer required more of the same. Beer supplies were short, driving up the cost of a pint, and the added expense was more than the colonists could bear.

Colonials responded with their first organized resistance to the Crown. It quickly became fashionable to drink homebrewed beer. From their meetingroom in the Green Dragon Tavern, the disgruntled and angered Sons of Liberty wrote to the other colonies suggesting the formation of a Stamp Act Congress. Imposing yet another tax on beer was just too much.

One of their ideas was a nonimportation agreement. Under the proposal, no one in England's North American settlements would purchase taxable goods from the motherland. This was their way of hitting the Crown where it most hurt. It was better to let the stamp-targeted goods rot on the dock. Not only would revenue from the stamps slow to a trickle, it would anger the English merchants who had come to rely upon trade with the colonies, who would then put pressure on Parliament to rescind the act. It was a convincing strategy.

As rhetoric grew more inflammatory, bordering on open rebellion, the colonists began to destroy the stamps. Frustrated by the colonists' response and the ineffectiveness of the tax, England eventually repealed the law. True, the reaction was against the expansive reach of the tax, but beer ignited emotions well beyond complaints about the cost of a tankard.

The colonists didn't have long to savor their accomplishment. Shortly after repeal of the Stamp Act, the Crown instituted the repressive and unpopular Townsend Acts in 1768. What the new law represented was bestowal of sweeping authority for search and seizure. Economic consequences were even more suffocating. As opposed to the Stamp Act's taxation of goods produced within the colony, this law placed a tax on imports, including beer. This prompted a switch to locally produced beer, providing a much-needed boost to American brewers.

James Otis.

Taxation, seizure of property, and invasion of privacy were provisions of the acts that, along with the impact on beer, prompted the revolutionary leader Samuel Adams and his ally, James Otis, a prominent attorney, to take action. Together, Adams and Otis drafted a letter, adopted by the Massachusetts Assembly, requesting the other colonies join them in formally protesting the Townsend Acts as a violation of the British Constitution.

On receiving news of the Adams-Otis proposal, the royal government demanded the Massachusetts assembly rescind the letter or face an official order to disband. In open defiance, the assembly voted 92 to 17 to refuse the Crown's order. In remembrance, "92" became Massachusetts's patriotic number.

As the situation heated up, citizens with recently awakened political awareness formed associations and groups for formal protest. Needing a place to meet, express views, report news, and form plans, they logically congregated at the community's social center. Within ale houses the seeds of liberty were planted and

Samuel Adams.

nurtured. Beer drinking and politics had an early marriage. In Winchester the protesters met at the Black Horse tavern. It became a frequent meeting place for Samuel Adams and his chief monetary backer, John Hancock. There, over tankards of beer, the idea of independence was born.

Samuel Adams was an austere, simply dressed man. A true American hero, his connection to beer started with his great grandfather, Joseph Adams. In a will dated July 18, 1694, Joseph Adams left the family business, a malt plant, to Samuel's grandfather Peter. Bequeathing the business from father to son was a tradition that eventually installed Samuel as owner. It was the malt house, next to the family home on Purchase Street, that tied Samuel Adams to brewing.

Born in 1722, young Samuel Adams entered Harvard in 1740, and it is difficult not to imagine him claiming his share of the beer. Samuel could speak for himself. A student of the classics, his motto was inspired by Ovid: "principii obsta" or "take a stand from the start."

Encumbered by a shaky hand and quivering voice, Samuel Adams was not destined for great oratory, but that unsteady hand was capable of great writing and planning. Working behind the scenes became Adams's strength. He wrote inflammatory articles and along the way plotted a little sedition. Considered by historians as one of the true masters of revolution, Adams was content to pull strings while encouraging other Sons of Liberty to do the speech-making. Among his peers were Joseph Warren, John Hancock, James Otis, and his cousin, John Adams.

Samuel's job was to plan the attack, secure financial backing, and organize followers. A revolutionary prototypical, he was known for his ability to pull in members and maintain their enthusiasm. Working for him were various rites and rituals he organized as an integral part of membership. Of all those he devised, the favorite was the century-old practice of drinking toasts. At each meeting the Sons of Liberty raised glasses and with zeal drank a ceremonial damnation to the British ministers. Whenever Samuel Adams asked, John Hancock was quick to fund a barrel of ale.

Frustrated by signs of resistance, England tried to make life difficult for the rabble rousers through a variety of methods, most directed at the ringleaders. Often as not, their choice of targets failed. One tactic that backfired was an attempt to financially cripple John Hancock by confiscating his sloop, *Liberty*.

A sloop rigged as a smallish cargo boat, *Liberty* was one of Hancock's profitable trading vessels, plying its trade along the coastal waterways. Commandeering the boat after it docked in Boston, royal officials trumped up charges accusing Hancock of smuggling. They might have succeeded with impounding the ship permanently, but beer stepped in the way.

After confiscating the *Liberty,* the Royal Navy dispatched two warships to Boston harbor. Arriving in Boston shorthanded, the captain of the HMS *Romney* resorted to a common practice for filling billets in the British navy. Ordering a landing party ashore, he directed his men to scour waterfront taverns on a mission to "impress" men into shipboard service. Refusal was equated with treason, so the *Romney*'s party set back to the ship with their unwilling, but thoroughly entrapped, "recruits."

Rallying in their defense, the Sons of Liberty gathered and fortified themselves with a few flagons of beer and rum, then descended on the port, intent upon freeing those impressed. Watching from the moored *Romney* in the harbor, the British captain compounded his mistake by ordering the ship's company to arm themselves and take aim at the crowd. Though they did not fire, this was the first time the English had leveled guns at their own colonists. Sensing the damage done, royal officials made a weak attempt to retain the *Liberty,* but eventually dropped all charges.[3] All in all, the incident further inflamed Bostonians' attitudes against the Crown.

British acts of retribution against the troublemakers got the authorities in London absolutely nowhere. They only served to unite the Americans further. In taverns throughout the colonies, kegs of beer inflamed spirits and emboldened other-wise loyal British subjects to new levels of resistance. Committees of correspondence soon bound the various colonies in agreements of nonimportation, once again endors-ing the plan to hurt the government where it mattered most: in the pocketbook.

Philadelphia was tempted to break the agreement early in its life, but the merchants did not falter. Direct confrontation with the homeland was prompted by a shipment of English malt. In July 1769, the *Charming Polly* tied up at the docks with a shipment addressed to Mr. Amos Strettell. Refusing the shipment, Strettell joined other merchants in a meeting to determine their course of action. On the day after its arrival the Philadelphia brewers issued a joint pledge: "wherein they engage that as the load of malt just arrived was contrary to the agreement of the merchants and traders they will not purchase any part of it, nor will they brew the same, or any part thereof, for any person whatsoever."[4]

Most colonial leaders bristled at the events in Massachusetts. In New Jersey conditions were a bit more complicated. Governor William Franklin was a British-sympathizing Tory whose political beliefs led his famous father, Benjamin, effectively to disown him. Ben Franklin thought his son had turned into a British puppet.

Governor Franklin was attempting to walk a political tightrope. His administration passed an act on December 6, 1769, intended to furnish the "Necessaries for Accommodating the King's Troops."[5] However, with boycotts of English goods and embargoes, colonists were quick to reserve local production of beer for their own use. Even William Franklin, always eager to please the Crown, waffled over giving up beer: "BE IT ENACTED That . . . In Lieu and Stead of Four Pints of Small Beer hereby allowed each Man per day it shall and may be lawful for the said Commissioners to provide and allow to the said troops a Quantity of Molasses not exceeding One Gallon to a Barrel of Small Beer."[6]

Again the local brewing industry reaped the benefits of the embargo. Frequent beer shortages inspired more people to open breweries, and despite their long reliance on imports, the maritime towns and cities were finally supporting the local beer industry. A waiting game developed, with the Crown expecting the colonials to crumble. It didn't happen. Nonimportation was working, and the ports experienced a decrease in business of 45 to 50 percent in Boston and up to 83 percent in New York.

By 1770 the British were starting to feel the pinch, and in a conciliatory gesture repealed the Townsend Acts, except for the tax on tea. Retaining the import tax on tea was a face-saving gesture, but Americans looked at it as a slap in the face. They understood the British point, that London would dictate all policy, and they didn't like it.

Peacefully drinking pints in meeting after meeting, the colonials plotted their response and took their time. Over glasses of beer on December 16, 1773, in the Green Dragon Tavern on Union Street in Boston, Samuel Adams and John Hancock met to conspire and incite. Over the past several months, they had singled out this night for their plot. Quiet settled over the city, bathed in the light of a full moon. One at a time, a band of the Sons of Liberty assembled in the tavern and donned a thin disguise, loosely resembling Indian garb.

Hancock had generously donated barrels of beer, and an enthusiastic following imbibed in preparation for the night's activities. Outside it was cool and brightly moonlit. Knowing that their clothes wouldn't conceal the fact that they were not Indians, they headed for the piers.

On reaching the docks, the company made directly for the ships laden with a cargo of tea. Boarding with the whoops of war cries, they threw the tea into the harbor, committing a physical, if not violent, act of overt rebellion. Though another beverage was the focus, the Boston Tea Party was conceived, planned, and organized over tankards of ale.

When British authorities heard the news, they took it exactly as the Americans intended. The Prime Minister, Lord North, was a master politician who normally maneuvered quietly to attain his desired results, but as events heated up, so did his temper.

North felt the rebellious offspring of North America needed a stern lesson, and that he was just the teacher. The Crown felt the message had to be both strong and have an impact on all colonists. London unleashed a royal "spanking" that became known as the Intolerable Acts. Smugly surrounded by the comforts of London, the King confidently wrote to Lord North, "The dye is now cast. The colonies must either submit or triumph."[7]

First among the Intolerable Acts was an edict called the Boston Port Act. It sealed the city in a commercial blockade intended to bring America's most impassioned colony to its senses. Rather than extinguishing the flames, the act fanned and stoked the fire. England declared the blockade would remain in effect until the colony made "satisfaction" for the ruined cargo and damages to the ships. British hard-liners were convinced the colonists would submit. They were wrong. Confident in their convictions, they ignored Edmund Burke, the great backer of colonial rights, when he spoke in Parliament of the peril in such a policy. He insisted that "rendering that means of subsistence of a whole city dependent upon the king's private pleasure, even after the payment of a fine and satisfaction made, was without precedent, and of a most dangerous Example."[8]

Burke was Parliament's most moderate and accurate voice regarding the American colonies. Perhaps Burke knew the inhabitants would prove even more testy when denied their beer.

In the southern colonies tempers also flared. With each new English demand, hostilities grew more likely. Reaction to the Stamp, Townsend, and Intolerable Acts paralleled those in the North. Southerners boiled in outrage. Drawn together to discuss options, they used the same techniques as had the protesters in Boston.

From the 1760s on, taverns were the hotbeds for political discussion. Long before the Revolution, a Virginian veteran of the British army was preparing to turn his back on former allegiances. Although not a firebrand on the order of Samuel Adams, he matched Adams's resolve, but with a more subdued approach. However, like Adams, he felt the best possible forum for political discussion was over a pint of porter, and in the comfortable confines of a tavern. Seeds of discontent had not merely sprouted, they had taken root. George Washington would see to it the tree grew straight and tall.

The closing of Boston's port and the subsequent boycott of imported goods joined the colonies together in a common cause.

In Virginia, the assembly, behind Patrick Henry, Richard Lee, George Mason, and Thomas Jefferson, along with Washington, designated June 1, 1774, the date the Port Act was to go into effect, as a day of "fasting, humiliation and prayer." Less than amused, the Royal Governor in Williamsburg was so enraged by the resolution that he proclaimed the assembly dissolved. Members left the chambers unfazed, and in short order reassembled at the nearby Raleigh Tavern. In actuality it was probably a much more enjoyable session, because the taps were close by. There, over beer they declared, "an attack on one of our sister colonies, to compel submission to arbitrary taxes, is an attack made on all British America."⁹ They further proclaimed, "That we will not hereafter, directly or indirectly import, or cause to be imported, from Great Britain, any of the goods here- after enumerated, either for sale or for our own use, . . . beer, ale, porter, malt."¹⁰

Bostonians bore up as best they could while the former sup- ply of beer dried up. In a way it was a blessing in disguise, because the shortage once again encouraged the growth of com- mercial brewing. Boston's crisis inspired the colonial committees of correspondence to take more vigorous action than ever before conceived: the call to convene the first Continental Congress.

Following the Boston Port Act, the committees of correspon- dence grew more active. First they rushed supplies to Boston's relief. Next they sent out the call for delegates. All colonies agreed to assemble, and in a move inspired more by reason than chance, they selected the beer-friendly city of Philadelphia for their meeting.

Throughout the deliberations they discussed ways to orga- nize resistance and persuade England to ease its grip. However, though considerably angered at the throne, they weren't quite ready to renounce their status as loyal Englishmen. What they needed was a way to convince England they weren't second- class citizens. They were seeking an acceptable path to both respectability and reconciliation.

Setting out from Boston, the Massachusetts delegates began the long, overland trip to Philadelphia. Boston was one of the leading cities of the times. Its reputation for firebrands and rabble rousing had gained Samuel Adams notoriety and a seat in the

Continental Congress. Traveling with him, his cousin John was another of the colony's delegates.

John Adams was a proud man who aspired to a lofty position. All too often, detractors labeled him as an admirer of the English aristocracy. It was true that John Adams looked forward to the benefits of an advanced station, and he did value the English way of life. But in reality, Adams had a strong affinity for the common man and a passion that burned to protect the rights of his fellow colonists.

Given a choice, John Adams had a fondness for madeira, but he also regularly enjoyed beer and cider. Adams was anxious to arrive in Philadelphia so he could begin deliberations with the brightest and most talented citizens of the colonies, and if his past activities are any indication, to debate in the tavern over a couple of pints.

In a practice repeated throughout the journey, Samuel and John visited taverns all along their route. In Connecticut they stopped at the Hartford Tavern and were entertained "with upwards of thirty Gentlemen of the first character in the place."[11]

They made similar stops, and took refreshment at taverns in New Haven, New York, Princeton, and finally, in Philadelphia.

Carpenters Hall, owned by the guild members of the city, played host to the convention and Samuel and John located it as their first priority. Arriving well ahead of the scheduled September 7, 1774, opening session, they were there before most of the other delegations arrived. Deciding on how to spend the time until the Congress was convened was easy.

With a parched throat and eager to talk politics, John headed where he knew satisfaction awaited for both, at the famous City Tavern.

John Adams must have loved taverns, for he seemed to declare each as being "the most genteel tavern in America." For him they were a place to debate political strategy and a source of good beer—everything he could want. Adams's journals and letters read as if important meetings and a couple of beers were synonymous. On September 2, 1774, he wrote of the arrival of the Virginia delegation and how he, with cousin Samuel, hurried to meet them at the City Tavern.[12] From the very start smoky tavern rooms and deals made over a couple of beers were part of the American political scene.

Observations by John Adams on early American drinking habits extended beyond the tavern and into some of the most prominent homes in the country. Following a dinner at Mr. Miers Fisher's of Philadelphia, John felt obliged to describe the meal. They feasted upon "ducks, hams, chickens, beef, pig, tarts, creams, custards, jellies, foods, trifles, floating islands, beer, porter."[13]

John Adams was not alone. Many of the delegates recorded similar accounts of the hospitality, food, and beer of Philadelphia. If the city's residents schemed to make a good showing, they succeeded. When it came time to determine a site for the Second Continental Congress, the choice was once again Philadelphia. Like the hosting of any other convention, the availability of places to unwind was a major selection factor.

Forming the Continental Congress was not an act of separation from England. It was intended as an act of union, with the purpose of reaching understandings and lasting agreements with the government in London.

But delegates from Massachusetts regarded the Congress differently. They thought the time had come for cutting the transatlantic ties by conducting their own affairs as a free and independent state.

After political compromise, thoughtful deliberations, and consideration of all available alternatives, the Congress did something uncharacteristic by later standards: they took action. Approving a variation of the nonimportation agreement, they constructed a nonconsumption accord to end imports from Great Britain on December 1, 1774. Subsequently, the Congress voted to encourage the population to abstain from imported tea, madeira, and port wine. Of course they granted an exemption for locally produced beer.

It was the punitive effects of the Boston Port Act, and its blockade, that drove southern colonies into alignment with their northern sisters. England's message was clear: the Crown wouldn't hesitate to deal with all colonies in a similar fashion. It was as if the colonies' frustrated leaders had collectively heard a call to arms. George Washington, Patrick Henry, Peyton Randolph, Robert Carter Nichols, and Richard Henry Lee were steadfastly in support of the nonconsumption agreement.

Samuel Adams posted the following bill in Boston:

It is to be hoped, that the Gentleman of the Town will endeavor to bring our own OCTOBER BEER into Fashion again, by that most prevailing Motive, EXAMPLE, so that

Philadelphia's State House in 1778.

we may no longer be beholden to "Foreigners" for a "Credible Liquor," which mayh be as successfully manufactured in this Country.[14]

Abstaining from the comforting supply and quality of English ale was a sacrifice. It must have been especially difficult for Washington, who was a devoted fan of English porter. Brewers benefited from the agreement as they had during the previous periods of disagreement with England. This was an opportunity to eat into the market share of British beers.

Southern colonies had the most to lose by consenting to the nonconsumption agreement. Though of limited capacity, the North had an established brewing industry. Colonists living below the Mason-Dixon line willingly placed their beer mugs in the hands of their fellow Americans.

Shortages became a way of life and the supply of beer reached a near crisis. The early dependence on British beer imports had retarded the growth of southern breweries, and the ominous signs of war foretold of inconsistent shipments from the North. With this in mind, the Virginia legislature concerned itself with the "advancement of American arts and manufactures." Among the recommendations was encouragement of hop and barley farming, because the production of local beer would "tend to render the consumption of foreign liquors less necessary."[15]

A revolution was brewing. Once again the colonies sent delegates to Philadelphia, and a Second Continental Congress was convened on May 10, 1775. Having outgrown the confines of Carpenters Hall, the delegates met up the street, in the Pennsylvania State House, now known as Independence Hall. Despite the growing tension, colonists continued to hope for a peaceful solution to their disagreements with England. They weren't as interested in breaking from the empire as they were in securing what they perceived as basic English rights.

Less than a month after the delegates from the Second Continental Congress met, fighting broke out at Lexington and Concord. Widening differences and growing tensions pushed a small group of alienated colonists into all-out warfare with the largest power in the world at Lexington and Concord. Fortunately, they had at least the making of a rudimentary military. Throughout the colonies' history, defense of the settlements had been the responsibility of volunteer militias. Regular British army troops were never present in large numbers, and when they were, they were preoccupied with chasing the French all over North America. Protecting the rural farms and villages was left to the inhabitants. An army enlisted and trained, with beer as the incentive for their participation.

After the battle of Bunker Hill on June 17, 1775, colonists made one last attempt to reconcile with Britain, offering London a compromise called the Olive Branch Petition, a proposal granting concessions in exchange for a more active role in government. It was rejected. Before them were hard times, suffering, defeats, and the challenge of creating a new government. They faced difficult decisions, but every night the Congressional delegates sought temporary relief from their responsibilities in Philadelphia's taverns.

Five

Beer and the Revolutionary War

Standing guard at the edge of camp was lonely duty. Four-hour shifts had all the appeal of watching grass grow. Once again the sentry checked his powder. Carefully cocking the musket, he flipped open the lock to check the pan, probably the thousandth time he had done it on this watch. While he was out there his fellows were getting their daily beer ration. What a distraction. It wasn't as though he'd get left out, the quartermaster would hold his share. He'd just rather have it now.

From what the young soldier had seen thus far, there was no glamour associated with service in the regular army. On the day he signed up it had seemed different. Standing on the tavern's porch, the recruiting officer had worn a blue uniform trimmed in buff, and his golden buttons had brightly reflected the light of the sun. With one hand resting on a new barrel of ale, the recruiter had urged them all to step forward and lift a tankard to the new army. "Join the Continental Line," he had shouted, "and fight for liberty!" Caught up in the moment, the young man and his friends had all joined. But where was the fighting?

The young soldier placed the musket down within easy reach and scanned the horizon again. Shifting his weight from foot to foot, he thought back on all the "action" he'd seen over the past several months. When the uniforms were first issued he couldn't have been prouder. In those first few weeks he learned all about army life, taught by a European volunteer. They were career officers from the Old World, and sure knew their stuff, but soon the routine of drill became boring. From his point of view, all they'd done was break camp, cross a few rivers, gather supplies, make camp, stand guard, and then repeat the entire process. How much action had he seen? It was more like inaction.

Conditions weren't as good as he had expected, either. Between encampments they slept in the open. Meals were often meager and the best ones were had by foraging. His uniform needed repair, the other members of his company were sick, and where was his relief? At least the army usually made good on its promise of beer.

At the snap of a twig he became alert. "Who goes there?" Adrenaline continued to pump after he heard the password. Why did the next watch always show up when he was daydreaming? No bother, at least it was time for a beer.

Thoughts like these have been common in the military for hundreds of years. Long before the sentry stood his watch, and long after, other soldiers would face the same boredom, and think about beer. Beer was just as important to the army as to society, in general. In colonial America, beer wasn't merely a ration, it was a recruiting tool, and great leaders knew the success of any army depended largely upon the force's ability to act as a unit. For the militia, the discipline and coordinated actions required for battlefield maneuvers were gained through the "drill day." Set aside for training the soldiers, it was an occasion for the outlying troops to gather and socialize.

Giving away beer was a standard colonial method of raising an army, but it had one inherent problem: the social aspect. In a community where the population was normally preoccupied with the constant struggle to maintain an existence, drill day meant a chance to relax and mingle with seldom-seen neighbors. Training day was also the chance to quaff a few beers.

Militiamen were required to study drill, observe military discipline, participate in field exercises, and do a bit of marching. Their second most favorite part of drill day was when they fired a few rounds from their flintlock rifles and muskets. However, the activity that came next was by far the most popular. When the drills were finished it was time for beer. Volunteer soldiers were always anxious to reach this part of the day; they were frequently treated to free beer. From a military viewpoint the actual training received, and the level of sobriety, were always questionable, but everyone in attendance agreed it was a first-rate party.

From the day the colonists landed, defense of their homes, farms, and settlements was a major concern. Far removed from the comforting security of the motherland's large standing army, they had to rely on themselves. As a result, the colonials formed militias, volunteer, part-time armies that would form up for defense in times of crisis. Whether serving in action against other colonial powers, such as in the French and Indian Wars, or stationed in a garrison, the militia expected beer as a guaranteed right in exchange for their service. Practically every soldier had the same thought: they were recruited with beer, they were trained with beer, and by golly they better well receive it when called to lay their lives on the line.

When supplies of beer ran short, the men often turned surly. John Boyd, a member of the militia, recorded the frustration felt by the Massachusetts militiamen, faced with a shortage, in a letter of protest to a government not honoring its commitment to supply beer. At issue was the authority's failure to provide even a crude form of beer:

> Whare as the Solders in Garison belonging to the Province of the Masechesets [sic] Bay have Refused to be at the trifiling Expence of two Pence Per Week Each Man for to have their Molases Brued into bear and have Insised upon haveing Molases Deliverd out to tham Under Protence thay Brew it tham Selues which thay have been Indulged in Some time that they Might So So and it a Pearing now that in Stid of Using the Molases in that way which the Gouernor aford Sd. Desined thay Eat it with thair Vittils to Pregeduce of Thair Helth Thair fore Nomore Molases is to be Deliverd to them.[1]

Troops like these felt beer was the least the colonial governors could provide. When they were cut off their response was close to mutiny.

Armed fighting first broke out between the British army and ordinary citizens, and there, too, beer was involved. On a late winter evening in 1770, a tavern crowd in Boston downed a few pints as they discussed the repressive nature of the latest English taxes. As the beer went down, tempers rose, and the mob spilled into the street. Antagonizing the sentries near Boston's Custom House, they began tossing snowballs and calling threats. Shots rang out and five of the throng fell dead. Legal defense of the soldiers rested upon the talents of John Adams and James Otis. The soldiers were exonerated, but in the process Adams and Otis clearly stated their position against English interference in colonial affairs. Shots had been fired, and there were more to follow. What the "Boston Massacre" made clear was the need for a strong colonial fighting group.

Recruiting and training part-time troops was certainly not the way to maintain an effective fighting force. Despite the enthusiastic attendance at the training day, with its high morale, the reputation of militia forces was poor.

Beer was an inducement, but it was also the root of a problem. Conducting a drill day without the troops falling into a state of unbridled inebriation would have been considered an unusual departure from the norm. Governor Winthrop of Massachusetts, witnessing a drill day conducted entirely sober, was as much surprised as he was overjoyed. Winthrop's satisfaction lasted only as long as it took to dismiss the soldiers from ranks. Immediately after securing the drill, they made for the beer with wild abandon. For the militiamen this was typical. Despite the more important reasons to meet, drill, and practice martial arts, they believed the objective was to make it through the day's drill to the inviting kegs of ale. The British always preferred to fight against the militias with this poor reputation, rather than against the more disciplined Continental Line.

As in the North, southern colonies were similarly disposed to the use of beer as a recruiting tool. Remarking on the nature of the militia, one commander in Virginia recommended the technique of supplying beer on drill day. He said his custom of supplying beer on drill day always prompted his troops to expressions of heart-felt gratitude. Understandably, the results of southern drills were every bit as sorrowful as those in the North.

America holds dear the image of the Minutemen standing defiantly in opposition to stronger British forces. In reality, they were saddled with rag-tag uniforms, inconsistent training, and inferior equipment. Militias represented a curious mix of the simple farmer, independent thinker, citizen-soldier, and patriot. But they had one thing in common: world-class thirst.

The morning after Paul Revere's famous ride borders on allegory. That morning, April 18, 1775, dawned with the British marching in lock step toward the undefended towns of Lexington and Concord. Ominous and threatening, the Redcoats seemed invincible. As they approached the village green of Lexington, a slight mist lifted, revealing a line of American colonists, waiting bravely, prepared to fight for their rights.

Even the best histories neglect to point out another important fact about the Lexington story. Captain Parker, in charge of the American forces, did not establish a headquarters on Lexington Green. Instead, he chose a more logical spot adjacent to the battlefield: the familiar and comforting surroundings of

Buckman's Tavern. Their first encounter showed they could match up against the king's army and bolstered confidence about the nearing hostilities in regards to their fighting ability. By sunset colonial troops had much to celebrate. It must have been a little unsettling. They were engaged in open rebellion against a super power.

At the opening of hostilities, beer's role in the military was not lost on the new Congress. Meeting in Philadelphia, delegates invited beer directly into Independence Hall. Their considerations reached well beyond declaring independence and setting up a new form of self-rule.

Part of the daunting task of fighting a war with England was raising, clothing, equipping, and arming troops. Familiar with the traditional method used in training militia, Congress discussed supplying beer to the soldiers. Positioned firmly as a part of the nation's diet and culture, beer was considered as much an item of war as bullets. Asking soldiers to leave their homes and family for a war of uncertain length was bad enough, asking them to do it without beer was unthinkable. Delegates viewed the issue of beer as a vital need for troops and included beer among the army's authorized rations.

So it was that despite the formidable matters engaging the delegates' attention, beer was on their minds. One of the first laws of the new country directed the army's quartermasters to ensure that each soldier receive a daily ration of beer. Representatives to the Continental Congress passed a resolution supporting that directive on November 4, 1775. It specified that the government was responsible for providing each man under

George Washington.

arms with "1 QT of Spruce beer, or Cider / man / day."[2]

In 1776, less than a year after fighting broke out, the army was completely adjusted to, and expecting, a daily ration of beer. While encamped in Brooklyn, New York brewers were busy satisfying a demand that reached a consumption level in excess of 300 gallons per day.

Later that year, after the colonials were driven from New York, the army settled in for the long, difficult winter at Valley Forge. Throughout the bitter conditions of 1776 and again the next year at Morristown, New Jersey, the army nearly dissolved when faced with inadequate shelter, sickness, and pitifully low supplies.

Fortunately, their leadership was exceptional. Earlier in 1776 the Continental Congress debated the question of who should act as commander of American forces. Their choice came down to two beer drinkers. One was the famous politician of Boston, John Hancock, who actively campaigned for the position. Representing the choice of the southern colonies was a 43-year-old veteran of the French and Indian Wars, George Washington. Selection of Washington was assured when John Adams of Massachusetts endorsed him. Adams may have backed Washington partially for political reasons (both courting and showing unity with the South), but the value he placed on Washington's military experience was one of the many great decisions Adams made during the formation of the country. It placed his personal relationship with Hancock at risk, but it was right for the country.

Quiet and reserved, Washington was a Virginian who had had limited success in his attempts at farming, soldiering, and business, but he had a sharp mind and was quick to analyze situations. His intellect and statuesque frame were invaluable in tavern sessions of politicking. Over tankards of porter and lively conversation, he soon gained a well-deserved reputation.

When considering Washington's many military accomplishments, none stands out more than his ability to hold the army together under miserable conditions. At times he did it by obtaining provisions with his own money. On all too many nights, despite exhaustion, the tired general penned an endless series of dispatches to Congress by candlelight. Each one listed

Landing troops in Boston.

the priorities for keeping his army in the field. His correspondence literally begged for food, clothing, guns, and beer.

Washington's forces weren't alone in their desperation. Early in the war British troops, too, felt the pinch. After Ethan Allen and his Green Mountain Boys captured Fort Ticonderoga, the fort's cannons were moved down country to encircle Boston. Washington, with the aid of the artillery, surrounded the city. Under siege, but not panicking, the British generals sought to calm the troops and maintain morale by establishing contracts with English brewers for shipment of up to 5,000 butts (540,000 gallons) of strong beer.

Eventually the British evacuated Boston, moving their troops to New York. When the city fell, Washington moved south and west into Pennsylvania. On the move, and with supplies stretched thin, a reliable supply of beer was elusive. Growing desperate, many of the soldiers were lured by the much more accessible whiskey. Washington knew morale was low, and nearly agreed to the substitution, but he hesitated, wavered briefly, and then disapproved the switch. Common belief held that consumption of whiskey in the winter was ruinous to the health. More than anything else, Washington was dedicated to the safety, health, and welfare of his army. Washington's temptation to allow whiskey has been described by historian Harry Wildes:

> fearing the effects of too abundant cheap liquor, then . . .
> To discourage the use of whiskey, rum and brandy, prices were raised to four shillings a quart; cider was increased to a shilling a quart; but beer was reduced in cost. Soldiers could buy "small beer" at the sutlery for a

shilling a quart instead of the old market price of a shilling tenpence. No other liquor selling was permitted within seven miles of the camp.[3]

Washington once again issued proclamations banning the sale of whiskey near camps, and remained dedicated to the idea of beer consumption and its healthful effects on the army. He was trying to a guard against drunkenness.

As in other wars, the continental army sometimes took supply and provisioning into its own hands. When pressed by shortages, the troops resorted to less than honorable methods of procurement. John Lowry, a Virginia plantation owner, filed a formal complaint against Colonel Dabney because his command had "taken and distroy'd a great deal of my barley w'ch . . . they have deprived me of the opp'ty of Brewing any Beer w'ch is the only way I had to get a little money to enable me to discharge my taxes. They took my Brewhouse and Break my locks whenever they are opposed."[4]

Sayings usually have at least some basis in truth. For the military, the old saw "an army travels on its stomach," fits. With beer considered a major source of nutrition, the colonial army demanded constant replenishment. Blockades were in place beginning after the first shots. Imports were virtually eliminated and colonial breweries rushed to make up the deficit. War-induced shortages contributed as much as or more than any other factor in creating the demand for locally produced beer. Blockades enforced by the English navy helped secure a future for the fledgling American brewing industry.

Appreciating the importance of a daily beer ration, the army granted that consideration on prisoners of war. In a humanitarian gesture, the Continental Army, when possible, provided beer to its captives. In Lancaster, Pennsylvania, a regimental paymaster visiting captured Hessian troops left an account of this in his report, dated May 31, 1777: "Of provisions, each prisoner receives daily, one pound of bread and one pound of meat, besides a weekly ration of six glasses of beer."[5]

Supply of the troops was, of course, often spotty. Throughout the war people were as occupied with obtaining a source of beer as they were with winning freedom. To ease the trouble of both civilians and army alike, Franklin proposed to solve a new problem with an old answer. He provided a home-brew recipe, obtained in France, for the production of spruce beer. (See his recipe in chapter 12.)

Essence of spruce was added in place of hops, which were also in short supply. Spruce, like hops, acted as a preservative and had the side benefit of an appealing aroma. As a substitute it was not unusual: ancient cultures and colonials alike commonly used herbs, spices, and tree bark to preserve and balance beer. Spruce achieved the same ends. (Some Nordic countries continue to use juniper in this method.) Hop harvesting in colonial America was dependent upon wild varieties growing in the woods and imports from England. With the overseas supply cut off, it was up to the locals to identify acceptable substitutes.

It seems natural for beer to have been on America's collective mind throughout the war, either how to get it or how to make money off it. Soldiers thought about beer while they drank daily rations, and thought about it more when the allowance didn't materialize. Some, like Thomas Peters, conceived of brewing operations that would make fortunes supplying the army. Peters completed his enlistment and started plans to build a large brewery in Baltimore. He was certain fortune lay in servicing the Continental and French troops. Years later he wrote of his plans:

> I then formed the plan, which I established in Baltimore, of a Brewery on the most extensive scale of any in America, for the purpose of brewing to serve the American and French troops, for which we had contracted to do, counting that the contest would be determined to the southward and that we could supply them by water.[6]

But others also recognized the potential profits to be made during the conflict, and sprang into action. Commercial brewery expansion and the end of hostilities ended Peters's dream before construction of his brewery could begin: "But all things prove the uncertainty of all sublunary things—before I could get to work, happily for my country, peace and independence took place—to the failure of my plans, as the brewery was by far upon too large a scale for the use of Baltimore."[7] Brewers unencumbered by army service stepped forward to fill the gap. Peters's moment had passed.

Warfare continued, and shifting battle lines, irregular supply routes, and expansion of breweries resulted in unpredictable inventories. On the home front, beer was usually available, but there were occasional disruptions in obtaining the daily liquid bread. John Hancock received provisions throughout the war.

His records show that between December 1778 and April 1783 beer was delivered by one Andrew Johonot. Hancock had a long and productive relationship with Johonot, and despite the fighting, purchased an average of more than 30 gallons of beer per month. Another proof of the availability of beer was a present George Washington received from Caleb Dais, Speaker of the House in Massachusetts. It was a sizable shipment of beer. Sincerely touched, the general took time from the busy pace around his Dobbs Ferry, New York, headquarters to write Davis of his delight and gratitude while satisfying his thirst.

Central to all the fighting was the "highway of America," the Hudson River. Before the war it was the one easy transportation route for moving goods economically and with greater payloads than all road shipping combined. Flowing from near Canada down past the island of Manhattan, the Hudson River was the king of hauling. During the war it was invaluable both for moving troops and shielding Washington from the British.

Though New York was blessed with the river, they weren't always able to take advantage of it to ship beer. In fact, it sometimes worked against them. Strategically important, control of the Hudson was coveted by each of the combatants. For both armies it was a way to rapidly deploy troops, and for tactically minded Washington, underrated as a general, it was one of the essential elements of his campaign. Survival of the American forces depended upon the careful selection of terrain, allowing Washington the advantage of dictating when and where battles were fought. Key to his war plan was the use of river hopping, which placed the geographical barrier of the river between the army and its British opponents.

During the fighting, availability of British imports, including beer, was wholly dependent on which side held the Hudson. But bigger issues were at stake. Washington was well aware that the Hudson River provided the English with "an easy pass to Canada" which they could use to effectively divide the country. The Hudson's importance as a supply route, its role in augmenting the quick movement of troops, and its location near the center of the colonies kept Washington on maneuvers in the area of New York and New Jersey throughout the war. As a result, the area north of Manhattan changed hands frequently. British supply dumps constantly restocked with imports of English beer became attractive targets. Washington could hardly be blamed if he evacuated each time the supply of beer ran low; why not let the British refill the fridge?

Working against Washington was the fact that the importance of the river to his campaign told the British exactly where to find the Continental Army. It provided them with opportunities to trap the rebels.

At the Battle of Brooklyn Heights, Washington remained a bit too long in Brooklyn, but through a series of brilliant maneuvers and rearguard actions, he managed to extricate his troops. Of course, leaving early would have meant walking away from beer. By this point in the war New York breweries, spurred on by a combination of patriotism and profit motive, had increased production to serve the army. Production in the city and immediate area easily matched the 200 to 300 barrels consumed by the army each day. For an army of 10,000, this amounts to about a gallon for each soldier per day. Soldiering worked up a powerfully dry throat.

Among Washington's least recognized but most valuable skills was locating his encampments within reach of a supply of beer. Though often limited, it was typically near at hand. On those occasions when troops couldn't obtain beer through the normal channel of the general mess, they were able to obtain it by a variety of other means. Soldiers in need of a beer usually found it in a tent pitched by an independent supplier. Called "suttlers," they operated as freelancers, under the premise of serving the army. In fact they were profiteers.

In New York, Washington was continuously troubled by volunteers from rural areas, who tended to purchase a bit too much from the "suttlers store." Frequently it was whiskey, not beer, that was the problem. Eventually things got so bad with whiskey and gin that Washington addressed the suttler problem directly. Time and again he was forced to issue a general order barring them from selling spirits near the camp. Each time, however, he exempted beer. Perhaps he was influenced by his own taste for porter and ale, or maybe he was convinced by the views of his personal physician, Dr. Benjamin Rush, who insisted that beer was one of the most healthful drinks a person could consume.

Beer was also present during the time when the Revolution came closest to taking Washington's life. Fraunces Tavern in New York was one of the general's favorite spots to unwind, both during and after the war. Phoebe Fraunces, daughter of owner Sam (a freed black), was credited with foiling an assassination attempt on Washington's life. She overheard the plotters as they overindulged and grew loud. Maintaining her composure, she made a quiet exit and informed the general's staff.

Fraunces was also the host when the New York Legislature invited the army's general staff to a closed-door session on June 8, 1776. Their receipt from the event lists purchases of "Porter 23/ -Cyder 37/- Spruce [beer] 4/6."[8] According to Captain Caleb Gibbs of Washington's staff, the evening consisted of festivities during which "many patriotic toasts were offered and drank with the greatest pleasure and decency. . . . all the under officers . . . seemed much animated. . . . Our good General Putnam got sick and went to his quarters before dinner was over."[9] (Putnam was well regarded for his beer-based recipe for flip.)

Soldiers fighting in the Revolution encountered a variety of hardships. The odds were stacked against them, and danger reached beyond the range of musket balls. Colonial troops were poorly equipped and inadequately provisioned, and had only the crudest of health care. Casualties from sickness far outnumbered deaths on the battlefield. Taking sick, even in the safety of camp, often proved fatal. Members of the general staff studied the reports and knew their greatest enemy was anything that attacked the health of their troops. For that reason, they attempted to provide the best conditions possible. Although quarters, clothing, and food were often poor, they did everything possible to ensure the army received the one thing they were sure was healthy: beer.

Beer's role in the army was understandable as a reflection of the value placed on it in society. North American culture followed the example set in England. Customs, beliefs, and values were the same on both continents. People knew beer was good. It was an irrefutable truth and it stuck with them, and comforted them, through the worst moments of the war. It would also last long after the fighting was over.

Although engaged against the world's largest super power, the colonials successfully carried out a guerrilla war—one fought on their own terrain and on their terms. As the fighting dragged on, Britain was bled dry by a war of attrition. English generals fought at the end of a fragile supply line that stretched over 3,000 miles of the Atlantic Ocean. Wholly dependent on England for replenishment, they were caught in an unwanted and costly fight.

When the colonies established an alliance with France, it signaled the end of British hopes for holding onto North America. Washington pinned down British General Cornwallis on the Yorktown Penninsula, and French warships insulated the British army from their supply line. Surrender was unavoidable.

When peace came, Washington remembered the warm hospitality of New York. Before heading for home and the benefits of liberty, Washington and his staff gathered together one last time. For their farewell celebration they chose Fraunces Tavern. Almost overcome with emotion, Washington conducted his famous farewell to arms amongst pints of beer. Washington might have been saddened at leaving such a comfortable taproom, but he'd be back.

Six

LIFE, LIBERTY, AND THE
PURSUIT OF PORTER

Postwar Beer

Daylight faded into darkness as the brewer closed the door. After latching it shut he turned toward home. It had been a long day in the brewery, and it was one of those days full of problems. Of course everything had somehow worked out, and despite all the trouble, and the fact that he faced a long night of work at home, his mood was chipper.

Though the walk from the brewery was short, it was nearly dark when he walked in the door. His wife greeted him with a customary peck on the cheek and a hasty hug. While putting away his things she outlined the evening's plans. Apologizing for the light meal, she reminded him that it was by his instructions, that he had told her there was a lot of preparation to complete. He smiled and reassured her that was correct, they'd dine quickly this evening and get to work.

When the table was cleared they pulled out sheets of paper and painted signs proclaiming the merits of locally made beer. Dried, they were tacked to a signboard he'd carry tomorrow. Next they selected his clothing. It was actually pretty simple: he was to wear an outfit similar to what the rest of his colleagues had decided upon. Still, they wanted to make sure everything looked just so. Out came his best black shoes with brass buckles, with them went a pair of brown pants, a white shirt, and a vest, all topped by a hat. Some barley and hops strung in a type of garland-like sash were the accessories. Festivities would be grand—after all, the worst was over. It was time for a celebration.

People like the brewer were ready for better days. Building a young country was a strain on everyone, but the benefits made it all worthwhile. True, the economy could have been more stable, and access to manufactured products easier, but they were no longer trapped in the yoke of serving a foreign power. In fact, liberation helped the economy, and people in jobs like brewing profited from a lingering backlash against England.

Disdain for English products, including beer, continued after the fighting. Retaining currency in America, by purchasing American goods, kept money in circulation and everyone profited. "Buy American" became one of the first official policies in the government.

Although the stage seemed set for breweries to expand rapidly, it was during the period directly following the Treaty with Britain that beer faced its biggest challenge. In one respect it was a domestic challenge, but viewed in another way it was foreign.

112

A cider mill.

From the earliest days of the colonies, farmers had difficulty growing English barley, and although American varieties were beginning to flourish, New Englanders saw an opportunity for an economical and tasty alternative. Occasionally beer was difficult to purchase, and they thought they had finally discovered a reasonable substitute. A relative of the rose, apples weren't native to America, but the trees took well and bore abundantly. What to do with the generous harvest got the New Englanders thinking.

Knowledge of cidermaking had come with them from the Old World. As a beverage there cider was well established and had a long history. Charlemagne had promoted cider as a healthy drink, and cidermaking developed in Europe parallel to beer brewing.

The American climate was perfect for apple trees. Better yet, it seemed ready made for cider drinking. New England's cold, crisp weather was ideal. It complemented cider and in the process, secured its position as a popular drink. Even without war-related shortages of malt, cider would undoubtedly have gained its share of popularity. Cider production was uncomplicated. Ease in manufacturing and a plentiful supply of apples made cider inexpensive and soon placed it on an equal footing with beer.

Production of hard cider expanded rapidly as orchards matured. For some regions, apples became the undisputed crop of choice. In 1721, one New England village consisting of only 40 families pressed and fermented more than 3,000 barrels of hard cider.

Although it never quite replaced beer as America's favorite alcoholic beverage, cider made serious inroads on beer's share of the market. Revolutionary leaders, famous for their love of beer, regularly imbibed a glass or two of cider. In the mid-1800s, when describing his grandfather John, Charles Francis Adams reported that the former president started every morning with a large tankard of cider as his breakfast draught.[1]

There was no reason to doubt Charles Francis Adams's report, John Adams mentioned it himself in diary entries made between July and August 1778. It was an unseasonably warm summer and his wife, Abigail, was worried that the scorching heat would ruin hopes of the orchard turning out even a single barrel of cider. For John the news was distressing, as they counted on a good apple crop.

Cider's appeal, like beer, was felt by all classes. Ben Franklin was best known for his love of wine and beer, but now and again he demonstrated a fondness for cider. John Hancock, another beer and wine drinker, followed a breakfast routine similar to that of Adams, tossing back a pint of cider each morning before breakfast. Although the orchards and presses were located primarily in New England, consumption was common throughout the country. Residents of the Mid-Atlantic states were every bit as likely to drink cider as their New England neighbors, and nicknamed their version "Jersey Lightning." People in Maryland and Virginia also drank cider, and it spread with the frontiersmen to outposts in Ohio and Tennessee.

Far-reaching though its influence became, New England was cider's real home. Long before cooking with beer became fashionable, cider was gracing Yankee tables. A favorite meal was baked ham in cider. This was made by "soaking the ham overnight in cider then placing in a 350° oven while basting with cider. Remove the skin and cover with a paste of brown sugar, mustard, dry bread crumbs, and stud with cloves. Return to the oven and bake 1/2 hour more basting again with cider."[2]

Another recipe was for chicken, "salted, peppered, dusted with flour, sautéed in butter 'till golden brown followed by stirring in cider, bringing the whole to a boil, adding one whole onion and simmer for forty minutes. Remove the onion, stir in two thirds cup of heavy cream and thicken."[3]

Consumption of cider, like beer, spread through the full spectrum of life and was visible at all the same occasions on which colonists served beer. Breakfast, lunch, dinner, funerals, weddings, meetings, and barn raisings were all acceptable times for a pitcher of cider. Because it was considered in the same category of healthy beverages as beer, new mothers frequently nursed their infants on cider.

Part One

James Madison.

Near the end of the 1700s cider had gained enough popularity in New England that it left some breweries with an excess of beer, which was shipped to southern states. All that changed rapidly in the early 1800s, when one of the country's several prohibition movements led to large-scale abandonment not only of cidermaking, but of entire orchards of apples.

Cider challenged, but never replaced, beer as king. Ale had a secure position, and what helped keep it there was the use of beer as a base for mixed drinks, essentially the 1700s version of a cocktail. Along with regular consumption of beer itself, beer drinks were a factor that contributed to the continued expansion of the brewing industry. Beer's future was assured by its enduring popularity, and by an unofficial endorsement as the favorite drink of Congress. Beer repaid the favor.

During the war years, members of Congress debated, deliberated, mused, and legislated in the State House during the day, and at taverns in the evening. Their job complete at the cessation of hostilities, they went home, but not for long. Soon they returned to Philadelphia, this time drawn together by the impossible difficulties resulting from the attempt to coordinate the actions of 13 independent-minded states adrift in a sea of self-interest.

116

Although bound by the Articles of Confederation from the end of the war on, the separate states slowly acknowledged that the paper government was toothless. Seeking a solution drew them back to another convention in Philadelphia. It opened in May 1787 for yet another try at forging a nation.

Arriving in Philadelphia, an ordinary looking delegate from Virginia selected the Indian Queen Tavern for his quarters. During the course of the convention he would sit either in the taproom or in his chambers at night and record the thoughts that made him the "diarist" of the Constitutional Convention. From May to September he recorded the great debate and dialogue leading to the establishment of one of the most remarkable constitutions ever devised.

James Madison described the manner in which delegates worked hard through every long, exhausting day. He also recorded the real progress accomplished at night.[4] Each evening weary delegates unwound in Philadelphia's taverns. That was where behind-the-scenes deals resolved many of the differences between states. Unofficial get-togethers in the barrooms of the City Tavern, the George, the Black Horse, and the Indian Queen were where the real agreements were reached. This made sense because it was the one time of day when the representatives put aside their differences and raised glasses of beer in friendship.

Eating and drinking served as the most significant social activity during the Constitutional Convention. Visiting Frenchman Moreau de Saint-Mery reported on what was typical:

At about two o'clock . . . Their dinner consists of broth, with a main dish of English roast surrounded by potatoes.

Following that are boiled green peas, on which they put
butter which the heat melts, or a spicy sauce; then baked
or fried eggs, boiled or fried fish, salad . . . pastries, sweets
. . . For desert they have a little fruit, some cheese and a
pudding. The entire meal is washed down with Cider,
weak or strong beer.[5]

Of all the after-hours meetings at the Constitutional
Convention, none was more important than the meeting that
took place downstairs from Madison's room on June 30, 1787. It
also ranks as one of the most significant meetings in American
history. Compromises from that meeting determined the structure of the U.S. government.

To the Federalists at the convention, the solution to the awk-
wardly running confederation was to merge the states into one
nation, strongly bound by a central seat of government.
Opposing this plan were the problems of individual identity and
political power.

Smaller states like Rhode Island, Connecticut, and Delaware
were wary of the influence wielded by the more populous states
of New York and Virginia, especially if representation in the government was based upon population. Larger states had no intention of granting equal power to their much smaller neighbors.

Delegates were stalled on this point, and in an attempt to
break the stalemate, representatives of each side came together
on the evening of June 30, 1787, in the Indian Queen tavern.
That night Roger Sherman of Connecticut was invited by John
Rutledge of Virginia to see if they could work out an agreement.
As described by the eminent historian, Charles Mee, in *The*

Genius of the People, the meeting took place "At the Indian Queen on the evening of June 30 . . . amidst the temptations of pipes and bowls, cards and dice, rum and beer."[6]

Roger Sherman.

The delegates arrived at a settlement that brought large and small states into agreement. The Indian Queen was the place where the idea for a legislative body consisting of a "house" and a "senate" was born. Smaller states felt safe knowing the Senate provided them equal power, while larger states had the house of representatives as the avenue to exert their influence. Thus, American government was designed and born among the pints at the Indian Queen ale house.

The framers of the Constitution surely realized they had accomplished something momentous. Some thought that undoubtedly events of that magnitude occurred but once in a millennium. After the members solemnly signed the document, General Washington, who presided over the affair, noted in his diary that delegates could think of no better way to conclude this auspicious occasion: "The business being closed, the members adjourned to the City Tavern."[7]

For what they had accomplished, the representatives deserved a beer. Only one obstacle remained. Their agreement specified that the plan had to be adopted (ratified) by at least three-quarters of the states. Ten states would have to approve of the constitution for the country to unite.

Ratification of the Constitution proceeded slowly, and with considerable debate. One by one the states voted. As each state approved the Constitution, excitement mounted. New Hampshire was the ninth state to ratify, and when news of that vote reached Philadelphia, plans to commemorate approval by the critical tenth state began.

Celebrations for ratification of the Constitution were planned as the biggest holiday the country had seen. Members of the organizing committee were drawn from every walk of life, and virtually every guild assisted in the planning. All that remained was a yes vote from one more state.

Finally, on the June 26, 1788, the City of Philadelphia learned that a group of Virginians led by George Washington, James Madison, Henry Lee, John Marshall, and Edmund Randolph had succeeded in obtaining the unconditional approval of the Constitution. Unbounded joy rolled through the city, and the party kicked off in a mood of patriotic fervor.

Dawn broke on a perfect day for the celebration. It was as clean, bright, and sunny a day as any could remember. Organizers looked upon the weather as a sign of divine consent. Bolstered by the cooperation of the elements, they started the day's first event.

Unequaled in North America at that time, the "Grand Procession" was a parade of bands, the militia, and assorted dignitaries that marched to the approval of the crowds. Interspersed were commemorative man- and horse-powered floats. Guildsmen also marched in groups according to trade.

Each group found a way to incorporate the magic number "10," representing the 10 states that had ratified. Floats captured this theme in a variety of ways. One float portrayed the facade of a great building, with 10 finished pillars and three more unfinished ones positioned to support the structure. Other groups, including the guilds, used the number in similar fashion.

Marching in position number 40, between the barbers and sugar refiners, were the brewers. To maintain the theme they numbered 10. Headed by Rueben Haines, each carried a malting shovel and mashing oar. In their hats were 10 shoots of barley and they wore sashes of hop vines. Among them was brewer Luke Morris, who carried a banner decorated with the brewers' arms, which displayed the motto "Homebrew'd is Best."

Dr. Benjamin Rush wrote to a friend that he was pleased to report it was a day completely void of spirituous liquors. Organizers had banned rum and whiskey; only beer and cider were permitted. After the parade ran its course the celebrants gathered at Bush Hill for a "Cold Collation" (a picnic) washed down with "American Porter, American Beer, and American Cider." Events ran with such smoothness that a newspaper report of July 23, 1788, was effusive in its praise:

> A correspondent wishes that a monument could be erected in Union Green with the following inscription . . . "In Honour of American Beer and Cyder, It is hereby recorded for the information of strangers and posterity that 17,000 assembled in this Green on the 4th of July 1788 to celebrate the establishment of the Constitution of the United States, and that they departed at an early hour without intoxication or a single quarrel. They drank nothing but Beer and Cyder." Learn Reader to prize these

121

invaluable liquors and to consider them as the companions of these virtues which can alone render our country free and reputable.[8]

Philadelphia remained a brewing power, and by 1790 it had breweries clustered around a street aptly named Brewers Alley, all ready to fill the needs of a thirsty and thankful population. Brewers in other parts of the country needed help, and it came from a strange source: a tax.

James Madison, during his congressional term in 1789, sought to increase support for U.S. brewers, and introduced legislation that imposed a tax on all foreign-made beers. This served a dual purpose by also raising revenue for the war-depleted treasury.

In spite of the change, old habits remained hard to break. People were accustomed to ordering their beer from the established breweries in England. With the conflict put aside, some people wanted to return to the old familiar routine. With beer it wasn't so much a matter of ending consumption as it was altering the source of supply. George Washington, who became the first U.S. president in April 1789, tried to modify his own purchasing practices. He fully supported the local effort, and described to his war-time friend, Lafayette, the types of goods available: "We have already been too long subject to British Prejudices. I use no porter or cheese in my family, but such as is made in America: both these articles may now be purchased of an excellent quality."[9]

Washington voluntarily continued to follow this policy throughout his presidency. Correspondence and records of purchases reveal Washington's favorite beer and brewery. From 1790 on, official letters frequently referred to Washington's preference.

From the capital his aide Tobias Lear directed buying for the president. Well-crafted porter was a priority. In preparing for one presidential vacation, Lear wrote, "Will you be so good as to desire Mr. Hare to have if he continues to make the best Porter in Philadelphia 3 gross of his best put up for Mount Vernon? As the President means to visit that place in the recess of Congress and it is proba-

The first presidential mansion, at Pearl and Cherry Streets in New York City.

ble there will be a large demand for Porter at that time."[10]

In the period immediately following the war, New York brewing ran at or above the rate of growth of other states. Government officials enjoyed the city's beer even as debate arose about the proper location for a national capital. Seeking to appease all parties and in the process hold together a shaky union, they struck a compromise: the North and the South selected a geographically central site. Situated on swampy ground, it was an unlikely place for the seat of a government. More than 10 years passed before a single building was completed, but elected officials were confident they were planning a city of monuments that would some day rival any capital in the world.

Selected to act as the temporary capital, New York was fully capable of meeting the beer-drinking demands of thirsty representatives. Not far from where Peter Stuyvesant had walked along the fortifications and contemplated North America's first beer tax, George Washington and John Adams were sworn in as the country's first team of top executives.

123

Samuel Fraunces's tavern.

The return to public service filled Washington with mixed feelings. He had spent too many years in the army and away from his farm in Virginia. Yet once again he was persuaded to answer a call to serve.

Taking the oath of office in New York, Washington recalled his best times and meals, and gratefully appointed Samuel Fraunces as first official steward for the presidential mansion.[11] Perhaps Washington knew he could count on Fraunces for a steady supply of his favorite drink, porter.

Samuel Fraunces's tavern remains in operation to this day in lower Manhattan. Now designated a national landmark, it continues to serve both food and beer. George Washington would feel right at home. Porter is served in the same room in which he used to plan military campaigns, reach political agreements, enjoy a beer, and take his meals.

While Washington ruled in the East, a large portion of the country was moving westward. As they did, brewers followed to supply the ever-growing population. At times the brewers arrived first, accurately anticipating where a population center would be built. On the western end of Pennsylvania, Pittsburgh was just such a town, poised to develop a brewing heritage as it built its city.

As early as 1795, following the Whiskey Rebellion, a Scotsman named Peter Shiras decided that Pittsburgh needed a brewery. His plan was to satisfy the seemingly unquenchable demand for ale and porter of both the city's residents and the passing tide of settlers heading west. Located at the confluence of the Allegheny and Monongahela Rivers, the brewery was constructed on the point of land where the rivers met. Within 20 years the city could boast four breweries and a street named Brewhouse Alley. Sadly, people attending Three Rivers Stadium have little awareness that the stadium sits on the old brewery site.

Boosting the profits of Pittsburgh were the swarms of settlers journeying down the Ohio River to western lands. Flat boats about to make the trip were loaded down with all manner of provisions, and in keeping with tradition, beer was included. Westward travel was a boon for the growing river town.

Downriver another city was born from similar origins. Cincinnati was founded on the banks of the river and located where the path of overland emigrants and flat boats intersected. It was a natural stop before heading on to the Mississippi River and westward up the Missouri River.

First settled in 1788, Cincinnati was built on land purchased by New Jersey Congressman John Cleves Symmes. Like others of his time, Symmes was speculating on the vast tracts of western lands. Congressman Symmes guessed correctly; the city grew rapidly. As did other brewing centers, Cincinnati based its brewery construction on the enthusiastic support provided by the many Germans who came to call the Ohio River town their home. One of the city's neighborhoods grew so populated it was nicknamed the "Over the Rhine" section of town.

With anxious customers waiting, breweries sprang up all over town. Davis Embree was the first to recognize the opportunity, and he opened Cincinnati's first brewery at 75 Water Street just prior to 1810. With customers in place, the brewery grew quickly. By 1816 it had a considerable output. David Thomas wrote of the operation: "Embree. The works now in a progressive state, are now sufficiently extensive to produce annually five thousand barrels of beer and porter, and the quality is excellent."[12]

Though credited as first, Embree wasn't alone for long. By the time Thomas visited in 1816, other breweries were beginning to appear. An 1815 report by Daniel Drake outlined the extent of the city's brewing: "Their products are beer, porter and ale, of a quality at least equal to that of the Atlantic States. Large quantities have been exported to the Mississippi, even as far as New Orleans, the climate of which they are found to bear very well."[13]

Though acquiring a considerable population, Cincinnati was never considered a terminus. It was a by-way that traders, pioneers, and businessmen passed through on the way west. Some turned north on their way to the area around southern Lake Michigan. An inviting place, the flat fertile land on the south shore of that Great Lake beckoned many farmers and settlers.

Even more valued was Lake Michigan's access to the rest of the interconnecting Great Lakes and a network of rivers that provided convenient transportation to a sizable portion of the interior frontier. In the coming century, two towns would develop on the western shore of Lake Michigan, one called Chicago and the other Milwaukee. As they grew famous, breweries would bring beer to them as well.

At the close of the century, the older American cities enjoyed an established brewing industry. New York brewers grew faster than any others, thanks to a large local following that was not as distracted by cider as were their neighbors in New England. They also shipped beer to southern colonies, which further bolstered business. The only thing that could hold New York brewers back was the limited supply of fresh water. And eventually, it did.

As the eighteenth century ended, commercial industry was growing, and beer had positioned itself, along with cider, as the country's favorite drink. In general, the public still held to several beliefs about beer drinking. First, that it was better than drinking water. Second, that beer was a foodstuff and a healthful supplement to the entire family's diet. And third, that beer drinking was an acceptable way to promote social discourse, with an overall positive impact on the community.

The end of the colonial period was by no means an end to the country's troubles. America had yet to face the development of an economy and establishment of foreign alliances. Many of these issues were hammered out by the Constitutional Convention in Philadelphia; through it all, beer was the one thing they agreed on.

Seven

THE NATION AND BREWERIES EXPAND

The Early 1800s

Rising from bed, the vice president dressed quickly. He was excited, for it wasn't every day a new century started, and Thomas Jefferson intended to enjoy every bit of it. Walking over to the window, he took in the view of a new age.

In the middle of his term in the country's number two position, Jefferson was disturbed by the deterioration of his friendship with the president, John Adams. Their disagreement over the scope and power of the central government had opened an ever-widening gulf between them. Eventually they would heal those wounds, but not until both were long out of office.

Jefferson took another look out of the window and headed downstairs to check on the plans for New Year's Day. Known mostly as a wine drinker, he was, however, an avid homebrewer. He planned on having a beer and thought about what the next hundred years held in store for the young nation. There were problems, things weren't perfect, but the vice president was excited about the country's prospects. They'd been through so much, surely destiny held something special for this land.

During the 1800s America experienced a period of remarkable change. Page Smith used the term "The Nation Comes of Age" in his extensive history of that era. Progressing from a loosely formed confederation of former colonies, the country grappled with difficulties in building an economy, formed a strong central government, embraced industrialization, received the first surge of immigrants from a strife-ravaged Europe, and struggled through divisive social issues. As it coped with these issues and more, the nation created the foundation that would launch it into the status of world power by the latter part of the century. At the same time, changes in American life shaped the beer drinking habits of citizens and overall consumption of the beverage.

Already firmly entrenched in American life, beer's popularity was increased by conditions in Germany. Political unrest and oppression drove thousands of Germans to seek relief from persecution in the United States. This group of new arrivals quickly assimilated into the new land, but hung on to the customs and tastes of home.

Americans welcomed the newcomers with reservations. Already the country was wrestling with the conflict arising between their ideals and their biases. Stumbling along, they accepted the immigrants, at times only reluctantly. To their credit, the Germans overcame the stigma of outsider quicker than most other ethnic groups.

Perhaps it was because they brought beer with them. From that time on many an American has been thankful they did.

In the first part of the century it was fashionable for Europeans to travel through the new country and make observations on its development. Visitors' journals described the countryside, customs, and culture of the people. They also reported on the best places to get a beer. One of the first in the wave of tourists landing on U.S. shores was Frenchman Louis Phillipe. In his *Diary of my Travels in America,* he recorded on April 12, 1797, how his party looked forward to visiting German settlements because "Beer is available in these German homes, and theirs are the only inns where we have been able to buy it."[1]

In general, the quality of homebrew was always suspicious, but the Germans had a well-deserved reputation for quality. The significance of Phillipe's observation was that he was probably drinking German alt-style beer, which owed much of its character to cold lagering. It was no doubt smoother in contrast to the more readily available ale and porter. Indeed, Americans' love affair with German beers began with those first sips of their homebrewed beer.

In early 1801 Jefferson was sworn in as the country's third president. His concern for the health of the nation extended well beyond the balance in the treasury and status of the army. Jefferson believed the state of a nation was directly tied to the welfare of its citizens, and he was concerned. He had noticed a disturbing trend in American drinking habits. Excessive consumption of whiskey seemed to have created a nation of drunkards. Jefferson was determined to undertake a course of corrective action. He was convinced all he need do was to increase production and availability of what his countrymen really wanted: beer. Writing about beer to a friend, he explained: "I wish to see this beverage become common instead of Whiskey which kills one third of our citizens and ruins their families."[2]

Jefferson, like many of his contemporaries, believed beer was a temperance drink. Shifting people back to the healthful benefits of beer and away from the debilitating effects of spirits seemed the most logical course of action. Jefferson invited a number of brewers from Bohemia, now the Czech Republic, to train brewers in the United States.

Although George Washington was a well-known lover of beer and had his own brewing recipe, the title of America's first brewer fits Jefferson more accurately. At Monticello the architectural drawings included space for a brewery. Designed by Jefferson's own hand, the brewery was located near the kitchen, under the south pavilion. Martha Jefferson undoubtedly was involved in its layout, including the large masonry fireplace.

After her mother's death, Martha, Jefferson's daughter, moved back into Monticello to look after her father. In addition to running the household and estate, she was the brewmaster. Her first batch brewed at Monticello was recorded shortly after her arrival there. Brewing's importance in her life was reflected in a notation dated September 17, 1813, which shows that she interrupted settling-in chores to brew 15 gallons of beer.

An accomplished brewer, Martha Jefferson's beer was probably one of the better examples of its day. She insisted on avoiding substitutes and aggressively sought supplies of hops. Her accounts for kitchen expenses list frequent purchases of hops, and she proudly noted bargains such as "bought 7 lbs of hops with an old shirt."[3]

Today the commercial bulk price for hops hovers near $3.50 a pound, and the trade of an old shirt for seven pounds of hops would still be a great bargain. Hops were an essential ingredient in what was most likely "small beer." Small beers were low in alcohol and intended as table beer. Brewed with wheat, they were aged a little less than a week, only long enough to ferment.

Well known and respected as a brewer, Martha Jefferson's beer was a treasured part of any visit to Monticello. So much was served to staff and guests that she made over 170 gallons in her first year there—enough for more than 1,800 glasses of beer. Possessed of an endlessly curious mind, Thomas Jefferson was considered the ultimate student and master of nearly everything he touched, but he came in second to his daughter as a brewer. Indeed, Martha Jefferson became so proficient a brewer that her famous father had a hard time keeping up, especially when it came to bottling.

By January 1814 Jefferson was nearly awash in beer. He was confronted with a problem that has always confounded home-brewers: not enough bottles. In Jefferson's time a severe shortage of glass made bottles scarce. Writing to friends, he mentioned the brewing of a year's supply of strong malt beer with no way to bottle it. Jefferson was actively involved in the search for bottles because Martha Jefferson had him hooked on brewing. Even as she excelled with beer, Thomas Jefferson unsuccessfully attempted to establish a winery. He was both appreciative and enthusiastic about her beer reserve, going so far as to mention it in correspondence inviting James Madison to a fall brewing session.[4]

Thomas Jefferson.

Interest in beer prompted Jefferson to pursue additional knowledge. Like his contemporaries Adams, Franklin, Washington, and others, Jefferson took pride in his library. Heavily laden shelves spanned a broad range of subjects. As brewing wedged its way into his life, he frequently sought new information on malting and brewing. As did many colonial readers, he relied upon word of mouth to learn of new titles and where to acquire them. Such was the case with a book that nearly led to the establishment of a national brewery. The work, *American Brewer and Maltster,* by Joseph Coppinger, contained a description of how to use Indian corn in beer. It was of particular interest and Jefferson's letters were full of attempts to locate and purchase a copy. Failure to obtain the book didn't stop Jefferson, who kept brewing and searching. Little did he know he and Coppinger would soon cross paths.

From the time Joseph Coppinger, a "porter brewer from Europe," first set foot in New York in 1802, he was on a mission for beer. Initially settling in western Pennsylvania, he teamed up with Peter Shiras to establish Pittsburgh's famous Point Brewery. Business was good and the city embraced the beer, but Coppinger had lofty ambitions and the small Allegheny River city couldn't hold him.

Relocating back to New York, Coppinger started pursuit of his real dream. On December 16, 1810, he contacted President James

134

Madison and launched his campaign, writing of his plan for "the establishment of a Brewing Company at Washington as a national object. It has in my view the greatest importance . . . to improve the quality of our Malt Liquors in every part of the Union."[5]

To bolster his case he exploited a deep-seated social belief: fear of drinking the polluted water of the day. He assured the president that a good supply of beer was essential for the health of the country. Beer, he said, would also "serve to counteract the baneful influence of ardent spirits on the health and morals of our fellow citizens."[6]

Coppinger knew how distrustful citizens were of the water supply, and he again used this tactic in his follow-up letter of December 20th: "those families who . . . [use] malt liquor freely as their common drink . . . keep and preserve their health while less fortunate . . . are the victims of fever and disease."[7]

There was no need to convince Madison, who remembered his days at the Indian Queen Tavern during the Constitutional Convention in Philadelphia. Madison boarded at the tavern and took many of his meals in the taproom. However, the president was then embroiled in a dispute with Great Britain over shipping and fishing rights off the Atlantic Coast. Though occupied with the pressing concerns of foreign affairs, the president believed the idea had merit, and he turned to a person he trusted as both a leader and a brewer, Thomas Jefferson.

Although Coppinger didn't know it, the referral was a break in his favor. Rather than a brush-off, it was a recommendation to an ex-president who, as a student of brewing, knew more about it than any other government official. While Jefferson was trying to locate a copy of Coppinger's book, fate was bringing

Coppinger to him. But just as things seemed promising, Coppinger's efforts stalled. War broke out with England.

Over the next several years America's fortunes hit a low point. With the exception of a few brilliant victories at sea, the War of 1812 was nearly the young country's swan song. Devastating defeats on land were no better demonstrated than by England's burning of the capital.

Americans fought back and slowly the tide turned. One bright spot was in Baltimore, where Francis Scott Key, on a mission to exchange prisoners, was inspired by the battle of Fort McHenry to write the Star Spangled Banner, amongst glasses of beer in Baltimore's Fountain Tavern.

In all, the war was bad timing for breweries. The delay rendered the nation's economy helpless and distracted citizens from any thoughts of improving industry. They were literally fighting to keep the country afloat. Thankfully, the continued European antics of Napoleon helped weaken British resolve.

Following the end of hostilities, Coppinger once again took up his campaign. His plan was to sell government "brewery" bonds to raise the $20,000 start-up costs. Coppinger's financial plan projected a 200 percent return on sales of porter and ale. This was surely tempting, but despite Jefferson's serious consideration, the former president was compelled to decline the offer, writing on April 25, 1815:

·The business of brewing is now so much introduced in every state, that it appears to me to need no other encouragement than to increase the number of customers. I do not think it is a case where a company need form itself merely on patriotic principles, because there is a sufficiency of private capital which would embark itself in the business if there were a demand.[8]

Matthew Vassar.

The time for Coppinger's dream of a national brewery had passed. If not for the unfortunate intervention of the war, the national brewery might have come about. Perhaps it might have been possible to stroll down Constitution Avenue, and there, across from the Smithsonian Institution, or maybe as part of it, would be the doorway to the national brewery's taproom. But it was never built.

Jefferson's observation that breweries were doing well on their own was most likely about the industry in general, but it could have been an observation about what was taking place up the Hudson River from New York City.

One of the breweries that defied war, economic upheaval, and the growing force of temperance was the Hudson Valley Brewery of Matthew Vassar. Born in England in 1792, Vassar made the crossing to the United States at the age of four. Young Matthew liked life on the farm but was always excited on market day, which meant taking a wagon trip with his father, and though the road was rough, a journey to town was worth any discomfort. Excursions to the market weren't for entertainment; the family loaded the wagon with produce. After a time they sought to further increase sales, and on one trip brought a "spare" barrel of beer. It was well received, and demand for their ale grew. Before long they needed a larger and more reliable supply of malt. Out of this need they introduced barley farming to the area surrounding Dutchess County, New York.

Sales of beer increased faster than the family could brew on their tiny farmhouse system, and over time they built a proper brewery. Watching the business grow from its birth, Matthew Vassar was the one his father entrusted with its operation. On November 15, 1810, at the tender age of 18, Matthew Vassar took over management of the brewery. An appraisal of the time listed assets of:

Ale & Beer	$1,200.00
Barley, Malt, Hops, etc	$1,800.00
The books accts	$1,500.00
Works & Mtrl's including brewery	$8,000.00
	$12,500.00[9]

Business continued to grow, and all seemed well. Then fate dealt the Vassars a hard blow: a fire destroyed the brewery on May 10, 1811. A common problem in early breweries, fires put many brewers out of business. In Vassar's situation there was added anxiety. Imagine losing your father's business within six months of assuming control. Fortunately, Matthew Vassar was made of stern stuff. Setting up temporary quarters in the dye-house of a relative, he began rebuilding with a modest output of only three barrels at a time.

As cash flow increased, the brewing operation slowly built up enough capital to move into its own quarters. Selection of a new home was easy enough. Vassar knew where there was a crowd, there was a market. Assessing the potential in downtown Poughkeepsie, he settled on a location that was a twist on the old colonial tavern. In the early days of the colonies, court was conducted in the local tavern, but in this case the tavern had traveled to the court. Vassar established his new taproom in the basement of the local courthouse. Advertisements declared a full return to brewing and promoted a product line of "London Brown Stout, Philadelphia Porter, and Poughkeepsie do and ale."[10] Watching expenses and plowing profits back into the business enabled Vassar, by 1813, to begin construction of a new brewery.

With the availability of locally abundant resources, the brewery acquired a large following, and Vassar earned a reputation as an honest businessman, dedicated to service and quality. Steering a course of conservative expansion, the company attained financial comfort and a size unprecedented in American brewing history.

Brisk sales forced Vassar to address an agreeable problem in 1836. Demand was running ahead of capacity—the brewery was too small. Vassar expanded the facilities by constructing a new brewery in Poughkeepsie. Sales increased further, and through the establishment of agencies Vassar's beer was made available up and down the East Coast. With distribution to every state, it was the first time a brewery had reached the milestone of nationwide sales, and it happened more than 50 years before any of the well-known names in national brewing arrived on the scene.

In retrospect, the most remarkable fact about Vassar's operation was the technological limits that restricted brewers in those days. It was an era before refrigeration and so Vassar, like his peers, concentrated on producing beer between mid-August and April. Despite the handicap of an abbreviated brewing year, national

139

production hit an annual capacity of 30,000 barrels by 1860. But that was long after Matthew Vassar had lost interest in brewing.

By 1850 Vassar had relinquished day-to-day operations of the business and set his sights on a new goal. His dream was to establish a women's institute of higher learning. Using part of his considerable wealth, he succeeded in opening Vassar Female College in 1861. Not only was it one of the nation's first colleges for women, it was also the beneficiary of a significant endowment. Modern beer ads routinely attract criticism for an insensitive portrayal of women, but it was a brewer who originally took up the standard for women's education. Vassar's legacy endured. In honor of its benefactor, the school changed its name to Vassar College in 1867, and to this day, each spring the students celebrate "Founder's Day" in tribute to an old ale brewer who had a vision of equality.

Conditions in the country were changing during the period when Vassar was building his empire. Even as he was acquiring his greatest wealth, forces were at work that would eventually cause the brewery to crumble. Most significant to brewing was an accelerated migration of Germans during the 1820s. As they landed in their adopted land it was quite natural for them to settle in German communities, towns, and neighborhoods.

As with earlier groups from Germany, the new arrivals found comfort in retaining as many of the customs and habits of the old country as possible. For enterprising members of their number it spelled success in an instant market for goods of the old country, especially for brewers. As historian Samuel Elliot Morison wrote: "The German didn't give up his beer, instead he made Milwaukee famous."[11]

Wisconsin and Missouri in particular were destinations for immigrants who hoped to settle in what they dreamed would become little German states. Milwaukee, along with Philadelphia, New York, Cincinnati, Chicago, and St. Louis, all became centers for both German populations and brewing. Beers produced by this new generation of Germans weren't limited to the ales and porters popular in America. They introduced the *alt* and *weiss* beer styles favored at home.

Up to the 1840s, the title "Brew Town USA" belonged to Philadelphia. New York had fallen behind after the turn of the century. Breweries in Manhattan declined because of a problem dating back to the early Dutch settlers: a fresh water supply. When the Dutch owned New York, lower Manhattan looked much like their homeland, with low-lying marshes. Inspired by the similarity, they promptly set about planting crops and digging canals. They even built a sturdy lock at the entrance of the biggest canal, which ran along today's Broad Street, to trap a supply of water for fire fighting during low tide. But nowhere did they locate an adequate supply of fresh water. Nevertheless, construction continued.

Large-scale relief from a continuing water shortage was first attempted by Aaron Burr in 1799. He formed a state-chartered water company. Built amidst controversy over possible misuse of funds (How very like New York!), an improved pump from a deeper well brought 691,000 gallons a day to a reservoir built above ground on Chambers Street, just behind what is now City Hall. A distribution system constructed out of 25 miles of wooden pipes eventually brought water to more than 2,000 houses. Once again, despite the poor quality, the inhabitants were happy. Unfortunately, the supply didn't last.

By the 1830s the lack of water was becoming an impossible situation. Finally, in 1837 the city and state were forced to seek a more substantial and permanent means to end the shortage. A request for proposals was issued, inviting bids on 23 sections of an aqueduct to provide the city with water from upstate. One of the most ambitious construction projects of its time, the schedule called for completion of the system within three years. Meanwhile, planners selected the Croton River as an adequate site for a reservoir. Even this part of the project went forward in typical New York fashion—land appraised at $65,400 was finally acquired for $257,198. However, within a few years, the bill looked like a bargain.

Under the watchful eye of Chief Engineer John B. Jervis, the aqueduct took shape. Constructed of stone and buried except where it spanned streams with stone bridges, it was an elliptical pipe 7.5 feet wide and 8 feet high, curving downward at a grade of 13 inches per mile. Over its course it traversed 33 miles from Croton to the Harlem River, which it crossed by means of the 1,450-foot High Bridge, which still stands today.

Entering Manhattan, the route continued in a wide sweeping arc to the Yorkville Receiving Reservoir, on the Great Lawn in Central Park. From there it traveled a final 2.25 miles to its terminal reservoir at Murray Hill.

In those days the city's population was confined to the area below Fourteenth Street and the reservoir's location between Fortieth and Forty-second Streets was considered to be "out in the boonies." Today this is the site of New York's public library, but back then the reservoir was built on a potter's field and constructed as an above-ground, fortresslike enclosure of stone.

142

Finally, at 5:00 A.M. on June 22, 1842, Croton water was directed into the aqueduct. As it rose it floated and then propelled a tiny boat christened *Croton Maid*. Carrying four of the commissioners, the boat sailed along the waters of this new river, and when it emerged at Yorkville it visibly demonstrated that water problems were over. On July 4 the waters were admitted to the Murray Hill facilities to the salute of a hundred cannons and the thrill of thousands of spectators. This was followed by a parade more than five miles long and a large "cold collation" (picnic). Philip Hone, the famous diarist of New York, proudly observed "not a drunken person was to be seen" but this didn't mean beer was absent, nor did it mean only water was on peoples' minds.

How much of an impact did the completion of the aqueduct have on New York's brewing industry? It was just in time. It brought an abundant supply of water to the breweries, precisely coinciding with the arrival of the just-discovered style of lager beer. At the same time, thousands of new German immigrants helped propel the brewing industry of New York to greatness. Its effect is no better seen than in the list of brewers who began making beer immediately after construction of the aqueduct was finished. It reads like a who's who of beer.

From 1820 through the 1830s almost one out of three immigrants was of German descent. But this was just a drop in the bucket. Events in Germany during the 1840s really got things going. Social upheavals, the Prussian Uprising, and poor economic conditions throughout the century drove the numbers of immigrants even higher.

The other significant event for brewing was the advent of the clipper ship. Yankee ingenuity and shipbuilding skills led to the development of the fastest vessels ever built. When these ships began shattering the records for transatlantic crossings, it made the trip short enough for brewers to import a new strain of yeast and make an entirely different style of beer. Soon lager's popularity would sweep the country. But not everyone took to it. Mark Twain related one conversation with an Irishman, who said of his fellows and lager: "They don't drink it, sir, they can't drink it, sir. Give an Irishman lager for a month, and he's a dead man."

The Irish not notwithstanding, lager beer had arrived and things were never going to be the same again. A light, crisp beer was ideally suited to the climate of America, and it was a hit from its introduction. At the same time, innovations in glassmaking produced inexpensive glasses that enhanced the presentation of the new, bright, sparkling clear beer, displacing the old pewter, wood, clay, or leather tankards that shielded crude and unattractive ales. Before long everybody wanted lager, and who could blame them?

Even New York City, which had lagged behind the rest of the country in establishing breweries, finally overcame the obstacle of a restricted water supply and became home to a large number of local breweries. The solution to the water problem coincided with the introduction of lager, and the Big Apple quickly made up for lost time.

Lager's only draw back was its dependence on cold temperatures, which drove brewers to search for caverns, tunnels, and supplies of ice. Generally the temperature restrictions of the yeast resulted in American brewers following the Bavarian seasons of brewing, which ran from Michaelmas, September 29, until St. George's Day, April 23.

These restrictions would soon disappear. Construction of aqueducts, application of technology, development of railroads, and expansion of industry all created an incubator for the American brewing industry. It was a time when the forces shaping the country also shaped the future of beer. While the innovations occurred in the second half of the 1800s, cornerstones were firmly set by the actions and progress of the period preceding 1840. Everything was coming together to make beer big business.

Eight

FAME AND FORTUNE: THE EMERGENCE OF THE BIG BREWERIES OF THE 1800S

Tired and thirsty, the office worker wanted nothing more than a beer. It was a lucky day; there was an open seat at the bar. Leaning forward, he attracted the attention of his regular bartender, who grabbed a familiar mug and spun toward the taps. Pouring it with the experience gained through a million repetitions, the barman topped it off, and after tossing a coaster on the bar, set down the freshly drawn beer.

After taking a long draught, the customer looked around the room. It was reassurance and stability in an often tumultuous world. Long a regular, he wasn't the first to have frequented this bar, not by a long shot. With a reputation bordering on legendary, it had been serving the city's beer drinkers for ages. Somehow, though popular, it had escaped the stigma of being "trendy." As long as he'd been drinking there it was simply a comfortable tavern.

Looking above the back bar as he'd done a thousand times before, his graze lingered on the framed lithographs that appeared to have hung there since the place opened. They looked as though they were pictures of factories. Calling the bartender over, he excused himself for not having ever inquired, and asked what they were. Smiling, the bartender nodded toward the taps and explained. They were once the most famous breweries in the area. Their owners were captains of industry, but only a few still survived. Some were only ghosts, torn down decades earlier. Some were abandoned, rotting hulks, their glory days a distant memory. But all of them were important, a part of history that started back around the early to mid-1800s. It was a shame more people didn't remember, or ask. Every old city had them.

BOSTON
Bunker Hill Brewing

Tracing the origin of a brewery often yields mixed results. Easiest to document are those that were originally constructed by the owner and are still in existence. Others are shrouded in the mystery of time and obscured by sparse documentation. So it is with the birth of Boston's Bunker Hill Brewery.

With what can be found, it seems the birth of the company dates to 1821. In that year two partners, John Cooper and Thomas Gould, constructed a small brick building in Charleston, near what is now 40 Alford Street. Not much is known of their motivation, but they did undertake the effort with the intent of brewing. In fact the facility, under various managers, produced beer at this location for over 30 years.

With a longevity of three decades it must have had some success, but it was probably moderate. There is reason to believe that at some point it operated under the name of the John Kent Mystic Lake Brewery, no doubt in reference to that nearby body of water. Through those early years the facility was at some point expanded to a four-story brick building with a stone cellar.

In 1860 the brewery's future would turn upon its sale. That was when William T. Van Nostrand bought a share of the business and changed the name to the Van Nostrand and Kent Brewery. Under the guidance of William and his son, A. G. Van Nostrand, the company embarked upon a program of steady expansion. Production, distribution, and sales all increased and the once tiny brewery began to thrive.

In 1886 sales justified the addition of a bottling line. A year later the brew house acquired what would become its signature feature.

The old Boylston Market, which dated back to 1809, closed its doors in 1877. With its passing, Van Nostrand surrendered to an urge, purchasing the belfry and clock tower of that once busy facility. Perhaps it was a symbol of his ownership, because in that same year Van Nostrand gained complete control of the brewery and changed its name to Wm. T. Van Nostrand and Co.

It was an unusual product line that gained the brewery respect among Boston's drinkers. During the era of lager's conquest of American taste, Van Nostrand secured customer loyalty with "P.B." Ale, "Old Musty Ale," "Old Stout," "Porter," "Half-and-Half," and finally "Bunker Hill Lager."

Bunker Hill Brewery.

By 1890 the brewery was ready for another change in name. This time it was proclaimed by a banner that flew from a rooftop flagstaff, announcing it as "Bunker Hill Brewery." It would continue as such, under the corporate name of "Bunker Hill Breweries, A. G. Van Nostrand," for the next 28 years.

Now operating the brewery by himself, A. G. Van Nostrand continued the strategy of steady expansion laid down by his father. In 1891 he purchased an ammonia ice machine to aid in the production of Bunker Hill Lager. In 1892 he built a lager brew house. This was quickly followed in 1895 by a "double" brew house that achieved an output of over 60,000 barrels per year.

Another landmark was affixed to the brewery in 1897, when it acquired the marvel of an electric sign, which declared it the home of "P.B. Ale." It was pride in "P.B. Ale" that ultimately forced the brewery to file a precedent-setting lawsuit. Irritated over the pirating of the "P.B. Ale" name by those ready to cash in

150

on its popularity, A. G. accused 11 "offenders" of damaging the brand by selling lesser beers under its name. In the first case of this sort heard before the Massachusetts Supreme Judicial Court, Van Nostrand secured permanent injunctions against these trademark violations.

At the dawn of the new century the brewery was operating at full capacity and the bottling line shipped 892,092 units of bottle-aged beer. During this period the brewery reached its largest size. The company grounds was made up of the brewery on Alford Street, a malting plant, a grain-drying facility on Arlington Avenue, and the bottling plant on West Street.

Bunker Hill beers remained a popular choice of Boston beer drinkers until Prohibition forced the brewery's closure. After Prohibition, two attempts were made to reopen the brewery. The first attempt, in 1933 under the Bunker Hill name, at 60 Alford Street, failed quickly. A second reopening in 1934 as "Van Nostrand Brewing" produced no beer, and by the end of 1934 all that was left of Bunker Hill was an empty building and memories.

NEW YORK
Jacob Ruppert Brewing

The Ruppert story begins in 1837, when Franz Ruppert started out as a grocer. Franz did well in that trade, and by 1845 he had earned enough money to quit the produce business and seek a new fortune. His ambition led him to the purchase of a malt house, and then in 1850 the Aktien Brauerei at 322 East Forty-fifth Street, near the intersection of First Avenue. That section of the city was known as Turtle Bay, and it was the name he adopted for his newly acquired brewery.

Just before leaving the grocery business, on March 4, 1842, his son Jacob (Sr.) was born, and a few years later he joined his father in the brew house. By 1863, at the young age of 21, Jacob was managing the entire operation.

By 1867 Jacob was feeling the urge to strike out on his own. At that time large sections of the city were still undeveloped. The area on Third Avenue between Ninety-first and Ninety-second Streets was one of these. Unlikely as it seems these days, Jacob was able to construct his brew house by purchasing a plot of timbered land, felling the trees, clearing the property and building the brew house with his own hands. While he was working on the brewery he married the daughter of another famous New York brewer, George Gillig, who was one of the country's first lager brewers. This further refined Jacob's brewing skills and soon his

beer was enjoying immense popularity. Franz Ruppert retired from brewing in 1869, selling the old Turtle Bay operation to brewer Jacob Robinson.

As is typical in stories of successful brewers, Jacob Ruppert's beer sold well enough that he quickly outgrew his first facility, so in 1874 he purchased land one block north, on Ninety-second Street and Third Avenue; a spot that would ever-after be associated with the Rupperts. As the appeal of lager grew during the late 1800s, so did Jacob's

Jacob Ruppert.

fortune. In his first year at Ninety-second Street he sold more than 5,000 barrels of beer. He wasn't yet in the league of Matthew Vassar, but he would be soon. In fact, he purchased a farm in Poughkeepsie not far from Vassar's.

Then came the invention that would revolutionize brewing and secure Ruppert's fortune: refrigeration. Jacob was one of the earliest brewers to embrace this new technology, building ice houses in 1877 and again in 1880 to take advantage of year-round brewing. His constant expansion made Ruppert's brewery one of the leading producers in the country, and he did it by relying solely on sales within the New York City region. Very little was ever shipped elsewhere.

Nothing could have made Jacob Ruppert Sr. more proud than the day his son, Jacob Jr., born in 1867, joined the business. And Jacob Jr. would bring the company even greater fame. Under Jacob Jr.'s guidance, the brewery continued to expand, and in 1916 was selling one million barrels per year, the first non-national brewer to achieve this milestone.

Jacob Jr. was a natural public relations man and knew associating with nonbrewing activities could help with beer sales. He was one of the first to grasp this concept and use it to his advantage. Thus it was that when Admiral Byrd made his second Antarctic expedition, Ruppert beer went along. Ruppert was a major contributor, and the expedition named their ship *The Jacob Ruppert*. Ruppert couldn't have been happier, and he sent along enough beer so that each of the 56 men had 21 cases: more than 1,200 cases total.

For New Yorkers the most significant date in Ruppert's history was 1915. That was when he cemented an image that is now

153

considered all-American. The marriage of beer and baseball can mark its anniversary as the date Jacob Ruppert Jr. and a partner, "Cap" Huston, purchased the New York Yankees for the sum of $460,000. By 1919 Ruppert was building the team into a baseball dynasty that would dominate four decades. Things really took off when he made a deal with the cash-strapped Boston Red Sox for a pitcher/outfielder named George Herman Ruth. Although no one can deny the role Ruth played in making baseball popular, it was a brewer that brought baseball into the modern age and the Bambino to New York. Rumor has it the Babe was so upset when he left Boston that he placed a jinx on the team to never again win a world series. Superstition or not, they haven't won since.

Ruppert would have rebuilt the team more quickly if it hadn't been for an interruption in his plans. World War I broke out and Jacob Ruppert Jr., who like his father was a member of the New York National Guard, came to the service of his country. Jacob Jr. had an exceptional war record and returned home with the rank of colonel. Even after serving three terms in the U.S. Congress, it was his military duty people remembered, and he was thereafter known as "the Colonel."

When Prohibition began shortly after the war, in 1919, Jacob Jr. made the best of those years. With the real estate holdings Jacob Sr. had acquired, the family was secure, and Jacob Jr. continued his sporting ways, including racing horses and sailing his yacht, *Albatross,* on Long Island Sound. It was also during Prohibition that Ruppert undertook what at that time was the largest private construction project in the world, the building of Yankee Stadium. It might be called the house that Ruth built, but it was actually built by Ruppert beer.

154

On repeal of Prohibition, Ruppert beer once again filled the barrooms of New York, but fate had taken a turn against this brewing giant. Part of the problem was Ruppert's failure to modernize the brewery as it lay idle during the 14 long years of Prohibition. The large national brewers had been busy upgrading their equipment and gaining the economic advantage. Their national base was another advantage they had over Ruppert. Over-reliance on the New York market had left the brewery in an unwitting position of vulnerability. A unionized brewery truckers' strike in 1949 signaled the end of the Ruppert dynasty. While Ruppert beer was kept out of the city's taprooms, the national brewers continued to be handled by the truckers, giving them a share of what had been a nearly exclusive market for local beer. The national suppliers never looked back, and eventually the once proud name of Ruppert disappeared from New York's bars.

Beadleston and Woerz Brewing

What could a Queen of England, James Cagney movies, the French Revolution, and a brewery possibly have in common? If it's Mary Queen of Scots, gangster films, and the Bastille, the answer is a prison, and surprisingly, that's also the connection to the Beadleston and Woerz brewery.

Brewers supplying New York City in the early 1800s defied that era's logic by locating their facilities well beyond the city limits. They had no choice. New York's water supply, unreliable and of poor quality, was insufficient for brewing until completion of the Croton Reservoir system in the 1840s. Thus it was that beer came from the north, up the Hudson, and by 1825 Matthew

New York State Prison.

Vassar was well on his way to riches by supplying a thirsty New York with shipments of beer from Poughkeepsie.

None of this was lost on Abraham Nash, who lived even farther upstream than Vassar, in Troy, across the river from Albany. A brewer of ale, Nash was experiencing modest success, but knew the path to real wealth led downriver. His problem was distance; he was located well beyond the easy one-day trip Vassar enjoyed. A more pressing problem was management: how could he run a brewery in Troy while servicing clients in Manhattan.

Nash solved his problem by employing a technique used many times in privately held companies. He turned to a trusted relative. So it was that in 1837 Ebenezer Beadleston was charged with running the New York office of the Nash brewery.

Beadleston was good at his job, and by 1840 the business was thriving. As a reward for these efforts he was admitted to the firm, which then became known as Nash, Beadleston and Company.

By 1845 New York's new water system was in full operation and fortune awaited those brewers who were ready to

156

build in the city. Beadleston began a search for an appropriate Manhattan location. Years earlier the state had built a prison up the river in Ossining to replace the facility it had used within the city since 1797. After Sing-Sing's completion in 1828, the old State Prison remained empty, until Beadleston acquired it in 1845. Situated on West Tenth Street, it was perfect for brewery operations, and by 1846 it was producing beer. Even the old cells had a function. Their damp nature was well suited to malting, which was carried on in those vaults for the next several decades.

Sales continued to grow and so did the brewery. It encompassed 17 city lots, and with this success came a name change to Empire Brewing. In 1856 the city location split away from that in Troy and was renamed Beadleston and Nash. Then in 1860 Nash retired, selling his interest to an employee named W. W. Price. With Nash removed from the brew house, the technical operations were assumed by E. G. Woerz, who had received his training at the famous Yuengling Brewery.

Woerz performed his duties in such an exemplary manner that he became a partner in 1865. When Ebeneezer Beadleston retired in 1871, he passed his share of the business on to his son William. By 1879 the demand for Beadleston and Woerz beer had far outgrown capacity at the old "prison" plant, and it was razed to make room for a new brewery that also included a 60-by-120-foot ice house on Washington Street. The last vestiges of the prison disappeared during a remodeling in 1881.

In 1889 the brewery was incorporated as "Beadleston and Woerz" and billed itself as makers of "ale, porter and lager beer." Profitable right up to the onset of Prohibition, it was, unfortunately,

Beadleston and Woerz.

one of those with insufficient capital to reopen after repeal. As in other sections of the county, old-timers in New York spoke fondly of the Beadleston and Woerz beer for decades after its closing, regretting the loss of another hometown brewery.

Schaefer Brewing Company

Imagine an immigrant arriving in New York City during the 1800s. As the boat pulls into the busy harbor, a young man leans on the rail, taking in his first view of the New World. He brings few possessions, but carries plenty of hope. He's an unknown in that year of 1838, but before long his name will be on everyone's lips. Such a description could fit any number of newcomers, but none better than Frederick Schaefer.

Fresh off the boat from Wetzler, Prussia, Schaefer wasted no time putting his brewing background to work. Soon after arriving the 21-year-old secured a position in the newly completed Manhattan brew house of Sebastian Sommers on Broadway, between Eighteenth and Nineteenth Streets. Determined to succeed, Schaefer launched a plan that began with diligent saving.

Stories of many brewers from this era have similar beginnings; however, rather than saving to purchase a brew house, Frederick was working to bring his brother over from Prussia. Then, when Maximilian Schaefer arrived a year later, the brothers worked together on their dream to own a brewery.

In only three years they had amassed a large enough sum to buy out their former employer, and from 1842 on the brewery would be known as F. M. Schaefer. Frederick's European training brought the brothers ever-growing sales, and by 1845 demand for Schaefer beer far outpaced the original facility's capacity. So it was that in 1845 they opened a new brew house on Seventh Avenue, between Sixteenth and Seventeenth Streets. There, in 1848, the new brewery produced the first batch of Schaefer's lager beer, placing Frederick and Maximilian among the country's pioneer lager brewers.

This was the period of lager beer's steamrolling popularity, and Schaefer beer sold even more briskly than before. In only four years the company had once again outgrown its facility. Resolving to avoid building too small, they selected a location uptown on Park Avenue (then called Fourth Avenue) between Fiftieth and Fifty-first Streets. Four stories tall, with extensive underground lagering cellars, it would operate there from 1849 to 1911. During that period the most significant development was in 1880, when they changed the name to F. M. Schaefer Brewing Company, with an address listed as 112/114 East Fifty-first Street. In 1911 another expansion engulfed Park Avenue from Fiftieth through Fifty-second Streets.

In 1912 Rudolph Schaefer assumed control of the company, and in 1916, blessed with ever-greater sales, he opened a new plant across the East River. With an address of 430 Kent Avenue and 2 South Ninth Street, Schaefer joined the honor role of Brooklyn breweries, at a location where beer would be produced continuously for the next 60 years.

The timing of the new plant's construction was significant. Idled by Prohibition, only those brewers with the most modern plants were able to reopen after the forced shutdown. From 1919 to 1933, Schaefer remained solvent by shifting to the production of ice and near beer. Of equal impact was the ascension of a new leader in the company. In 1927, young Rudy Schaefer took over the reigns of power. At 27 years of age, the youngest brewery president in the United States, he capably steered the company through the remaining no-beer years.

F. M. Shaefer.

After Prohibition was repealed, Rudy correctly assessed the company's strengths and weaknesses and reopened only the Brooklyn plant. While other brewers struggled with plants 30 years old or older, Schaefer beer picked up right where it left off.

Over the next several years the company embarked on a controlled expansion based upon the acquisition of existing breweries in targeted markets. With this strategy they bought Albany's Beverwyck

Brewery, Baltimore's Gunther Brewery from Theodore Hamm, and the Standard Brewing Company of Cleveland.

With a network of plants throughout the northeast population centers, Schaefer survived while other pre-Prohibition notables suffered a lingering death. By the 1960s Schaefer had initiated a phased shutdown of its older facilities. Then, in a move opposing the prevailing trend, Schaefer constructed a modern brewery near Allentown, Pennsylvania, in 1972. Schaefer had once more defied the odds, and in doing so had become the eighth largest brewery in the United States.

By the mid-1970s regional breweries had become targets of national houses looking to secure their positions. Thus, in 1976 Stroh purchased the company and subsequently shut down the Brooklyn plant. No doubt that young shipboard immigrant of 1838 would have mixed feelings about this. Though the company was neither a separate entity, nor New York–based, a loyal following would still be drinking Schaefer beer more than 150 years after he first set foot in America.

PHILADELPHIA
Robert Hare Brewery

Ask people for nominations to a Philadelphia brewers' hall of fame, and the lists would look remarkably alike. Most people would cite Schmidt, Ortlieb, Poth, Bergdoll, and Schemm. Few would petition for Robert Hare, yet in his day he was the leading brewer of the city.

Robert Hare is reported to have learned the art of brewing as the son of a porter brewer in Limehouse, England. With a gift of

1,500 pounds from his father, he set out to make his own fortune. Immigrating to the American colony of Pennsylvania in 1773, he settled in Philadelphia. In 1775 he entered a business arrangement with John Warren to build and operate a brewery. This was the first porter brewery in Philadelphia, and some historians argue that it was the first in America.

Establishing one of the city's early breweries is quite an accomplishment, but that accomplishment is even more significant when the beer produced is considered the benchmark for its style. During the first and second Continental Congresses, George Washington became a big fan of Hare's porter, and he carried the memory of that beer with him throughout the war. In fact, Hare's porter was itself only a memory from 1777 to 1778, when brewing was interrupted by British occupation of the city.

Upon reopening of the brewery, George Washington renewed his status as a loyal customer. The relationship would continue for years. In 1788 he placed an order with his agent, writing, "I beg you to send me a gross of Mr. Hairs [*sic*] best bottled Porter if the price is not much enhanced by the copious droughts you took of it at the late procession."[1] It must have been a beer with considerable impact. In 1789 Martha Washington expressed her thanks to Hare for continuously keeping her husband in good spirits. On passing through the city she hosted a party, with Hare among her invited guests. Of course it could have been Martha's crafty play for the 10 bottles of porter he brought with him.

Tragedy interrupted brewing when the facility was destroyed by fire in 1790, an event that also brought an end to Hare's partnership with John Warren. Hare immediately reconstructed the brew house at 35 Callowhill Street. Reopening had no apparent effect on the quality of his product, and customers like Washington once again lined up to purchase Hare's famous porter. One such order was placed for the president by his secretary, Tobias Lear, in 1790: "Will you be so good as to desire Mr. Hare to have if he continues to make the best Porter in Philadelphia 3 gross of his best put up for Mt.Vernon?"[2]

In 1800 Hare was joined in the concern by his son, Robert Jr., who would become a scientist of some note in the 1800s. Operating as Hare and Son, they set up business at 155 Chestnut Street from 1800 to 1804 and then at 401/421 Market and Callowhill from 1805 to 1817. Robert Hare passed away in 1810 and Robert Jr. continued the business, but sold out to Jacob Smith in 1817.

Jacob Smith ran the operation until 1823. After passing through various hands, it became part of the Betz Brewery in 1869. By 1878 Betz ranked third among the city's 85 operating breweries. Shut down in 1920 by Prohibition, it reopened in 1933 and continued brewing until its final closing in 1939. Although now gone, the Robert Hare Brewery wasn't just a pioneer on the Philadelphia scene, it also became one of the largest in a great brewing city.

Lauer Brewing Company

To become one of the most important figures in U.S. brewing didn't require a large brewery, great fortune, scientific discovery, or even being well known; it required only a love of beer. Such was the case with Fredrick Lauer.

Part One

Lauer Brewing Company.

Born on October 14, 1810, in Gleisweiler, Bavaria, Fredrick Lauer was an early immigrant to America. Landing in Baltimore in 1822, his family soon found its way to Reading, Pennsylvania.

The original Lauer brewery was established under rather primitive circumstances by Fredrick's father. Located on Third and Chestnut Streets, it was established in a log cabin rumored to have been built by a local Indian called "Old Red," who lived there until the day the brewery was installed. Before long Fredrick took over the business and immediately embarked on a continuous program of upgrading and expanding the equipment and facilities. His perseverance paid off, and although the brewery was never among the national leaders, he did attain the respectable status of third largest brewery in Pennsylvania.

By 1844 Lauer was making lager beer, thus becoming one of the country's early brewers of that style, which secured him a comfortable income. His volunteer work assisting Reading's incorporation as a city won him a nomination to run for Congress, but he respectfully turned down that offer because of

164

the business in which he was engaged; he felt there would have been a conflict of interest. He did, however, accept a position as a member of the 1860 presidential convention, during which he vigorously pursued a party platform endorsing abolition. Later, during the Civil War, he equipped an entire company of the Pennsylvania 104th at his own expense.

Funding of any war is difficult, but it's even more so when civil strife rips apart the fragile structure of an economy. One of the financial methods pursued by the Lincoln administration was the creation of alternate taxing schemes, and among them was a significant tax on brewery output. It was this aspect of the war that brought Lauer lasting fame.

On November 12, 1862, brewers from throughout the country held a convention in New York City. There they discussed the new taxes and developed a unified response to that immediate threat as well as future government proposals affecting the industry. They elected Frederick Lauer as first president of the United States Brewers Association, and Lauer accepted the position in much the same manner he undertook other civic duties, fully immersing himself. Lauer cheerfully performed the delicate job of balancing national and industry interests by forging agreements that each side found acceptable.

Establishing fair and reasonable taxation schemes might have been enough for many people, but Lauer took his job even farther. Over the next five years, in his role of president he would guide the association through its formative years. Its ever-growing membership laid the foundation for an organization that would establish standards for the industry, self-assess their labor practices, and eventually create a highly respected brewers' academy.

Meanwhile the brewery in Reading continued with consistent, if modest, success, and expanded two additional times under the watchful eye of its loving owner. Even after Lauer left the leadership of the United States Brewers Association, he remained active. Others frequently remarked on how easy it was to tell Fredrick's location during the convention by the number of smiles concentrated on the convention floor.

Actively running his business for more than 40 years, Fredrick Lauer finally relinquished operation of the brewery to his sons, Frank P. and George F., in 1882. Shortly thereafter, on September 12, 1883, Lauer passed away at age 74. But this is not the end of the story. The impact Fredrick Lauer had on his fellow brewers and his legacy at the United States Brewers Association continued to play upon the thoughts of the members, who were constantly reminded of his warmth, dedication, perseverance, and friendliness. Thus it was that after their annual meeting in 1885, the members traveled from their convention site in New York to Fredrick's beloved adopted city of Reading. On May 23, in a ceremony charged with emotion, they unveiled a monument capped with a life-sized bronze statue of none other than their comrade, Fredrick Lauer.

Lauer's life demonstrates that one needn't be the biggest, best, wealthiest, or most flamboyant to make history. Fredrick Lauer's brewery is but a shadowy memory in U.S. brewing, but the statue commemorating his work remains a lasting tribute in Reading.

Bergner and Engel

The introduction of lager beer changed beer drinking in the United States. Seldom had a new beer style had such an immediate and

166

dramatic impact. The quick ascent of lager was nothing short of meteoric, and a pair of brewers from Philadelphia were leaders in that rise.

Charles Engel came to America in 1840 after working at breweries in France and Germany. He was a childhood friend of Philadelphian Charles C. Wolf, and it was this connection that led him to the city. The year was 1844 and Wolf, owner of a Philadelphia sugar refinery, offered Engel employment. Soon after they began brewing together. Within a year Engel struck out on his own and established a brew house in Lewisburg, producing *schenk-bier* (small beer). However, his brewing venture wasn't meant to be, and only a short while later the brewery was destroyed by fire. Coincidentally, as Engel was losing his business, fire also consumed part of Wolf's sugar warehouse. Thus, fate drew them together again, and the result was construction of a new lager brewery at 352-4 Dillwyn Street.

By chance Engel had made acquaintance with Philadelphia brewer John Wagner, and it was a supply of Wagner's yeast that enabled Wolf and Engel to begin brewing. Wolf, in his later years, credited John Wagner of Philadelphia as the first American brewer to produce lager beer.

Even in that day, establishing a business followed the familiar three simple rules: "location, location, location." For Wolf and Engel, their choice met all three perfectly. Their brew house on Dillwyn Street was, at that time, in something of a resort area for the city's German population, and those thirsty masses, longing for a taste of the homeland, flocked to the brewery's beer garden. Wolf cheerfully reported that on more than one occasion these customers virtually drank the brewery dry. When this

Charles Engel.

happened the partners would simply apologize as they posted the date the next batch of beer would be available.

Although they were pleased to have such an enthusiastic and devoted following, selling out of beer was a clear signal that demand had far outdistanced production. Thus, in 1849, the pair began planning for a new brewery. This led them to obtain a tract of city land known as Fountain Green.

Retaining the original brew house on Dillwyn Street, they devised a rather innovative way to expand. Wort (unfinished beer) was produced at the old brewery and transported by teams of oxen to Fountain Green, where it was fermented and aged. More simple than it sounds, the arrangement worked so well that the brewery operated in this manner until 1870, when the city took possession of the property at Fountain Green.

While Wolf and Engel were building their operation, another Philadelphia brewer was gaining an equally impressive reputation. Gustavus Bergner first made beer in 1854 in a small facility located at 586 North Street. He too enjoyed the rapid pace with which Philadelphia's sizable German population lapped up lager, and in 1857 he increased capacity by constructing a new facility at Thirty-second and Thompson Streets.

When the city seized Wolf and Engel's property at Fountain Green, Wolf decided to retire from the business. This prompted Engel to search for a new partner. He found the person he was looking for in Gustavus Bergner, and Bergner's plant on Thompson Street was transformed into the firm of Bergner and Engel in 1870.

Sales of lager continued briskly, and the company flourished. By 1877 production at Bergner and Engel had reached well over 120,000 barrels per year, which vaulted them into third place among American breweries. They incorporated under the name of "Bergner and Engel" in 1879. Gustavus Bergner died May 6, 1883, but his shares remained in the Bergner family, and the company continued operating under the Bergner and Engel name. Sales continued to grow, and in 1895 they opened a second brewery at Thirty-third Street and Pennsylvania Avenue, increasing production to more than 250,000 barrels per year. Although sales increased, they didn't keep pace with other breweries. Bergner and Engel relied heavily on local trade and never developed markets beyond the immediate area of Philadelphia. As did other successful, but short-sighted, regional brewers, they failed to see the future in the development of a national distribution system. While they were number three in the nation in 1877, they had dropped to the fifteenth spot by 1895.

Seventeen years after the death of Bergner, in 1900, Charles Engel passed away and operation of the company was assumed by C. W. Bergner, Gustavus Bergner's son. At the onset of Prohibition the brewery shut down. It reopened after Prohibition ended, but like many other breweries, it suffered from outmoded equipment and lack of a broad-based distribution system. It closed forever shortly thereafter, and Philadelphia lost a brewery that once was a national leader and always one of the city's friends.

Yuengling

Of all the breweries still operating in the United States, the oldest is located in Pottsville, Pennsylvania. In 1806 David Yuengling was born in Germany. At the age of 22 he crossed the Atlantic. His search for clean brewing water led him to his new home west of Philadelphia. Just a year after his arrival, he was already running his own brewery. Like Matthew Vassar, Yuengling endured destruction of his brewery by a fire that struck in 1831, and just like Vassar he rebuilt the operation and continued on. Yuengling became highly regarded for its beers, and guided by David, who ran the company until his death in 1876, it achieved a ranking of eighteenth among the country's brewers. This was at a time when Pennsylvania had more than 360 breweries, each carving out its own market.

David's son Fredrick G. and his brothers had entered the company in 1873, and its name was changed to D. G. Yuengling and Sons. Fredrick rose among his siblings to assume operation at his father's death, and guided the company well despite failed attempts to expand by merging with two New York City breweries in the late 1800s. Both facilities were located on 128th Street, one at Fifth Avenue and the other at Tenth Avenue. Unfortunately both operated at a loss from the time they were established until their closing in 1884 and 1897, respectively. Despite these problems,

Yuengling.

the Pottsville brewery remained strong, and during Prohibition the company survived by producing near beer and other cereal-based beverages. It remains in operation, and the popularity of the beer led the brewery to an expansion in 1998.

Robert Smith Brewing Company

Long before the man arrived, the brewery was there. It had a connection to one of the world's most renowned breweries and would become famous in its own right for bucking a trend.

Joseph Potts had built the original brew house on a tract of land located at 2/4 South Fifth and Minor Streets. In 1774 it was one of many opening in America's most established city, but although it would continue operations for almost a century and a half, Potts was forced to shut down brewing only three years after opening. The occasion for this interruption was the city's role as seat of the revolutionary government. As such it became a military

171

target, and was captured by the British in 1777. For Potts the occupation was literal: his brew house became a barracks for the invading British troops.

Once the brewery was back in American hands, the beer again flowed, and Potts directed the business until 1786, when he sold it to Henry Pepper and Son. It operated under this name from 1786 to 1807, eventually passing into the hands of George and David Pepper and their partner, Fredrick Sickel. This team ran the brewery until 1837.

More than 60 years after its opening, the man who would make the brewery famous arrived on the scene. Robert Smith received his brewing training at Burton-on-Trent, England, in the Bass brewery. He bought into a partnership with Sickel, eventually taking full ownership in 1849. Smith's considerable skill was, of course, based in ale production, and despite the sudden

Robert Smith Brewing Company.

and overwhelming popularity of lager in the mid-1800s, Robert Smith stuck with what he knew: ale. This turned out to be quite a good decision. Under Smith's control, sales increased, and by 1887 construction of a new brew house was necessary. It was in this facility at Thirty-eighth Street and Girard Avenue that production hit 40,000 barrels per year. It was then he changed the name to the Robert Smith India Pale Ale Brewing Company.

In 1893 Smith died, and with him went the ability to make a go of ale in a lager market. By 1896 it became necessary to reorganize the company; later that same year the company was acquired by Christian Schmidt. The name Robert Smith was so well regarded in Philadelphia that it was retained as the brand name. Unfortunately, as had happened to so many others, Prohibition brought an end to what was a cornerstone of Philadelphia brewing. In 1920 the brew house closed.

CHICAGO

Land in what used to be considered the Old Northwest was irresistible, and soon after the first settlers arrived, they began building one of America's great cities. Chicago would become known as the hog slayer of the world, the city of broad shoulders, the home of the first American saint, and the site of the first nuclear reactor and chain reaction. It was also a home to beer.

Recognition for being the city's first brewer goes to either Adolph Mueller or William Lill, in 1833. Of these two, Lill is more widely credited, mostly because of his success. Beer and Chicago—the two are nearly synonymous. From the city's earliest origins, beer was there. In fact, two taverns were among the first of the city's buildings. These were establishments run by Elijah Wentworth and Samuel Miller, who sold beer at 6 1/4 cents per pint (a price we wish had been frozen).

Most of the breweries built in the city were located on the north side, because brewers had discovered that area was most favorable to building cool, underground aging rooms. But the earliest brewery was established on the west side of town. A business association of William Haas and William Lill began brewing in 1833, and they continued their venture until 1839, when Chicago's first mayor, William Ogden, bought into the operation. Thus was established the long and legendary link between Chicago politics and beer.

Brewing operations moved at about that same time, to a tenement building at Pine Street and Chicago Avenue. This new facility enabled the company to expand production to 450 barrels per year. Far from being an absentee owner, Mayor Ogden was actively involved in the business. His letters imply an obsession with the procurement of hops, which he purchased from New York's famous hop-growing region of the Finger Lakes. A milkman headquartered in the same building bought into Ogden's interest when he divested himself of his part of the business in 1842.

In 1842 Michael Diversey, an immigrant from Alsace-Lorraine, joined the partnership. The name was changed to Lill and Diversey from 1863 to 1871. Other names it would operate under concurrently included Lill's Chicago Brewery (1867–69) and Lill's Cream Ale Brewery (1846–71). Under the direction of these two well-known partners, the brewery underwent continuous expansion until it covered more than two city blocks. By

Lill and Diversey.

1860 annual sales had hit 44,780 barrels, and they were shipping beer east to Buffalo, north to St. Paul, south to New Orleans, and west to St. Joseph, Missouri.

Also counted among Chicago's first brewers was James Carney, a grocer, who in 1840 built and operated a brew house at 39-63 South Water Street between State and Wabash Streets. Another was Jacob Gauch, who had an operation on Indiana Street between Pine and St. Clair Streets, which he established in 1845. Later he moved the brewery, which became Gauch and Brahm, brewing at Rush Street and Chicago Avenue during 1855.

But of all the early brewers, Lill and Diversey are the names that are most enduring. Diversey passed away in 1869, leaving operations to Lill, who lived until 1875. Unlike so many other breweries in the United States, which succumbed to Prohibition, Lill's brewery closed at the hands of another historical tragedy: the Great Chicago Fire, in 1871. It was one of five breweries destroyed in that conflagration. Although it is now long gone, its name lives on in the city's streets and it gets credit for helping develop Chicago into one of the world's great beer-loving towns.

MILWAUKEE

If ever a city was destined to become a brewing center, it was Milwaukee. Ask nineteenth-century brewers the ideal location for a brewery, and Milwaukee would make nearly everyone's short list. What tempted the brewers were exactly the same characteristics that attracted settlers to the area of southeast Wisconsin.

Newcomers to the Cream City were greeted by a good harbor, coupled with access to plentiful ice. More appealing to the brewers was a strata of subterranean rock studded with caves. Cool temperatures were essential to the fermentation of beer, and brewers in the era before refrigeration relied heavily on ice and caves to extend the brewing season. Finally, there was the matter of customers. Here, too, Milwaukee was a winner, surrounded as it was by settlements of German immigrants. Indeed, it had everything brewers desired.

Despite the high concentration of Germans, the city's first brewery was neither owned nor run by any of their number. It was three Welshmen who earned the title "first."

Richard Owens, William Pallet, and John Davis opened an English-style brew house, producing ales in 1840. Inspired by civic pride, they named their enterprise the Milwaukee Brewery. When compared to the standard brew house of the day, their facility was crude at best. Lacking proper equipment, they began brewing with a makeshift brew kettle fashioned from a copper-lined wooden box. In spite of their unsophisticated equipment, the brewery had a brew capacity of five barrels.

Owens was the driving force behind the Milwaukee Brewery, and late in the first year he secured a traditional brew kettle from

Chicago. Output soon doubled. By 1845 Owens was ready to run the brewery alone, so he bought out his partners and changed the name to the Lake Brewery.

Eventually tiring of the long brew days, Owens rented out the facility to Powell and Pritchard of Chicago. The new partners continued to brew ale only until the business died of financial causes in 1880. If the deceased brewery had been given an autopsy, the cause of death would have read the same as what ailed other breweries around the country: a competing style of beer—lager. At the time it closed it was the last remaining ale brewery in Milwaukee.

Sad as it was that lager beer brought about the demise of the city's oldest brewery, it did lead Milwaukee to the title of Beer City, USA. Lager brewing was the path to fortune for the nation's brewers, and three of America's four largest lager brewers (Schlitz, Pabst, and Miller) would call Milwaukee home.

ST. LOUIS
William J. Lemp Brewing Company

Adam Lemp built the family's first brew house in 1840 and began by producing ales. Switching to lager sometime between 1840 and 1842, he has been credited by some historians with being the first commercial lager brewer in America. If not the country's first, he was certainly the first west of the Mississippi. Of even greater note, Lemp was the first national brewer, shipping his beer throughout the United States. In 1877 the brewery ranked nineteenth in the nation and was the largest in St.

Louis. By 1895 it held the number eight spot, but it was soon overshadowed by Anheuser-Busch. Its most famous label was Falstaff. Growing outmoded by the eve of Prohibition, its lack of modern equipment doomed the brewery. It did not reopen following repeal.

The breweries that opened in the early 1800s were instrumental in ensuring that the United States remained the same beer-loving country it had been at its founding. Over the course of the nineteenth century, America experienced nearly inconceivable growth. A strong economy and great industries developed. The West was opened and tamed, and the country took its first tentative strides as a world power. Paralleling the growth each step of the way was beer. From humble, often tenuous beginnings, breweries reached for greatness.

Lemp's brew house.

The late 1800s was the time of greatest change for the industry, but it was all built upon the solid foundation of beer drinking established by the discoverers, settlers, pioneers, frontiersmen, soldiers, and statesmen of America. They made beer an inseparable part of their lives, setting the emergence of breweries as big business in motion.

Part Two

Factors Influencing
Beer Drinking and
Brewing in the
Colonial Period

Nine

THE GOVERNMENT TAKES A BITE OUT
OF BEER: TAXATION

Wind-whipped waves carried a chill off New York Harbor directly into the face of the figure silhouetted in the sunset. Lost in thought, he pulled his frock coat tight to rebuff the biting cold. As he walked the battery, people living nearby could, if they listened, hear his peg leg thumping along as he tried to think. Pausing, he leaned against the battery's wooden breastworks and looked north, toward the wall that had been built as a fortification.

Nagging problems caused Peter Stuyvesant to take to his unsettled evening walk. Somewhat of a tyrant, Stuyvesant was a demanding governor, and when he made up his mind he expected strict adherence to his decisions. But this time the people of the colony weren't paying attention. Mulling over a possible course of action, he thought back over the short history of New Amsterdam.

When Wouteer Van Twiller, nephew of Kiliaen Van Rensselaer, was replaced as governor of New Amsterdam by Wilhelm Krieft in 1638, it was a dark day. Within the next few years Krieft would deal beer, and the inhabitants of New Amsterdam, a terrible blow.

By 1644 the ill-tempered Krieft was trapped in an impossible situation. Debts that piled up during the Indian Wars had all but bankrupt the West India Company. Responsible for the administration of the settlement, the company lacked adequate funds to run the colony. Krieft was desperate to find a solution. New Amsterdam's fort was in disrepair and the garrison was destitute. Backed into a corner, Krieft reached for what he intended as a "temporary" fix: a new tax.

If Krieft had studied history, he could have predicted the experiment's failure. Ancient civilizations and kings could have told him it wouldn't work. Aside from his autocratic philosophy

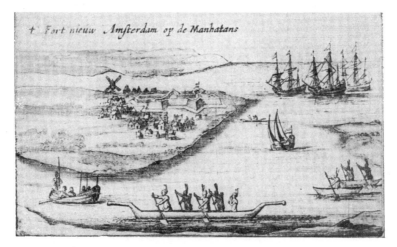

New Amsterdam.

and bad temper (that offended even his patrons), the tax itself was a bad idea. When combined with the large customs duties he enacted it was a disaster. Instead of raising cash, the law drove away traders and completely alienated residents. It wasn't long until most were ignoring the law.

Krieft was already unpopular when he placed an excise tax on beer, but after ignoring the advice of citizen representatives, he became the least-liked person in the New World. After his declaration the duty on beer was established "on each half vat (or barrel) of beer tapt by the tavern-keepers two guilders, half to be paid by the brewer and half by the tapster."[1]

Dutch reinforcements from Curaçao arrived in the settlement that fall. This should have helped the situation, but instead it complicated matters. Far from being a relief to the community, these troops also required extensive provisioning, including food, clothing, and guns. To pay for this, Krieft again turned to a beer tax. On October 28, 1644, he ordered the tax extended. It was set at three guilders per tun. Furthermore, brewers were forced to report how much beer they made before obtaining approval to sell it. To ensure the tax was collected, Krieft appointed a receiver, who was awarded a commission of 5 percent on each successful collection. Reaction was quick and entirely negative. Public spirit was aroused over the injustice of imposing a tax without first consulting the citizenry.

First the citizens sent a letter to the company. In it they outlined the abrupt manner in which Krieft had acted:

> The Director demanded that some new taxes and excise should be imposed on the Commonality. . . . Whereupon

185

we remonstrated that it was impossible for us to raise means from the people . . . that such must first be considered by a higher authority (to-wit, by the Lords Majors.) Hereat the Director became much enraged. . . . With all that the Director . . . without our knowledge . . . demanded . . . two guilders for every tun of beer, from the breweries as well as from the tapsters . . . this will probably have to be paid by the poor, who are unable to procure beer for the sick and wounded except by the can. . . .

Honored Lords! This is what we have, in the sorrow of our hearts, to complain of—that one man . . . should dispose here of our lives and properties at his will and pleasure, in a manner so arbitrary that a King dare not legally do the like.

—Done Manatans this 28th October, 1644[2]

Formally protesting, the "Ninemen," literally nine men who were representing the inhabitants, drew up their grievances for presentation to the Director-General. Three of the most respected of the Ninemen, including brewer Jacob van Couwenhoven, delivered a document they called the Remonstrance to Krieft. It was more than the first organized tax protest in North America, it was the beginning of colonial objections to taxation without representation.

Throughout the settlement people voiced their opposition and pointed out that a tax placed on the brewers would ultimately rest on the citizens. Brewers were in no mood to continue with what was originally proposed as a "temporary tax," and in opposition to Krieft they refused to pay. Krieft ordered his *schout fiscaal* (tax collector) to forcibly, if necessary, collect the owed tax. Refusing to submit, the brewers withheld payment.

Incensed, Krieft ordered the brewers prosecuted. Hauled before the court, they stood trial. Krieft had the advantage because New Amsterdam's court consisted of Krieft and the council (positions that Krieft appointed). Enraged by the brewers' refusal to pay taxes, the court ordered

Peter Stuyvesant.

confiscation of all the beer in the breweries' cellars. In a show of strength they removed it, and awarded it to the garrison, inflaming public opinion. With a voice loud enough to be heard back in Holland, the disgruntled colonials forced the company to replace Krieft.

Officials back in the Hague watched the situation with increasing concern. Growing public unrest and dissatisfaction with their New Amsterdam Director-General were reaching a crisis. Faced with overwhelmingly negative public opinion, the administrators yielded. Recalling Krieft in 1647, they replaced him with Peter Stuyvesant.

The new governor also worried about how to pay for civic improvements and defense. At times the problems seemed insoluble. As he reviewed the obstacles to building the perfect city (and he was a perfectionist), he thought of the recent report about the uninhibited spread of drinking.

Stuyvesant found the excessive Sunday drinking morally offensive, and instituted laws prohibiting sales on the Lord's day. His first attempt to inhibit consumption was a restriction on the traditional celebration of Shrovetide and the "Feast of Bacchus." Public response was similar to what Krieft had experienced. People resented the fact that Stuyvesant, without consulting the representatives of the people, had interfered with the holiday, he had "interdicted and forbidden certain farmers' servants to ride the goose at the Feast of Bacchus and Shrovetide [as an act] altogether unprofitable, unnecessary and criminal for subjects and neighbors to celebrate."³

To the people it seemed as though replacing Krieft would gain them little. Ignoring their protests, Stuyvesant continued with his agenda, but other efforts at curbing beer drinking fared just as poorly. Laws passed in 1648, 1651, and 1658 were dismal flops. In 1651 Stuyvesant fumed about the city's makeup, observing that upwards of one-quarter of its buildings were devoted to brandy, tobacco, or beer shops. Even a law of 1662 that attempted to dissuade citizens from pawning their possessions to buy beer didn't work.

Of concern to Director-General Stuyvesant, as to Krieft before him, was the colony's defense. Convinced that there was only one answer to his problem, Stuyvesant repeated Krieft's mistake. He continued the excise tax on beer. From his first moments in New Amsterdam he had irritated the citizenry, causing them again to write home:

After the public calamity—we mean, the rash war—was brought upon us, and effort was made to impose a beer excise . . . Director Krieft promised it should continue only until the arrival of a company ship, a new Director, or until the end of the war. And though nearly all doubted this, and it was not agreed to, yet he introduced it by force. The beer belonging to the brewers who would not consent to an excise was distributed among the soldiers as a prize, and so it has continued; but it has produced great strife and discontent . . . instead of abolishing the beer excise, his first act was to superadd thereto a wine excise and other intolerable burdens.[4]

For his part Stuyvesant believed he had acted prudently. He wasn't finished with the tax. New Netherland's treasury had dropped to perilously low levels in 1653, and Stuyvesant decided to find relief on a road well traveled. He turned again to taxation, but attempted to place the blame on the representatives of the people:

The Director-General and Council stand by their verbal promise given upon the proposition and reciprocal promise of the Burgomasters and Schepens on the 11th inst., to-wit, that the Director-General and Council shall provisionally and, subject to the approval of the Lords-Directors, cede and grant to the Burgomasters and Schepens the collection of the common excise on wine and beer consumed within this city; provided the Burgomasters and Schepens . . . furnish means for the maintenance of public works in the city and the subsistence of the ecclesiastical and political officers of the

Company, and that the excise shall be . . . according to the custom of the Fatherland.

—New Amsterdam, Novbr 25, 1653
By order of the Director-General and Council[5]

Revenue collected helped provision the military, but Stuyvesant needed additional funding to complete the colony's fortifications. Finally, having learned a lesson about including the citizens in decisions, he appointed brewers William Beekman and Peter van Couwenhoven, along with his representative De la Montagne, as a commission to complete the wall he envisioned as a protective breastworks across the entire north end of the settlement. They completed the task with a series of earthworks, ditches,

Peter Stuyvesant inspecting a tavern.

and palisades. No trace of that wall remains, except for the alley that ran along the inside. That exists to this day, and still bears the name of the old Dutch fortification. New Yorkers call it Wall Street.

Impressive as the wall was, it never deflected invaders. In 1665 the English took possession of the colony. They would learn that their laws held no more water, or beer, than those of the Dutch. Consumption of beer remained high, despite Stuyvesant's attempts to dry up the city. When the British arrived, they inherited a community in which there was one brew house or tavern for every 160 people. An impressive number, it seems more amazing when considering that it did not account for the majority, who brewed at home, or bought directly from overseas. New York's experience with taxation illustrates the problems encountered repeatedly throughout the colonies and later the United States.

Dutch Governors of New York may have been the first to implement beer taxes, but other colonies followed. Massachusetts received its beer tax in 1692, when the Puritans imposed a tax of one-sixth shilling on each barrel of beer. It was followed in 1702 by a law that stated: "every brewer commonly brewing beer or ale for sale, shall pay an excise for each barrel of strong beer or ale by him brewed, the sum of one shilling, and so proportionately for greater or lesser quantities."[6]

The law was designed to prevent cheating by requiring the brewer to make the payments on a weekly basis. To the relief of the common people, homebrewed beer was exempted from the law.

Taxation on beer continued throughout the colonial period, as Great Britain sought ways to pay for the costly wars fought in North America and elsewhere. Varying in application, at times the taxes represented an excise placed directly on beer. In other instances an indirect tax was applied, as in the case of the Stamp Act, under which the brewer paid a "fee" for the stamps that had to appear on the product.

When Americans revolted, and formed their own government, they too would turn to a tax on beer. What made it different to them was that they had made the decision to impose the tax through their own representatives. One such tax was introduced by the New Jersey Legislature in 1799. It specified that "all brew houses that brew for sale or hire, shall be rated at the discretion of the Assessors and chosen Freeholders any sum not exceeding one hundred pounds."[7]

What governors and colonial leaders failed to understand was the effect of beer taxes. They also broke two prime rules of tax legislation. First, never place a new tax on a necessity. Second, make sure people don't perceive the tax target as a necessity.

Administrators in the colonies were in a position identical to that of everyone who has ever placed a tax on beer. They were completely out of touch with public sentiments. Resistance, protest, and ultimately rebellion resulted because the taxes were exceedingly regressive. Taxes on beer struck people where it hurt most. It hit them with a fee on what they viewed as a necessity, never as a luxury. Nevertheless, such taxes were attractive to politicians because so many people engaged in the trade and consumption of beer. To them it was irresistible.

Tariffs, duties, import fees, excise taxes, and other forms of imposed revenues continued on beer. Whether used as a device to curb drunkenness (often termed a sin tax) or simply as a means to benefit the treasury, beer helped build the United States.

Ten

BEER'S HOME: THE TAVERN

English colonists in North America had to brew their own beer. What other choice did they have? Commercially produced beer was available only via the long supply route from Europe. The expense involved in importing beer in that age was prohibitive for most colonists. The problem was further compounded by the critically low levels of currency circulating in the colonial economy. Introduction of a tavern, especially to interior lands, stimulated a local economy, provided a focal point for social interaction, and a place for the government to carry on its affairs.

The location of a tavern was an important consideration. Random placement would have led to a settlement in an undesired location. The position of a town was strategically vital to the interests of the government, so the placement of a tavern wasn't left to chance. The government specified that the tavern's site be

Inn keepers.

close to the local meeting hall. For example, in 1651 Boston
granted permission for a new tavern, provided the owner "keepe
it neare the new meeting house."[1] At times the association
between the two buildings was more than just physical proxim-
ity. In Cambridge, Massachusetts, the innkeeper, owner of the
town's first "house of intertainment," was also deacon of the
church and later was appointed Steward of Harvard.

In a few instances the tavern and church were, oddly enough,
in the same building. In 1633, the former Massachusetts home of
Governor Winthrop was transformed into a religious meeting house
that later became a tavern operating under the name Three Cranes.[2]
In Fitchburg, Massachusetts, the tavern also served as the church on
the Sabbath.[3] From those innocent beginnings the church and tavern in America began their uncomfortable relationship.

194

When a tavern came to a region, it often played host to the church, with religious services conducted inside its communal walls. Not surprisingly, local citizens often preferred the warmth and good spirit found in the tavern over the cold and uncomfortable appointments of the meeting hall. At one point, villages in Massachusetts discovered more parishioners in the tavern on Sunday than in church. This prompted a colony-wide ordinance requiring innkeepers, during hours that services were conducted, to ask those present to kindly attend church. Finally, suffering from the competition for their members' attention, Massachusetts church leaders were successful in introducing a law in 1656 that made not only selling alcohol, but also drinking it, illegal on the Sabbath.

Although inns and taverns were quite spartan by today's standards, they did provide shelter for wayfarers. Colonial travelers slogging along crude, rutted roads could spot taverns by a variety of means. In the earliest days owners marked their establishments by imitating an old English custom. When commercial beer was first introduced, tavern owners erected an "ale stake" to identify their business. An ale stake was nothing more than a pole with a bush tied to the top. Illiterate customers (there were plenty in that time) could easily read the "sign language" that proclaimed "beer." The next generation of tavern signs also was wordless. Their design and shape, commonly portraying the likeness of a famous person or of beer itself on a hanging sign, beckoned the thirsty. Eventually signs with words to indicate the type and name of the business were introduced in the mid- to late-1700s.

Most colonies adopted laws that required inns to display a painted sign within their first 30 days of operation. Before long tavern signs became a common part of the colonial landscape. For one young sign painter, the tavern provided a stepping stone to a much grander vocation. Benjamin West, America's first well-known artist, began his career as a tavern sign painter, composing advertising boards for scores of inns and taverns up and down the East Coast.

On approaching an inn in nice weather, it was common to see several people gathered outside the tavern door. Typically they were the brewer, owner, and regular customers, all seated on an ale bench engaged in conversation and generally enjoying the day.

By the end of the 1700s an average tavern consisted of a main room with sanded floors. At one end stood a large fireplace and near it were several tables and chairs for dining. Along one wall stood a bar.

As in most businesses, there were uniform tools of the trade that all respected colonial bars possessed. Considered odd in later days, the most common were fireplace-oriented beer utensils. A large earthen vessel called a "muller" attracted the attention of all who entered the taproom. From its position on the mantle, a muller proclaimed that the barkeep could replicate the popular drinks of the day. It was shaped like an extra large beer mug or pitcher and functioned like a mixing bowl. In those times beer served as the basis for a number of popular mixed drinks, and the muller was the vessel in which those early "cocktails" were prepared. Well-equipped bars always had a "bar spoon" ready for use with the muller.

Another essential piece of fireplace-related bar equipment was the "mullet." It was funnel-shaped, with the narrow end

196

closed. Set into the grate of the fireplace, and among the coals, it was used to heat beer for the drinks called "cups."

Behind the bar was a "scantling," a type of cradle, made of crossed timbers, which held a cask of beer. In more popular taverns three and up to four casks of different beers were stocked to meet customers' preferences. Beneath the taproom floor better inns had a full cellar. In the days before refrigeration, the best place to keep beer cool was below ground. The insulating properties of the ground kept the temperature stable for a long period of time and allowed extended storage. To this day the term "cellar temperature" refers to the approximately 50 degrees Fahrenheit found in most cellars.

Upstairs a small staff attended to customers' needs, taking orders and serving freshly pulled beers. While delivering beer to the tables, the staff kept running totals of what was consumed, similar to the modern practice of running a tab. Ever-watchful

Night scene.

197

owners reminded the staff to track the bill. Occasionally, especially during raucous and crowded hours, the proprietor would
regularly remind the staff to pay close attention to business with
the phrase "mind your P's and Q's." Common tavern slang, this
was verbal shorthand for "Remember to keep an accurate tally of
your served Pints and Quarts." Eventually the phrase reached
beyond the tavern walls and evolved into a way of telling people
to "mind their own business."

In the average tavern, the taproom was the focal point, and
owners placed an emphasis on its appointments. Sleeping accommodations were a bit more rustic, with several visitors sharing a
common sleeping area. Dr. Wayland F. Dunway described what
he considered an adequate tavern of the day: "The better taverns
were usually built of stone, and their accommodations and tables
were a constant source of pride to the owners. Whatever the class
of tavern, however, its one indisputable feature was the bar,
which provided liquid refreshments not only for jaded travelers
but also the inhabitants of the countryside."[4]

The more affluent taverns would have a parlor, separate from
the taproom, as an exclusive section reserved for the most
wealthy and influential patrons. Functioning as combination
hotels and restaurants, taverns drew currency into a region.

Important as a tavern might be to travelers and the community,
it was even more critical in the plans of the authorities. There
was a only a small budget for public works, and government
buildings in the colonies were virtually nonexistent. Still, it was
essential for any effective colony to have a firm grounding in the
practice of English law. The method used to bring government

to outlying areas was a system of traveling jurists. They moved from town to town settling disputes and administering justice, and this practice became known as "riding the circuit." The authority of the Crown traveled with them. What better way to administer the law than in the center of a community, in a building that could be used at no expense? It seemed as though there was scarcely a pause between the time a tavern was opened and court was in session. Holding court in the tavern not only made riding the circuit a bit more appealing, it further established the tavern as a center of any rural community.

Serving as both a legal and commercial center, the tavern had unparalleled impact on colonial development. Growth and conduct of a region's affairs were invariably tied to the opening of taverns, and it wasn't long until the local tavern also became the social focus of a region. Travelers spending the night carried news and information from throughout the colony, and by this system the colonials also maintained contact with the mother country.

All this activity increased the demand for commercially brewed beer. As the number of taverns multiplied, it became increasingly clear that it was impractical to maintain a supply from England. Colonial breweries filled the void. At first they were inhibited by a lack of brewing's raw materials, malt and hops, but with the introduction of barley strains compatible with the Yankee climate and development of cultivated hopyards, this also changed.

As trade with England and the monetary system further developed, taverns solidified their standing as community centers. No town of any size was without one. Though the colonial

199

administrators were pleased with the results, local events soon tempered their enthusiasm.

Arguably a tavern was one of the most important buildings in a community. It filled the social needs of settlers struggling with an often harsh existence. They were the motels, restaurants, and shopping malls of their day. Among those who relished a good tavern was a circuit riding judge named Samuel Sewall. Coming into a town, Sewall did exactly as his peers did: the first thing he looked for was the tavern.

Use of the tavern was a matter of practicality. More often than not the only communal building was the local tavern. From the 1680s on, the tavern of John Turner hosted so many sessions of the Boston court that he actually designated one of the rooms as court chambers. In those times a barrister needn't travel far to celebrate a successful case; the convenience was in the next room. Judge Sewall (who didn't patronize taverns within Boston) was nonetheless often in the town's ale houses. He presided over many cases heard in the court chamber of George Monck's tavern.

This tradition of conducting a trial in the local watering hole continued for more than a century. Years after Sewall's career the ever-proper John Adams was himself riding the circuit and gladly visited many a tavern. He recorded his impressions of them for posterity, but his ratings should be looked upon with skepticism, for Adams described almost each tavern he visited as the "most genteel."[5]

The first serious threat to the tavern business in the colonies came at the beginning of the eighteenth century, and the cause of it all was a gesture of friendliness. As early as the mid-1650s, the government had been alarmed by intemperance among its citizens. However, complete abstinence was never one of their goals; they just wanted to keep things under control. Yet they did have reason for concern. Springing from one of the new social drinking rituals was a habit that gave them no end of grief: the drinking of toasts.

John Winthrop.

The custom began innocently enough. Raising a glass to someone's health was a means of promoting good spirit and a routine that gathered everyone together in a tavern's main room. What better way to cement a new friendship than over a mug of foamy ale? Unfortunately, the government was given reason to believe that things were getting out of hand. People were raising a mug not only to each others health but also to the King, the Queen, the royal offspring, the colonial governor, his spouse and offspring, and on down to the royal dog catcher.

This was all becoming just too much, and something had to be done. Governor Winthrop of Massachusetts recorded his opposition to toasts, writing, "The Governor, upon consideration of the inconveniences which had grown in England by drinking one to another, restrained it at his own table, and wished others to do the like."[6]

Winthrop was ignored. Equally ineffective was legislation. First attempts to impose "proper" behavior were woefully toothless. Enacted from the 1640s on, drinking and consumption laws were largely disregarded. It wasn't until 1712, when the Act Against Intemperance, Immorality and Prophaneness, and for Reformation of Manners put some power into enforcement. In reality it wasn't the act itself that made the difference, but rather the conscientious deeds of a dedicated law man, a lone protector who attempted to impose order on the chaos.

The night of February 6, 1714, was typical of Boston in midwinter. Shops had long since closed and shuttered their windows. Even at an early hour the streets were relatively empty, but that didn't mean everyone was asleep. A group had gathered in John Wallis's tavern to commemorate the Queen's birthday, and as they began their festivities they anticipated the arrival of a distinguished guest, none other than a member of the Governor's Council and esteemed justice of the Superior Court.

On entering the tavern their guest of honor was warmly greeted. All raised a glass to the Queen's health and jubilantly followed it with a toast to his. Their guest's reaction was exactly what they anticipated. Instead of pleasing him, they had only succeeded in raising his ire. It seems they were violating one of the colony's newest laws, and the guest was not amused. Judge Samuel Sewall was angry.

It was this "tavern disorder" that had prompted a constable to call Sewall away from the warmth of his fire. On arriving he lost no time in calling for the band of revelers to disperse. To Sewall's dismay, instead of following his directive, the group protested and stood their ground. After more than an hour of heated debate, the celebrants left the tavern, but any hope Sewall had of a quick return to his bed immediately evaporated. Merrily regrouping, the party simply relocated their festivities nearby in a home belonging to one of their number. After settling in they called for the colonial equivalent of a beer to go.

Such open defiance of the law was more than Sewall could endure. He obtained the help of his associate justice, Edward Bromfield, who threatened them with calling out the militia. Not yet impressed, the party continued to infuriate Sewall by jokingly spelling their names for his future use in court. Then they compounded the insult by insisting the colonial government was incapable of passing even "one good law." Sewall would see they had their day in court.[7]

It should not be assumed that Sewall was against tipping a glass of beer. In fact, he was known to partake freely of not only beer but also wine and cider. His journal recounts many evenings of hoisting a beer. He even owned a malt house. But the law was the law.

Sewall's encounter illustrates the curious paradox created by colonial lawmakers. There was no question that the establishment of taverns was beneficial to commerce, but the authorities also saw a problem in people gathering and drinking. Also, although people may have gathered initially for a social purpose, inevitably their conversation turned to politics. These political discussions made the Royal Governors nervous, because they questioned both the Crown's wisdom and its authority.

In typical government fashion, the governors' response was the same as putting out a kitchen fire by knocking down the house. Ostensibly they prohibited the drinking of toasts, but their intent was to inhibit what were becoming political gatherings. On the one hand the government was encouraging the growth of taverns, but on the other they concurrently enacted laws to discourage their use.

Unfortunately the encouragement of rural communities to open local taverns worked much better than the attempts to limit the behavior inside those structures. Economic development stimulated by tavern building reached well beyond the expectations of the most optimistic governor. With such unbridled success, the colonial governments couldn't order taverns to close. Politically this would have been the equivalent of shooting oneself in the foot.

As the taverns grew in community stature, they brought an unthought-of advantage, of such importance that it equaled and in some instances exceeded the economic benefit. The tavern provided a means to control vast tracts of the new continent.

Communities soon understood that taverns played an essential role in providing a means of common defense. In colonial times the ordinary citizenry banded together into an armed force. The militia was in effect a volunteer army. In times of Indian raids or threats from French Canada, the militia was called out to protect British settlements. The main problem with relying on a militia was

"WE DRANK THE KING HEALTH IN CHAMPAGNE AND FIRED A VOLLEY, ·∩·∩·
THE PRINCE'I HEALTH IN BURGUNDY AND FIRED A VOLLEY,
·∩·∩· AND ALL THE REET OF THE ROYAL FAMILY IN CLARET AND A VOLLEY."
FROM THE JOURNAL OF M⸰ FONTAINE·OF·THE·PARTY

Training day.

variation in both the ability and experience of its members. Regular army officers unfortunate enough to receive assignments to colonial posts viewed the militia ranks with skepticism at best, and usually with scorn. However, with problems of its own back on the continent, London was reluctant to station a standing army of any size in the Americas.

Thus it was up to the colonists to provide their own defense. The plan seemed simple enough, except that when faced with a choice, most militia members avoided the supposedly mandatory training days. Service in the militia didn't pay, so why drill? Their attitude seemed to be "Well of course I'll take this seriously . . . when I'm faced with certain death." It was exactly this attitude that nearly drove regular officers mad. An army is ineffective and subject to slaughter if it can't maneuver in the field with speed and discipline. Neither pleas nor demands to the Royal Governors could bring about satisfactory attendance. Frontier farmers and traders simply had better fish to fry. They habitually refused to show up for training.

Finally, the administrators turned to a solution that had succeeded with other colonial problems: beer. Need to turn out the population of a region? Easy, underwrite a few barrels of beer at the local tavern. This was an immediate success. Able-bodied "militiamen" literally leapt from the colonial woodwork. It was amazing what a little free ale could do.

With the aid of free ale, it wasn't long until drill day became a not-to-be-missed social function of the North American frontier. Long days of hard work carving a farm out of wilderness meant isolation. Settlers saw a chance to meet neighbors in a relatively relaxing setting, with free beer.

Militia training day became a smashing success. Soon wives and families wanted in on the act, and people started to show up early in order to pursue a little extra socializing before the drill.

Through each assembly of the troops beer flowed freely, sometimes to the detriment of the next day's drill. Thus, despite initial success in calling out the volunteers for drill, officers of the regular army were once again driven nearly to insanity. Was this throng uncontrollable? Eventually they came up with a solution: delay the release of free beer until the training was complete. For once a new policy worked. In New York a particularly well-conducted drill so pleased Governor Crosby that he expressed his gratitude by purchasing 12 barrels of ale for the troops.

A larger problem was brewing. The citizen soldiers were learning a few things. First and foremost, they realized they could function on their own. Second, the militia junior officers were learning to command. They also learned as a unit to assemble and then operate from a central point, the tavern. It is no coincidence that the earliest organized protest to English rule came from the tavern room. That was where political dissent was born and where disobedience to the Crown originated. John Adams described an experience he had in 1774: "I stopped one night at a tavern in Shrewsbury about forty miles from Boston, and . . . There presently came in, one after another, half a dozen, or half a score substantial yeoman of the neighborhood, who, sitting down to the fire after lighting their pipes, began a lively conversation of politics."[8]

Indeed, it was from a tavern that a mob spilled out to provoke Boston's British garrison into what became known as "the

Boston Massacre." Fortunately for the garrison, beer drinker John Adams successfully defended the Red Coats' actions in the trial that followed.

Later, John's cousin, revolutionary protagonist Samuel Adams, directed another group reinforced by the liquid courage of beer. From a planning and command post in Boston's Green Dragon Tavern, an institution that Daniel Webster described as the headquarters of the Revolution, Adams and his compatriots launched a protest to taxes that became known as the Boston Tea Party. Their attack on British cargo ships was in the thin disguise of Indians. Once at the docks they ransacked the tea, throwing it overboard. Such disregard for property by an organized mob pushed the Crown to the limits of its tolerance and set the stage for military action.

When the colonists and the British Army met in Lexington, Massachusetts, the colonists' headquarters was in the nearby Buckman Tavern. Military training and preparation, rewarded by beer, was certainly one factor that led to the colonists flexing their muscles.

Another factor that added to the success of taverns was the primitive state of communications. In those days news was circulated by word of mouth or through the rare newspaper shared by all. It's not hard to imagine, after a hard day's work, spending the evening in a candlelit tavern room. With their tankards (or Jacks) of ale, the locals gathered around a newspaper, listening to one of the inhabitants who could read. Thus in America, as in England, the tavern was much more than a quaint drinking establishment. It provided a community with a focal point for its social life, a news center, and a business hub. More than that, it was the place where people began to talk about politics.

Through their own efforts to develop a promising land, the British authorities set their demise in motion. The rapid growth of taverns and their popularity among the settlers would prove disastrous to the rulers, who did not realize that the solution to development of the colonies, encouraging the growth of taverns, would eventually lead to the end of British Colonial America.

Eleven

BEER DRINKS: THE COLONIAL COCKTAIL

Stepping from behind the bar, the tavern keeper walked over to the flickering hearth. Embers of the hardwood fire burned brightly, filling the room with warmth. Bending over, he picked up the jug he had placed on the brick floor close to the bed of coals. Inside the beer was just beginning to steam.

How many times had he done this since opening this inn? Hundreds? No, thousands. It was one of his most popular drinks. Customers never seemed to tire of ordering it, and he had a certain amount of pride in its preparation.

Placing the earthen jug near the fire was the first step. Then, while it heated, he returned to the bar to scoop his secret mixture into a large tankard. Actually, it wasn't that much of a secret. Tavern keepers all over the country made the same drink, but this was a personal variation. He thought back on preparing

209

it earlier in the day. To the fresh eggs, beaten into a froth, he had added brown sugar and a touch of rum. Others varied the basic recipe by substituting gin; he stuck with the traditional base. His version was unique in what came next. Rather than nutmeg, he added cinnamon, blended with a little apple and pumpkin to create an appealing accent that cut through the richness of the eggs. It made the drink taste distinctly different from the way it did in other taverns, and that was what brought people back here instead.

From the jug the tavern keeper poured the steaming beer into the tankard, swirling it with a spoon to dissolve the mixture. Bending over again, he picked up a poker. Its other end had been thrust into the coals nearly a quarter of an hour ago, and when he pulled it from the fire it glowed bright red. Then he thrust it into the tankard. With a hiss it threw off a small cloud of steam, and boiled the mixed drink into a thick, rocky head. Caramelizing the sugars, it heated the beer further, and cast an aroma of sweet spice throughout the room.

As he approached his customers smiled in anticipation. Perhaps making the drink was a little time consuming, but a result like this made it all worthwhile.

Beyond the sweet and spicy taste, the drink appealed to people for more than the flavor and aroma. They considered it healthy. For thousands of years both professional physicians and disciples of home cures had used beer as a base in their medicines. Of course drinking beer was unquestionably better than drinking water, which was considered vile. But over the years physicians had come to believe that warm beer was best of all. They thought warm liquids were easier to digest, and because

210

beer was considered healthy, there was nothing better than beer-based mixed drinks.

Modern-day cocktails employ a wide range of ingredients, producing a spectrum of characteristics. Use of soda waters became common practice during Prohibition in the 1920s, when inferior bootleg spirits were abundant, but beer supplies, harder to conceal and transport, had dried up. The cocktail owes its existence to the practice of mixing drinks with a base of beer, and in colonial America the beer mixed drink was king. Often as not they were served warm.

Influenced by the recommendations of physicians and folklore, colonial beer drinkers were as likely to order a warmed, mixed beer as a tall, cold one. Pokers called "logger heads," large mixing jugs, and long-handled bar spoons were all common pieces of equipment found in the ale houses, inns, and taverns of early North America.

Names for the mixed beer drinks varied as much as the ingredients. Initially the word "hum" was used generically to describe any sort of heated ale and beer mixture. Typically sold in small measures, it was presented in what was known as a "hum-glass." Hum was sometimes used medicinally: "What a cold I have over my stomach; would I'd some hum."[1] Eventually evolving into a beer laced with a spirit and then heated, hum was said to have been of considerable strength.

As time went by recipes utilizing other ingredients evolved. The earliest recorded beer cocktails included eggs. Egg recipes called for half the beer as a base. Once thoroughly mixed with the other ingredients, it was heated. Well blended, the remaining beer was added and the drink was served immediately.

211

Part Two

Throughout colonial times the most frequently mentioned beer drink was "flip." Undoubtedly of British origin, it was in America that flip gained its stature as a first-rate bar drink. While riding the circuit as a judge, John Adams reported that a person spending a day in the tavern would find it full of people drinking tankards of flip, carousing, and swearing.[2] Though it was reportedly mixed throughout the colonial period, the earliest mention of flip is from 1690. In 1704 the *New England Almanac* described its standing among the popular drinks of the time:

> *The days are short, the weather's cold,*
> *By tavern fires tales are told.*
> *Some ask for dram when first come in,*
> *Others with flip and bounce begin.*[3]

Recipes for flip, as for other foods and drinks, varied from town to town. Fortunately, a significant number of the recipes were printed. Despite the variations, all exhibited common roots. Generally the formulation called for "a great pewter mug or earthen pitcher filled two-thirds full of strong beer; sweetened with sugar, molasses, or dried pumpkin, according to individual taste or capabilities; and flavored with 'a dash'—about a gill—of New England rum. Into this mixture a red hot loggerhead, made of iron and heated in the fire, was thrust."[4]

Another formulation began with four pounds of sugar mixed with four beaten eggs; to this was added one pint of cream. Chilled, it "aged" for two days. When people ordered a flip, a mug was filled two-thirds full with warmed beer, to which the egg, cream, and sugar mixture was added to taste. Finally, a hot logger-head was thrust into the mix. It was topped with a half cup of rum.

Orders for flip appear in the journals of most of the Founding Fathers and frequently punctuate General Washington's expense account. Wherever a revolutionary fire burned, the tavern keeper kept a loggerhead heated and ready. A customary part of the tap-room scene, it was an essential fireplace tool. James Lowell thought it important enough to praise in verse:

> *Where dozed a fire of beechen logs that bred*
> *Strange fancies in its embers golden-red,*
> *And nursed the loggerhead, whose hissing dip,*
> *timed by wise instinct, creamed the bowl of flip*[5]

There were other slang names for both the tools and the drink. Some referred to the loggerhead as a hottle, while others called it a flip-dog. In the book *Cook's Oracle,* flip was listed as a "yard of flannel." Another source insisted that yard of flannel was similar in nature to flip, but distinctly different; although looking at the ingredient list of heated ale, brandy or rum, beer, brown sugar, ginger, lemon peel, and beaten whole eggs, it closely resembles flip.

Modifications of the flip theme appeared with recurring fre-quency. One used fresh rather than an aged egg-and-sugar mixture. When it was beaten into the mixture immediately before serving, it was considered different enough to earn the name "Bellowstop." As the loggerhead hit the fresh egg mix, it had the same effect as with flip, foaming over the top of the mug to the delight of every-one except the person who had to clean up the mess. Flip remained such a fashion that it was regularly served in American bars well into the mid-1800s.

Though flip was certainly one of the most frequently ordered beer cocktails, it was by no means the only one. Thrifty New Englanders devised assorted methods of serving beer, including beer that had gone bad. "Whistle (or whip)-belly-vengeance" was one. Originating in Salem, Massachusetts, it started with a base of sour household beer, simmered in a kettle. The barkeep or housewife then added molasses to offset the tartness and crumbs of "ryneinjun" bread to thicken. It was served piping hot. Dean Swift mentioned it in his "Polite Conversations," when discrediting a local brew as an offensive imitation of beer:

> *Hostess (offering ale to Sir John Linger)*: I never taste malt-liquor, but they say ours is well-hopp'd.
> *Sir John*: Hopp'd why if it had hopp'd a little further, it would have hopp'd into the river.
> *Hostess*: I was told ours was very strong.
> *Sir John*: Yes! strong of water. I believe the brewer forgot the malt, or the river was too near him. Faith! it is more whip-belly-vengeance; he that drinks most has the worst share.[6]

Reportedly as unappetizing as it sounds, this drink was a short-lived fad. Yet another of the warm beer drinks, a "brown Betty," also used bread. It was made from ale, to which the barkeep added brandy, spices, and a piece of toast, then served it hot.

"Egg hot" was another generic name for all types of spiced beers mixed with eggs. Popular from the mid-1600s to the late-1700s, an egg hot was made from one pint of "good ale," to which three eggs, two ounces of sugar, nutmeg, and ginger were added. Another of the same type of drink was called "egg posset" and was made as follows:

> Beat up well the yolks of eight eggs with refined sugar pulverized and a nutmeg grated; then extract the juice from the rind of a lemon by rubbing loaf sugar upon it, and put the sugar with a piece of cinnamon and a quart of strong home-brewed beer into a saucepan, place it on the fire, and when it boils take it off, then add a single glass of gin, or this may be left out, put the liquor into a spouted jug, and pour it gradually among the yolks of eggs, &c. All must be kept well stirred with a spoon while the liquor is being poured in. If it be not sweet enough add loaf sugar. In the university this beverage is frequently given to servants at Christmas and other high festivals.[7]

Other favored drinks of the period included "calibogus" or "bogus," which consisted of rum and unsweetened beer, a colonial version of a shot and a beer, or boiler maker.

Yet another mixed beer drink was "mumm." Not related to the champagne, mumm was a flat (uncarbonated) ale made from fermented oat and wheat malt.

If all this didn't tickle a colonist's fancy, there were other beer-based drinks. One was "ebulum" (also known as ebulam), an ale-based drink prepared from juniper, ginger, elderberries, and assorted spices. It was produced as follows:

215

In a hogshead of the first and strongest wort was boiled one bushel of ripe elderberries. The wort was then strained and, when cold, worked [fermented] in a hogshead (not an open tun or tub.) Having lain in cask for about a year it was bottled. Some persons added an infusion of hops by way of preservative and some like-wise hung a small bag of bruised spices in the vessel.[8]

Another version, made from pale malt and white elderber-ries, was known as "white ebulum."

Also from the colonial dairy case came milk ale. Not a beer made from milk, it was another of the mixed drinks based on beer. It was made from one quart of ale combined with a pinch each of grated dried ginger and nutmeg. While it heated slowly, one large spoon of sugar was added. In a separate pan a quart of milk was heated to just below boiling and then blended with the ale mixture. It was served immediately after mixing.

Buttered ale reached the height of its popularity in the 1500s. Made in the days before hops were added to beer, it was reputed to have been a strong, unhopped beer to which they added sugar, spice, butter, and an egg yolk. No doubt it was a close relative of flip.

On occasion the names for some of the beer drinks were extremely misleading. Aleberry, dating from the 1600s, was a term used to describe a hopped ale, as opposed to the early "beer" that was unhopped. No berries were added to the beer. Beer was the base of all the previously listed concoctions:

Their ale-berries, cawdles and possets each one,
    And sullabubs made at the milking pail,

216

> *Although they be many, Beer comes not in any*
> *But all are composed with a Pot of Good Ale.*[9]

Later the term *aleberry* indicated a type of gruel or soup made with warm ale, oatmeal, sugar, bread, and flavorings such as lemon juice and nutmeg.

Mentioned in the poem above, and in many other writings of the era was "posset." All through the 1600s and into the following century, posset was served as another warmed beer drink. In one, the bartender combined warm curdled milk and ale with nutmeg.

Among the drinks brought over from England were the many "beer cups." Generally they followed a fairly uniform pattern. Starting with a quart of mild ale, a glass each of white wine, brandy, and capillaire (sweetened syrup) was added, along with the juice of a lemon and a thin slice of its peel, grated nutmeg, and a piece of bread. It also went by the name "cool tankard" and was consumed with regularity throughout the 1600s.

A cool tankard was made by extracting the juice from the peel of one lemon by rubbing it on a loaf of sugar. Next, two additional lemons were thinly sliced and combined with one-quarter pound of sugar, a half pint of brandy, and a quart of cold water. After mixing in a large container, a pint of white wine and a quart of strong beer, ale, perry, or cider were blended in. Finally, it was sweetened to taste with the capillaire, or sugar, and a handful each of balm and borage (an herb with a blue flower used in place of hops in some primitive colonial beers) were added. It was let to cool and set for one hour.

Another of the many cups was a "grace cup." This was ceremonially featured at corporation dinners. Sounding remarkably like the standard beer cup, the greatest difference between it and others appears to have been the use and name. It was prepared as follows:

> Extract the juice from the peeling of a lemon and cut the remainder into thin slices; put it into a jug or bowl, and pour on it three half pints of strong home-brewed beer and a [cup] of mountain wine: grate a nutmeg into it; sweeten it to your taste; stir it till the sugar is dissolved, and then add three or four slices of bread toasted brown. Let it stand two hours, and then strain off into the Grace Cup.[10]

A "parting cup" was another beer-based drink made for a specific purpose. In this case it was served on occasions of parting. It was also known as a "stirrup cup" because it was offered as a person sat on horseback, preparing to depart. People partook of "parting cups" as a sign of friendship; it was a way of saying that parting was almost too much to bear.

> *With those that drink before they dine —*
> *With him that apes the grunting swine,*
> *Who fills his page with low abuse,*
> *And strives to act the gabbling goose*
> *Turned out by fate to feed on grass —*
> *"Boy, give me quick, the parting glass."*
>
> *The man, whose friendship is sincere,*
> *Who knows no guilt, and feels no fear: —*
> *It would require a heart of brass*
> *With him to take the parting glass.*

With him, who quaffs his pot of ale;
Who holds to all an even scale;
Who hates a knave, in each disguise,
And fears him not—whate'er his size —
With him, well pleased my days to pass,
May heaven forbid the PARTING GLASS.

—Philip Freneau (1752–1832) [11]

To make a parting glass nowadays, begin by darkly browning or toasting two pieces of bread. Add them to a quart of mild ale mixed with two-thirds of a bottle of sherry. Grate in nutmeg, then sweeten the ale mixture with simple syrup (sugar and water mixed together). Immediately before serving, pour in one bottle of soda water.

Though used in any matter of celebration or recognition, beer cups were most commonly presented as a form of folk or home cure. Throughout the ages beer has supplied the basis for medicinal cures. Translations of the remedies listed in the ancient Egyptian book of the dead identify over 100 recipes based on beer. Ben Johnson, in his *Alchemist*, written in the 1500s, noted the use of ale in medicine of the period: "Yes, faith, she dwells in Sea-coal lane, did cure me With sodden ale."[12]

One cup, called Dr. Brown's ale, was made from an infusion of ale with various spices and "medicines." Invented by the court physician to King James, it incorporated everything he thought necessary to rid a patient of coughs and other aliments:

Take Senna and Polypedium, each four ounces, Sarseperilla two ounces, Agrimony and Maidenhair of each a small handful, scurvy grass a quarter of a peck, bruise them grossly in a stone mortar, put them into a thin canvass bag, and hang the bag in nine or ten gallons of ale; when it is well worked and when it is three or four days old, it is ripe enough to be drawn off and bottled, or as you see fit.[13]

Cups were often served as a summer drink, and were frequently spiced with mint, citrus, or other fruit. No set recipe existed, people concocted their own favorite blends. The Duchess of St. Albans was reported to have one she called "The Ale of Health and Strength," made from small beer in which she steeped herbs from her garden. Period writings offered advice as to its consumption:

> *Three cups of this a prudent man may take;*
> *The first of these for constitutions sake,*
> *The second to the girl he loves the best,*
> *The third and last to lull him to rest.*[14]

Going by any number of names, beer cups in different regions were called humpty dumpty, clamber-clown, hugmatee, stickback, cock ale, stiffe, blind pinneaux, stephony, northdown, and knock-me-down.

As the types of beer cups were perfected, they were designated as remedies for specific ailments. Patients might be directed to mix specific types as follows:

For pains in the knees—Muddle (pound and mix) woodwax and hedge-rife, then add to ale. A remedy devised by the Saxons, this was applied both internally and externally.

For those low with sickness—Take two pounds of dates and wash them clean in ale, then cut them and take out the stones and white skins, then cut them small, and beat them in a mortar, till they begin to work like wax, and then take a quart of clarified Honey or sugar, and a half an ounce of the Podder of Long Pepper, as much of Mace of Cloves, Nutmegs, and Cinnamon, of each one Drachm, as much of the Powder of Lignum Aloes; beat all the Spies together and Seeth the Dates with the sugar or Honey with an easie fire, and let it seeth . . . then eat little every morning and evening . . . and it will renew and restore.

—From the *Book of Notable Things*

For good against the devil—Mix a handful of sedge and gladden in a pan, pour in a bowlful of ale, boil the mixture, and "rub" in 25 libcorns.

For lunacy—Work (stir) herbs into clear ale, say 7 masses over the worts, add garlic and holy water, then have the patient suffering from lunacy drink it out of a church bell.

For lung disease—Avoid drinking sweet ale, but drink instead a clear ale in which young oak rind was boiled.

For consumption—Recommended in "The London County Brewer" of 1744, a brown ale called "stich" was administered to the unfortunates suffering from consumption. It was brewed from the first running off the malt and thereby was of considerable strength.

221

For black jaundice—To prepare a cure required a base made from a pint of honey and a gallon of ale. To that they added about half a cup of red nettles and some saffron and then boiled it. They skimmed it as it boiled, strained it, and let it cool. Over a period of two weeks they administered it to the patient every morning.

For coughs—Add a handful of red sage to a quart of ale and boil it, strain it, and then add a quarter pound of treacle. It was consumed warm immediately before bed.

For coughs and shortness of wind—Use "buttered beer." To prepare a batch, take a quart of strong beer and add a good piece of fresh butter, sugar candy, liquorice, and grated ginger.

For hiccups—Pound the root of jarrow, work it into a good beer, and serve it to the patient lukewarm. It was also alleged to be effective against all manner of other internal disturbances.[15]

Finally, if all else failed, a person could opt for the "Freemason's cup." A potent type, it was made from one pint of scotch ale and another of mild. To that they added one-half pint of brandy, a pint of sherry, half a pound of loaf sugar, and a generous amount of ground nutmeg, all blended together right before drinking.

Colonials observed Christmas, but with nothing like the festivities that began in the second half of the 1800s. To them the holiday was usually a quiet time at home. Still, they devised special seasonal drinks for the winter. "Jingle" was one of the traditional mixtures. Its recipe calls for ale, sweetened with sugar and flavored with nutmeg and apples. Reportedly it had a taste like that of another drink, named "lambswool." Popular in the 1700s, it was served at the beginning of November to celebrate the harvest of fruits and seeds. It was traditionally served through the remainder of the winter season as a form of strong drink:

> *Doubt not, then said the King, my promist secresye:*
> *The King shall never know more on't for mee.*
> *A cupp of lambswool they dranke unto him then,*
> *And to their bedds they past presentlie.*[16]

Tavern owners and others prepared lambswool by warming a strong (old) ale while mixing in grated nutmeg, ginger, and sugar. Apples were then roasted until the skins burst and were added to the warm beer mixture before serving.

Finally, there was "purl." Fortified with gin and bitters, purl was often prepared in advance, and allowed to cellar and mature for up to a year. Some versions used spices, and variations added Roman wormwood, gentian root, calamus aromaticus, horse radish, dried orange peel, juniper berries, and seeds soaked in the beer. When ready to serve it was heated, then cooled to a temperature at which a person could consume it in a single draught.

Colonial mixed drinks were created for a number of reasons. First, they served as a substitute for the fashionable but expensive wines of the day. They were also, as noted, valued as homemade medicines. Additionally, they may have been considered a way to "save" the often poorly made homebrewed beers of the era. Possessing only rudimentary equipment, and often forced to improvise ingredients and procedures, the beers were nothing like those consumed after the introduction of technology.

There is also circumstantial evidence supporting the theory that beer-based mixed drinks were designed as a way to save terrible beer. As brewing's raw materials, equipment, instruments, procedures, and science advanced in the 1800s, beer mixed drinks faded from popularity and all but disappeared. They did not outlast the period when the quantity of beer was greatest and its quality poorest.

A few of the beer mixed drinks have enjoyed a revival. Winter warmers and Christmas beers are a direct link back through time to the days of colonial drinking, and spicing, of beer.

Twelve

HOMEBREWING:
AMERICA'S BEER HERITAGE

Cool darkness greeted the farm wife on opening the milk-house door. This was a good sign. Farm wives like her always worried about the temperature, because the beer never seemed right when it got too warm. With so much time and work invested, there was reason to worry. Months before, she had completed the long process of malting the grain, and had dried it carefully over smokeless coals. Weeks ago, she had crushed the grain and added boiling water to soak it in a mash.

Draining produced a rich liquid laced with sugars from the malt. Stoking the fire beneath her largest kettle brought it to a vigorous boil, then she added hops. Last fall they had been lucky. A family trip to the woods had yielded a bountiful harvest of wild hops. In bad years she added fresh oak chips to offset the malt's sweetness, a trick she had learned from her mother. Cooling the pot after boiling took longer than she liked, but the barm (yeast) went quickly to work.

After what she estimated to be the proper amount of time, the farm wife had bottled the beer. Once over the next few days she wondered aloud if the timing had been correct. Her husband overheard, but said nothing. He knew nothing about brewing, that was woman's work.

Over the years she had had some bad batches of beer. However, she always managed to save it in some fashion. Once she added molasses. Another time roasted apples rescued a sharply sour beer. Her good beers were more memorable. She remembered the pride they had in the beer at the barn raising, and of course there was the beer they had brought to the church social. People always seemed to share their best.

Carrying a jug of beer to the kitchen, she made a little wish for it to be well balanced, strong, hoppy, and well conditioned. When she uncaged it and freed the cork, a wisp of pressure escaped. Her family would be happy. She smiled.

New settlements built brew houses soon after settling, and in a noncommercial effort of cooperation they made beer for the entire community. Later, as they were able to build proper houses, they continued brewing in their own kitchens. Making beer was as much a part of their households as cleaning and cooking.

Shortages of beer and the lack of hard currency encouraged continued homebrewing for most rural New Englanders, and it became a tradition that lasted well over three centuries. However, the beer was somewhat different from today's. Households were often confounded by economic conditions that prevented buying raw materials (much as they blocked the purchase of commercially produced beer). By no means did resourceful Yankees abstain—they simply made adjustments and compromises. Robert Beverly, the early colonial historian, observed:

> Their small drink is either wine or water, beer. . . . Their richer sort generally brew their small beer with malt, which they have from England, though barley grows there very well; but for the convenience of malt-houses, the inhabitants take no care to sow it. The poorer sort brew their beer with molasses and bran; with Indian corn malted with drying in a stove: with persimmons dried in a cake and baked; with potatoes with the green stalks of Indian corn cut small and bruised, with pompions, with the Jerusalem artichoke which some people plant purposely for that use, but this is the least esteemed.[1]

Using corn to augment or replace malt in brewing was practiced as early as 1584. Englishman Thomas Hariot wrote of it in his "Narrative of the First English Plantation of Virginia," published in 1588. His description thoroughly detailed the manner in which corn was used to brew beer, and described its character.

Substitution for traditional ingredients was practiced by commercial and homebrewers alike. During the formative years in the New World malt was scarce, and the strange, native plant that became known as corn ably filled the void in brewing. Almost two centuries after Hariot's description of homebrew, on February 14, 1775, journalist London Carter wrote of corn's use in the *Virginia Gazette*:

The stalks, green as they were, as soon as pulled up, were carried to a convenient trough, then chopped and pounded so much, that, by boiling, all the juice could be extracted out of them; which juice every planter almost knows is of as saccharine a quality almost as any thing can be, and that any thing of a luxuriant corn stalk is very full of it . . . After . . . the stalks and all were put into a large copper, there lowered down in its sweetness with water, to an equality with common observations in malt wort, and then boiled, till the liquor in a glass is seen to break, as the brewers term it; after that it is strained, and boiled again with hops. The beer I drank had been made above twenty days, and bottled off about four days.[2]

Articles like those by Carter were common, and often were supplemented by pamphlets. One of the same period described itself as "Every Man His Own Brewer, a practical treatise, explaining the art and mystery of brewing porter, ale, two-penney and table beer, intended to reduce the expense of families, by Samuel Child, brewer."[3] Child outlined the process and provided recipes of his own formulation. Patterned after the popular beer styles of the day, his booklet focused on ales and featured instructions on making porter: "One quarter of malt, 8 lbs. hops, 9 lbs. treacle, 8 lbs. licorice root, 8 lbs. essentia bina, 8 lbs. color; capsicum,

A primitive mash tub.

1/2 oz.; Spanish Liquorice, 2 oz.; cocculus indicus, 1/4 oz.; ginger, 3 oz.; lime 4 oz., slacked; linseed, 1 oz.; cinnamon, 2 drachms."[4]

Settlers in Connecticut began making beer shortly after their arrival, with homebrewing documented from the mid-1630s on. Without doubt it was common practice after 1634, when a party dispatched from the colony of Massachusetts settled in the area that became New Haven.

In Providence, Rhode Island, in the early 1700s, Major Thomas Fenner was well known for his homebrew. It is a classic example of substitution: "One ounce of Sentry Suckery or Sulindine one handful Red Sage or Large 1/4 Pound Shells of Iron Brused fine take 10 quarts of Water Steep it away to Seven and a quart of Molasses Wheat Brand Baked Hard. One quart of Malt one handful Sweeat Balm Take it as Soone as it is worked."[5]

A British writer in the 1730s described homebrew in the colony of Maryland. He explained that the people there grew very little malt, and so improvised: "The beer they brew is excellent, which they make in great Quantities, of Prsimmons, &c., of Molasses; for few of them are Come to malting their corn, of any kind, at which I was much surprised; [sic] as even the Indian Grain, as I have found experimentally, will produce an wholesome and generous Liquor."[6]

Georgian settlers from Salzburg wrote letters back to Germany about the brewing conditions in that colony as it existed in 1751. Their pastor, Johann Martin Bolzius, described the practice of homebrewing: "A brewer is not needed for as yet too little barley is grown; and the inhabitants who have the ability cook a healthy beer for themselves out of syrup, Indian corn and hops, or the tops of the white water firs, which is very cheap. Strong barley comes from New York, at times also from England."[7]

During the War for Independence homebrewing caught on again, and the attitudes formed during the war years prevailed for decades. Almost everyone seemed to have a way to make up the shortage of ingredients. Ben Franklin had his recipe for spruce beer, acquired while serving on the peace treaty commission in Paris. On his return, Franklin shared it with his fellow Americans:

> For a Cask containing 80 bottles, take one Pot of Essence [of spruce] and 13 pounds of Molasses.—or the same amount of unrefined Loaf Sugar; mix them well together in 20 pints of hot Water: Stir together until they make a Foam, then pour it into the Cask you will then fill with Water: add a Pint of good Yeast, stir it well together and let it stand 2 or 3 Days to ferment, after which close the Cask, and after a few days it will be ready to be put into Bottles, that must be tightly corked. Leave them 10 or 12 Days in a cool Cellar, after which the Beer will be good to drink.[8]

With no supply of hops, North Americans throughout the colonial period enjoyed and perfected spruce beers. It seemed everyone had their own special recipe. General Jeffrey Amherst, governor-general of British North America, produced a recipe in 1760:

> Take 7 Pounds of good Spruce & boil it well till the bark peels off, then take the Spruce out & put three Gallons of Molasses to the Liquor & boil it again, scum

it well as it boils, then take it
out the kettle & put it into a
cooler, boil the remained of
the water sufficient for a
Barrel of thirty Gallons, if the
kettle is not large enough to
boil it together, when milk-
warm in the Cooler put a
Pint of Yest [sic] into it and
mix well. Then put in the
Barrel and let it work for two
or three days, keep filling it
up as it works out. When
done working, bung it up

Jeffrey Amherst.

with a Tent Peg in the Barrel to give it vent every now
and then. It may be used in two or three days after. If
wanted to be bottled it should stand a fortnight in the
Cask. It will keep a great while.[9]

As colonials replaced hops with spruce, so too they found an
alternative for malt. Members of the American Philosophical
Society published a formula for pumpkin ale in 1771: "The
expressed Juice of the [pumpkin] is to be boiled in Copper . . .
that there may be no Remains of the fibrous Part of the Pulp.
After that Intention is answered let the Liquor be hopped cooled
fermented & c. as Malt Beer."[10]

Used only in desperation, pumpkin ale never attained great
popularity. As opposed to modern pumpkin beer, in which the
pumpkin only adds flavor, for colonials the pumpkin was a source

of fermentable sugar. Pumpkin ale of the colonial era, as a result, was said to have a noticeable "tang" unless aged for a few years.

George Washington recorded another formula for a beer made with a sizable substitution of molasses while on duty with the British in the French and Indian War. His homebrewed small beer was easily reproduced, all the brewer needed to do was to

> take a large Siffer full of Bran Hops to your taste—Boil these 3 hours hen strain out 30 Gallns into a cooler put in 3 Gallns molasses while the beer is scalding hot or rather draw the molasses into the cooler & strain the beer on it while boiling hot. Let this stand till it is little more than Blood warm then put in a quart of yeast if the weather is very cold cover it over with a blanket & let it work in the Cooler 24 hours then put it into the Cask—leave it the Bung open till it is almost don[e] Working—Bottle it that day [the next] Week [after] it was Brewed.[11]

Washington was more than the first president, he was a beer lover of the first order. His interest in homebrew illustrates the degree to which homebrewing was instilled in every walk of life.

Joseph Clarke, general treasurer of the Rhode Island colony, described his own method of brewing in 1775:

> You are first to have ready the following Implements, a mash Vat, to put your malt in; a Vessel under this to receive the Wort in; a Copper to boil it in; a Rudder to stir your malt with, and Vessels to cool your Liquor in.

First then fill your Copper with water, take then 6 Bushels of Malt and put into your mash Vat, leaving about a Peck to sprinkle over the Liquor when in, Let your water simper, and be in the next degree of boiling but not boil; lay it on upon the Malt well ground, and when you have laid on such a quantity as you can draw off a Barrel sprinkle the remaining Peck of Malt over all covering it up with Cloths and draw off a pail full or two; and lay it on again to clear your tap hole.

This done the next Business is to boil a Copper of Water, to scald your other Vessels with; always taking care to have a Copper of Liquor hot to lay on, upon the malt when you draw off the first Wort, and this will be for small Beer.

The three hours now expired; let go (as the Term is) which is let the first wort run off, putting into Vessel which receives it a pound of Hops; when all drawn off lay on the hot Liquor for your small Beer, clean out your Copper and put the wort, Hops and all into the Copper and boil it for two hours; strain it then off thro: a Sieve into your Vessels to cool it; and put your small Beer into Copper and the same hops that come out of the first Beer and boil it an hour.

When both are almost cool add Yeast to them; to set it to work, breaking the head in every time it rises; till it works itself clear and tun it; Bung it up with Clay and keep it in your Cellar, in three months you may bottle the Strong Beer, the other in a weeks time will be fit to drink.[12]

Along with providing advice on brewing recipes and techniques, publications described the materials and equipment that improved the quality of homebrew. At the start of the 1800s, I. E. Boardley published his "Essays and Notes on Husbandry and Rural Affairs." In the section on homebrewing Boardley explained

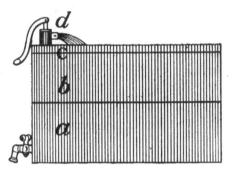

The Boardley family's brewing vessel.

the construction and operation of the "Tripartite" brewery. One vessel, separated by false bottoms into three separate sections, made up an advanced homebrewing mash tun.

Tripartite systems were built 40 inches long and 20 inches wide. Two inches from the top sat the first false bottom, a crude version of a colander. Set nine inches below the first false bottom was a second, the equivalent of a screen at the bottom of a modern commercial mash tun, leaving a void of 13 inches at the bottom of the tun.

Homebrewers placed a layer of malt in the center section of the tun and mashed in. Connected to the lowest void space was a pipe that allowed either pumping back to the top section, or draining to a vessel, and the liquid was then poured over the top. Homebrewers using the system repeated the process until the sweet liquor ran clear from the bottom. They then drained it to a brew kettle, added hops, and continued brewing in conventional fashion. Interest in these articles and improved homebrewing equipment continued for years.

234

Well into the 1800s and beyond, North Americans home-brewed, originally because of the severely limited distribution area of commercial breweries. Later, as city dwellers switched to purchasing beers from local breweries, homebrewing continued in the hamlets, villages, and farms of less-populated areas.

Gradually ingredients improved, as Americans started growing larger quantities of barley and hops. Homebrewing remained the major source of beer in the agricultural regions of the Americas until the latter half of the 1800s, when technological advances brought more rapid transportation, mass production of glass and mass bottling became practical, pasteurization lengthened beer's shelf life, and brewers perfected manufacturing techniques to assure beer stability.

Thirteen

Beer Under Fire: Temperance and Prohibition

As dark settled in, the driver leaned forward in his seat. Wrinkles deepened around his eyes as he unconsciously squinted at the road ahead of him. His grip tightened a little bit, and before long he would feel the results of that involuntary action as a knot forming between his shoulder blades.

Far from the comforting lights of town, the freighter was feeling a little nervous. He had good reason. Outside the village the thoroughfare deteriorated rapidly, road signs vanished, and assistance was scarce. None of those obstacles was his greatest challenge, however. What he worried about most was a potentially fatal problem: gangs hijacking loads were becoming more and more frequent.

Deserted stretches of road were the most dangerous, and it was just such an area he was passing through. Narrow and winding, with blind curves, at times the road sank between high banks as it cut through the rolling hills. It was the perfect spot for an easy ambush. Worse yet, the driver was carrying a targeted load: beer. Each foot of the road passed in agonizingly slow motion. If it weren't for the big payoff, he'd have never taken the job, and at times he swore each run would be his last.

Since Prohibition had been enacted, many of his kind had been victimized along similar stretches of road, and on the water the business of moving alcohol was equally hazardous. Transporting a forbidden cargo lowered the risk for thieves. They knew the victim would never report the crime, because the lonely drivers were also breaking the law. All of them were engaged in a deadly game of cat and mouse, all trying to make big money, and fast.

Profits were easy. The population did not support the law. In fact, the general public held it in contempt. True, magazines published stories and poems decrying the evils of alcohol, portraying broken homes, wrecked lives, and deplorable poverty. The fact was, few believed it. People wanted a drink. The effort to get one was turning nearly everyone into a law breaker. As restrictions tightened, the crime rate escalated, a result of the demand for illegal alcohol.

Sound like the first part of the twentieth century? Sure it does. From today's vantage point this little story of hijacking brings to mind visions of the Roaring Twenties, with gangsters and deception mixing in black-and-white images of bootlegging and rum running. In reality, this scene reaches much farther back in U.S. history. Scenes like this took place when localities, and sometimes states, outlawed alcohol. Prohibition movements first appeared in the early 1800s, but its roots dated to the time when European settlers first landed on the North American continent.

Settlers brought all aspects of their culture to the New World. Most of it was the solid stuff vital to keeping a young community together. Celebrations, religion, law, and heritage formed a blanket of security in a strange, foreign land. Hardships were more easily borne if the citizenry had the familiar to console them. Beer drinking was one of the things that bound them together. It was a communal drink, and as such had a respected role in the colonies. But not all alcoholic beverages were so readily embraced. A collective social memory recalled the tragedy of overindulgence and alcoholism that plagued England in former times.

It is easy to see how the settlers were confronted with opposing memories, beliefs, biases, and fears. Water was unsafe, but Old World lessons taught them alcohol could lead to social problems. They struggled with the question, "To drink, or not to drink?" and decided to drink. But as they did the issue of whether or not it was acceptable tore at the souls of the young settlements.

Nowadays the concept called separation of church and state is a natural part of our social philosophy. Things were different in colonial times. Rights and freedoms were important, but in a different way. Religious freedom meant the right to select and practice a religion not endorsed by the government. Unfortunately, in their efforts to escape the oppressiveness of the dominant European religions, settlers created their new communities in exactly the image they were escaping, especially in New England.

Leaders of the new settlements were often the ranking clergy who had guided their flocks on the long crossing to America. Their religion was cleansed of anything remotely resembling fun. It was this outlook which led to clashes with alcohol. How, they thought, could anything like alcohol be good when church teachings discounted nearly all forms of fun and self-indulgence. Alcohol was at odds with America's religions from the very start.

It wasn't only on alcohol that the church cast an eye of disapproval. Colonial clerics were the original "fun police." Skip church and you risked a fine of five shillings. Bring a deck of cards into the colony, and not only were they confiscated, but you also paid a penalty of five pounds for your error. No tobacco was allowed unless you were on a journey of over 10 miles. Single men could not live alone, and all games were outlawed. This was all part of the plan to reach a higher level of spirituality. From just outside the colony, economics tugged at the flock. Taverns were opening interior lands by stimulating the economy.

Not able to suppress the business of alcohol, church leaders sought other methods of control. Any number of strange restrictions followed. For example, innkeepers were prohibited from making games available, because church leaders believed bar games would waste "valuable time" and distract the citizenry. Conducting business on the Sabbath was considered entirely unforgivable. From early attempts to control alcohol came the "blue laws," now unfathomable ordinances banning the sale of alcoholic beverages on Sundays.

Throughout the colonial period the authorities struggled with the issue of alcohol. On the one hand, they believed it a necessity and referred to it as "the good creature of God," using it as a tool for financial development. At the same time, excessive consumption was considered a very real threat to the very fiber of society. From this conflict the early temperance movements were born. Control of alcohol and its consumption was the initial objective, not prohibition, but the original intent was a source of constant self-doubt, conflicting policies, and mixed messages to the populace. The indecision and paranoia led to the evolution of an uniquely American social schizophrenia, apparent at nearly every public discussion about alcohol.

Early efforts at alcohol regulation reveal an uneasy compromise of obligatory coexistence. When restrictions interfered with the desires of the populace, those affected, as was the custom in the Old World, found alternate supplies. Speakeasies, closely associated with the 1920s, were first introduced in the colonial era. Likewise, high tariffs, instituted for the dual purpose of generating revenue and controlling drinking, led to moonshining and smuggling. However, during the entire formation of the country, beer was not at issue. Authorities considered it largely benign. There was a bigger threat.

From the late 1600s on, the merchants of New England had developed trading routes with the British West Indies. Molasses, and its offspring, rum, was a solid part of the business. Eventually the New Englanders built their own distilleries, importing the molasses to make their own rum, and with it huge profits. Over time the practice became the lucrative "triangle trade" in which New England rum was exchanged in Africa for slaves who were sold in the South. The currency was used to purchase more West Indies molasses, which in turn was distilled in the North.

Riches reaped from the triangle trade propelled many colonial businessmen up the ladder of wealth. At its peak an estimated 600,000 gallons of the "demon rum" was shipped in a single year.

If the use of rum had been confined to the slave trade, there would have been little concern over its manufacture, but colonists in the North and South alike soon developed a taste for the spirit. Rum worked its way into every aspect of life and was threatening to displace beer and cider as the drink of choice. With the growing popularity of rum came increasing drunkenness. This problem was the basis of the first American temperance movement.

Georgia was settled much later than the other colonies. James Oglethorpe didn't receive a charter until 1733, and when he did one of his first concerns was about productivity. Oglethorpe knew it was challenge enough to hack civilization out of the wilderness, and he wanted distractions at a minimum. At his request the authorities in London issued a proclamation in 1733: "As it appears by your letters that the sickness among the people is owing to the excessive drinking of rum punch, the Trustees do absolutely forbid their drinking, or even having any rum." Along with their letter they provided copies of "Dr. Hale's Friendly Admonition to the Drinkers of Brandy."[1] This pamphlet provides insight into the relationship of distilled spirits, fermented beverages (beer), and prohibition. Dr. Hale did not advocate total abstinence. In fact, he suggested the use of beer over other alcohol. Beer was not the target.

Average residents of Georgia viewed the attempts at prohibition with scorn. Their response was to ignore the proclamation. King George II countered in 1737 by approving an act that forbade

242

the importation and sale of rum in the colony. This too was ignored. "Rum runners" landed the illegal cargo in South Carolina and concealed its transfer into Georgia. With no power to enforce the law, and unable to prevent the illegal traffic, the government abandoned the prohibition on rum in 1742. The consequences of smuggling, bootlegging, homebrewing, and rum running were a lesson lost on later generations. Studying its ineffectiveness and the trouble it created could have provided leaders of later years with valuable knowledge of failed approaches. Instead, they made more ill-fated attempts to separate the public from beer.

"Demon rum" was eventually defeated, but not in a way that anyone could have imagined. When the situation seemed most intolerable, colonial politics provided an unrelated solution. War was declared on Great Britain.

With supplies of molasses cut off, distilling came to an abrupt stop. Shifting direction in one fluid motion, the revolutionary government went from attempting to control rum to begging for a supply. The reason was that a daily ration of rum had been promised to the fledgling army. Suddenly none was to be had, leaving the army (and the new government) in a quandary.

At Valley Forge, Washington's troops complained loud and often of no pay, clothing, food, or rum. At times their dissatisfaction approached mutiny. Over time the rum ration was replaced by another spirit, American corn and rye whiskey, but until it gained acceptance the colonial quartermasters searched for rum, and substituted with beer.

While thankful that a supply of whiskey grew to replace rum, the army leadership grew wary of the practice of troops consuming up to a pint of spirits a day. Up until that time it was considered prudent to fortify a person with alcohol, the general belief being that it would refresh and revitalize the body. One man studied this belief in depth.

Thirty years old at the outbreak of the revolution, Philadelphia's Dr. Benjamin Rush was the University of Pennsylvania's first professor of medicine. Through his service in the Continental Congress he became well regarded and was appointed as Physician-General of the Continental Army. One of his early conclusions about the health of the troops was that alcohol was severely limiting their fighting ability. In 1778 he published his theories in a pamphlet titled "Directions for Preserving the Health of Soldiers." Among other recommendations, he dismissed the notion of taking hard liquors for health as totally fictitious.

Following the war, Rush continued his study of the alcohol problem. He came to the same conclusion from each investigation: excessive consumption was indeed a detriment to health. However, Rush did not propose total abstinence.

Releasing his findings in 1784 in a booklet entitled "Inquiry into the Effects of Spiritous Liquors on the Human Body and Mind," he set the drinking world on its ear. Contradicting the popularly held notion that spirits augmented health, he described the opposite effect, backing up his assertions with scientific observations. Throughout, it was a condemnation of the practice of heavy drinking, but it held one surprise.

Rush devised what he called a "A Moral and Physical Thermometer." Running up the scale, he listed the various beers, wines, ciders, and spirits. Across the scale he listed their effects on the human body. Worst on his list was what in that period were called the "ardent spirits." Rush claimed that these would

244

make a person resemble an animal: "in stupidity, an ass; in roaring, a mad bull; in quarreling and fighting, a dog; in cruelty, a tiger; in fetor, a skunk; in filthiness, a hog; in obesity, a he-goat."[2] At the bottom of the list were beer, cider, and water. Doctor Rush described that portion of the thermometer as leading to a long, healthy, and happy life. More than 200 years later, the U.S. government, through the department of agriculture, verified that moderate drinking of beer was a beneficial practice in the promotion of health.

Although he was never the leader of a temperance movement, Rush and his work did influence others. At the start of the 1800s, pious citizens and clerical leaders throughout the young country were concerned about the morals of their communities. It was a period of increased religious influence, which has always coincided with a temperance movement in America.

One of the first organized groups was founded in New York State. It began when a small town doctor named William Clark voiced anxiety to his minister about drunkenness in their rural town. Shortly before their meeting, Clark had finished reading the pamphlet written by Benjamin Rush. Gathering together the notable members of the town, they discussed the problem, and on April 30, 1808, established the Union Temperance Society of Moreau and Northumberland. It was the first formal temperance group in the United States. Others soon followed, each with at least a portion of its roots in religion.

Reverend Lyman Beecher, father of Harriet Beecher Stowe, was another who read Dr. Rush's booklet. He took aim at alcohol abuse and in 1813 was one of the founders and head of the Connecticut Society for the Reformation of Morals. His mission was aided by the Reverend Mason Locke Weems, most famous as inventor of the George Washington cherry tree story. Weems, inspired by Rush, wrote an essay titled "The Drunkards Looking Glass."

More clergy joined the movement. Reverend Justin Edwards of Boston founded the American Society for Prohibition (ASP) on February 13, 1826. Assisted by Reverend Nathaniel Hewitt of Fairfield, Connecticut, he developed the society into a national power with more than 1,000 branches.

By 1832 temperance movements had recruited enough members to begin meeting in a national forum. Prompted by Reverend Edwards, the national organization of the ASP suggested gathering the various chapter members at a national convention in Philadelphia. Delegates were confident that national prohibition was within reach, and with high spirits they formed the American Temperance Union. Their intention was to develop and approve a common leadership, responsible for instituting a uniform strategy.

At first the American Temperance Union provided an image of solidarity. Organizers reveled in a wave of new memberships. For a time their growth and success seemed assured, which of course attracted the attention of Congress. Ever-savvy politicians were ready to hear the opinion of any group representing such a large block of voters, and eventually Reverend Edwards was invited to address both houses on the subject of national temperance.

Drinkers must have braced themselves for the inevitable. However, as the anti-drinkers' influence was reaching its peak, their leaders made a critical error. Though holding the full attention of legislators, they failed to ask for national legislation. Instead they were content to request elected officials to merely set examples for their constituents. Not pushing for a national law set the movement up for failure.

Fortunately for beer drinkers, the various temperance societies and associated chapters were only loosely organized. When nondrinking ordinances were enforced in a locality, smuggling appeared. Often as not, the government was incapable of presenting a unified position on the degree of abstention from alcohol. Some groups supported a partial elimination, allowing the use of wine and beer. Others campaigned for a total ban.

Indecision among the faithful over the depth and scope of temperance was reflected in a word that remains a part of the American language. Often incorrectly associated with the 1920s, it actually originated in the 1830s. The word is "tee-total." Before it was corrupted, the root of this word was "T-totalism," which some insist was a title applied to those who would only drink tea. A more likely explanation comes from the actions taken by organizers of a temperance convention held in 1836 at Hector, New York. During the meeting members were identified by a badge which signified which "pledge" they took. The single letter "T" indicated a total abstainer.

The original aim of the societies was temperance, not prohibition. As previously stated, they were interested in curbing drunkenness and abuse, and did not push prohibition. As a result they expected no more from their associates than they did from the rest of the country. Members were not strictly bound to refrain from imbibing, and some swore to abstain only from spirits (hard liquors). This was the original oath or pledge of most societies, and members who supported this approach were marked with the letters "OP," which indicated their observance of the old pledge.

Zealous newer members pledged total abstinence, and proudly wore the letter "T." From that variation of a convention-eer's "Hello my name is . . . " lapel tag came the term teetotaler. Though odd sounding, the meaning of the word remains much the same a century and a half after its origin. A teetotaler is a person who refrains from consuming any alcohol.

Through the 1830s temperance organizations flirted with controlling the moral mood of the entire country. Never quite forcing their issue, they could never gather the last bit of strength to push them over the top to greater influence.

One example of how close the movement almost came to instituting national prohibition in the mid-nineteenth century is the story of the Washingtonians. In April 1840, six old friends were engaged in their daily practice. Sitting in a Baltimore tavern, afternoon became late evening as they were achieving yet another night of complete inebriation. Round after round was drained, the small crowd growing more bois-terous with each, cheering each new glass. Jokes, teasing, and good-natured ribbing followed the usual course of merrymak-ing. It was a good time for all. Then, one of them informed the group that Reverend Matthew Smith was visiting a local church, delivering a temperance sermon. Inspiration flashed through them as one—what fun it would be to attend the meeting—and with that off they went.

Six drunken old friends stumbled into the meeting. Thinking they'd later leave with their heads full of funny material, they, as were so many others around the nation, were unexpectedly caught up in the moment. Following the meeting, they swore to each other that they would give up all intoxicating liquor. With utmost sincerity they named their new organization after their most revered American hero, and thus the Washingtonians were born.

By an informal vote the original six chose tailor William Mitchell to write up their pledge. As part of the oath, the original six members promised to bring a new member to their next meeting. Each of those new members was to then recruit another new member, and in theory the organization would double at each assembly.

At the onset Baltimore's newspapers took great delight in poking fun at the Washingtonians, but within a short time their meetings required a rental hall, and meeting after meeting their numbers swelled. Part of their appeal and success was that they had designed the Washingtonians as a self-help group, run by reformed drunks to help reform other drunks. At the early meetings, only reformed drunks were allowed to speak, inspiring others by their testimonials.

Within a year the movement was spreading to other U.S. cities. At one meeting in New York's City Hall Park, the Washingtonians administered their oath simultaneously to over 2,000 new members. Celebrating the organization's first anniversary in Baltimore, a parade was followed by a convention. It attracted the largest number of temperance supporters the country had ever seen. Over 6,000 delegates rejoiced in the revival-like atmosphere, and on their departure went home to form other branches of the society. As rallies were held throughout the country, their numbers multiplied.

Thankfully, movements like the Washingtonians faded as quickly as they grew. Like most temperance societies of that time, they did not pursue their advantages. When a temperance organization first hit town, the citizens would become enraptured with the emotional impact of the experience. Pledging in unison, a whole town could be converted, yet soon after the organizers left reality would set in. As the emotional high subsided, the townspeople were left to maintain their pledges without a support group, and before long life would return to normal.

Time and again the pattern was repeated. Without a national organization and strong links to local chapters, it was impossible for a temperance group to retain momentum. One after another the temperance societies failed in their mission. Although both local and state prohibition laws were adopted over the next decade, few were enforceable and all were repealed shortly after passage.

It would be more than a half century before temperance groups would gain the connections, experience, and organization to implement a nationwide program. But what they learned in the early 1800s provided a solid basis for the future. Many of the techniques used in the early twentieth-century prohibition movements were borrowed directly from the work done by their predecessors. Washingtonians and the other teetotalers of the 1830s and 1840s never lived to see national prohibition, but the eighteenth amendment to the constitution, a beer drinker's nightmare, has its roots in their work.

Fourteen

COLONIAL BREWING TECHNOLOGY

Steam rose off the mash, obscuring the view of the brewer. With the wave of his hand he cleared away the steam so that he could see the grain he had milled the night before. It was a bright day, but the closed door kept it dim near the mash tun. More light would have made it easier to see, but he hesitated to open the door; it was cold out, and he would risk lowering the mash temperature. He reached into the mash. Was the temperature correct?

All morning the fire had been stoked, heating water to near boiling. When it hit the malt it confirmed that he had guessed right about the water's temperature. He had seen the steam rise off in exactly that manner before, it had even smelled the same, and as he remembered, it had made a very good batch of beer. Too bad the beer didn't turn out like that every time. It was this kind of encouragement that kept him going, that told him that he was a good brewer. Word got around town quick about that batch, and it had sold out quickly. Reaching back into the tun, his hand slipped into the mash. Good, it still felt warm.

Wiping off his grain-covered hands, the brewer went back to heating more water. It was almost time to rinse the sugars from the mash and transfer it to the brew kettle. He wished there were more hops for this brew, but on the last trip to the docks he had come up empty; no new shipments had arrived from England. What remained of the hops, mixed with buds of spruce, would have to do. It had worked before, but something wasn't quite right.

All day the nagging feeling had persisted, ever since, during the morning check on the aging cellar, he had found the brewery's cat, dead. Good mousers didn't come along every day. At least the beer was all right. For the past day it had been actively fermenting. Shaking off the thought he went back to work. This would be the first brew of the new year, 1770 was just around the corner.

Brewing in the 1700s was uncertain. It lacked any exact measurements and brewing supplies were erratic. Brewers had virtually no knowledge of the brewing process. They didn't know what caused fermentation and were unaware that colorless, odorless, carbon dioxide was a by-product of fermentation that could kill humans (or the brewery cat). Making things even more difficult, the equipment was primitive; then again, all colonial industry suffered equally from that problem.

North American industry of the colonial era was practically nonexistent. Generally unsophisticated, it bordered on crude and

252

had little impact on the period's economy. Colonials wanted and needed all types of tools, machinery, equipment, and supplies. Access was the problem. In part they were limited by a lack of capital, but there was a larger problem: England's trade policy. Gripping the colonies in a technological stranglehold, Britain deliberately stifled the development of colonial industry by blocking the transfer of any technology into the colonies. A self-serving policy, it was enacted both to ensure a flow of raw materials back to the homeland and to keep the colonists dependent on the mother country for products. Only taxation was a greater hindrance.

Descriptions of commercial breweries in this period are fairly similar. An account of common dimensions and a layout were provided by Victor Clark of Virginia, who described a typical facility in the 1700s as sized in proportion to its distribution area. Brew houses averaged 70 by 40 feet, a size that matched capacity with consumption. Often the brewery had a cellar of cut stone, with an above-ground structure of wood frame construction.[1]

As a self-contained operation, the brewery processed the barley it needed in a malting cellar of approximately 70 by 14 feet, with the remainder set aside for fermentation and aging vats. A brew kettle of about 20 barrels and a horse-powered mill completed the list of primary operating equipment.

Auxiliary equipment and tools were often made of wood, including the pumps, mash tun, forks, rakes, shovels and buckets. This made brewing a labor-intensive proposition. Worse, lack of precision measuring devices left brewers guessing during most of the critical steps in the brewing process.

When brewing first began, all brew vessels, like the tools of the trade, were made of wood. The earliest types were carved from a

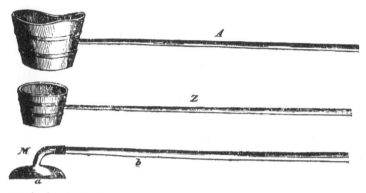

Wooden brewing tools.

single block of wood, like those recovered in Sweden. The pre-medieval Celts were credited with first building barrels and vessels of wooden staves. Wooden tuns continued in use up through the colonial era and beyond. In Virginia the colony's assembly granted permission to operate a brewery on November 25, 1652, stating, "Mr. George Fletcher shall have to himself, his heires, ex'rs and adm'rs. Liberty to distill and brew in wooden vessels."[2]

At the time North America was settled by Europeans, barrel hoops were made of bent wood, with iron hoops a relatively new innovation. Many breweries, when offered iron hoops, stuck with wood. All wood construction required more hoops, which in turn offered a greater degree of protection. If any single hoop of wood broke, the remaining hoops held the staves in place. With iron, fewer hoops were used and a broken hoop often resulted in a burst barrel. Iron-hooped barrels only replaced wood when the quality, reliability, and cost rendered the maintenance of wooden hoop barrels impractical. By 1621 settlers were advising new arrivals "Let your casks for beer be iron-bound."

Although smaller breweries and homes used wood for their tuns, commercial brew kettles were made of slightly more advanced material. Known as "coppers," they were named after the metal from which they were constructed. Acquisition of a brew kettle was an important event in the life of a colony. In 1633 Emmanuel Doling wrote to John Winthrop in Massachusetts Bay Colony, describing his purchase of a "furnace for brewinge [*sic*] . . . promised to send it to the plantation wh [*sic*] he has done."[3]

Likewise, Kiliaen van Rensselaer of Albany wrote happily of obtaining a kettle in 1637: "as soon as there is a supply of grain on hand, I intend to erect a brewery to provide all New Netherland with beer, for which purpose there is already a brew kettle there."[4]

As breweries expanded, two coppers were required, one for boiling the wort and the other to heat water. Those used exclusively for heating were called "hot water tubs." Regardless of the number or type, they were fueled by wood, peat, or, in the better breweries, hard coal.

Two-kettle brew houses were of either English or German design. English-style coppers had a thick bottom, two to three times thicker than what was required to bear the weight of the kettle and wort (unfermented beer). Supporting the rounded bottom was a brickwork cradle that formed the firebox. Kettles from Germany were configured in a square shape and built of either copper or iron. Brewers argued in favor of either design, but the English kettle had one distinct difference, a connection that allowed gravity draining. German kettles relied on the old method of dipping out the wort with wooden buckets attached to the end of long handles.

Kettle design fueled a dispute about brewing technique. English brewers used a closed kettle, while their German counterparts insisted an open kettle was best. Each side argued that its design was best for boiling hops. The debate continued for decades. English kettles, designed with closed tops, were most popular until the emergence of lager beer. The German's use of open boiling then gained favor. Finally, after scientific research on the makeup of hops, the English design resurfaced as the preferred style.

The greatest innovation of the period was introduced by Dr. Richard Shannon in 1798. Shannon's kettle was of an oblong shape and was heated by several smaller fires rather than one central flame. His configuration used less fuel to boil and saved energy, thus boosting profits. Later that year he unveiled a steam-jacketed mash tun.

Steam applications in the brew house were initially pursued solely as a means of heating. Documentation from 1828 indicates that the brewery of John Beveridge and Company at Newburgh,

A brew kettle.

New York, used steam to heat and operate the mashing equipment,[5] but pinpointing the first use of steam as a heating element is difficult. Many breweries in the early 1800s experimented with makeshift coils of piping that they inserted into existing kettles as a means of extracting heat from the steam engine's exhaust.

Another use of steam heating was applied to the production of hop extract. The first patent was obtained by William Kerr of England in 1788. His was a "closed" system, which cooked the hops in a boiler/steamer. Vapor from the steaming hops was directed to a heat exchanger, where it was cooled and condensed. Hop oil was separated from water in the condensed liquid, and brewers later added the hop extract to the boiling wort as they would hops. Hot water recovered in the process of condensing the hop vapor was saved in a tank for use with the next brew. Used in association with the mash, or to manufacture hop extract, heating was only a preview of steam's capabilities. When applied to brewery machinery, the steam engine enabled owners to construct breweries on a scale previously unimagined.

Early attempts to install steam engines were pioneered in America by Oliver Evans, an inventor, in 1803. Evans believed the engine was capable of performing a variety of tasks, including the powering of brewery machinery. Evans bought advertising specifically to promote his engine to brewers: "This powerful agent can on the new principles happily applied by Mr. Evans, serve with profit, all the various purposes of machinery; particularly Breweries."[6]

Evans recognized that breweries had different capacities and in response offered another "very small engine . . . for distilleries and breweries." Though unsuccessful in selling an engine of his own to breweries, another engine, copying Evans's design, was installed in a brew house owned by Thomas Jefferson.

Steam as a power supply for brewing was first introduced in Philadelphia. Built by Thomas Holloway, it was installed in the Vine Street brewery of Francis Perot during 1819: "It is believed to be the oldest stationary steam engine in America, and . . . developed about ten horsepower."[7]

Widespread use of steam engines in America didn't develop until the 1850s, when breweries grew into significant industrial operations. Visitors from Great Britain in the early 1800s judged American use of steam as lagging behind England by 50 years. It wasn't that U.S. brewers were uninterested, it was more a matter of population density driving the market.

In England, towns and cities were well established and a sizable population was within a horse-drawn wagon's delivery range. Sparsely settled America was a different story. Breweries remained small. There was no pressing need for steam-operated machinery because of the limited distribution. It wasn't until the midpoint of the century that breweries refitted with steam, when population centers had grown and transportation improved.

Equally innovative as steam heating was cooling. Though brewers didn't understand why, the quick cooling of wort to the temperature best for "pitching" (adding) yeast made for better beer. As more breweries were built and competition increased, the desire to improve the quality of the product motivated brewers to experiment with new methods and techniques, more efficient and effective cooling among them.

The earliest coolers were large, shallow pans. Made of wood and lined with sheet metal, they worked by spreading the wort

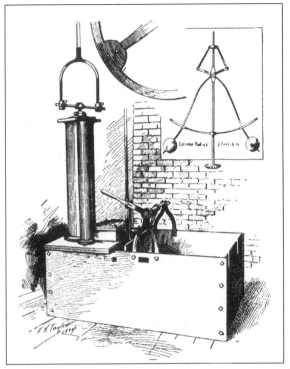

A steam engine.

over a large surface area. It takes beer in a brew kettle a long time to cool. Heat from the very middle of the pot requires a lengthy time to reach equilibrium. Pouring the same pot of hot water into a pan speeds up the cooling, because the liquid is spread over a large surface area and exposed to the much cooler air above. This is how coolers in brew houses worked. In Germany, where the pans were inverted, they were called *Kuhlschiffen*, which in America became "cool ship."

German brewers stacked the cool ships to sit one atop of the other. In that configuration wort was passed from the upper to the lower cool ship, increasing the cooling as it flowed. Typically,

259

wort was only a couple of inches deep in the cool ship, which cut the cooling time to six or seven hours.

Searching for a better way to cool the wort, brewers borrowed the idea of steam heating coils. Once again they tried using loops of metal piping. In one design, brewers placed the pipes in the kettle, following the boil, and ran cool water inside the pipes. In another type, wort drained from the kettle was directed through pipes immersed in a tub of cool water. Both styles were crude, but are direct ancestors of modern heat exchangers. In the steam era the design and fabrication of coolers and heat exchangers advanced as scientists sought ways to further maximize engine efficiency.

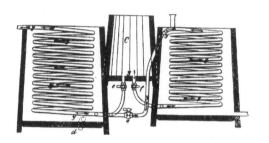

A wort cooler.

Primitive equipment and systems affected brewing in the colonial era equally with the lack of knowledge about the brewing process. Basic principles were understood, such as the need for both rapid boiling and cooling, and all acknowledged the importance of fermentation, but brewers had only an elementary understanding of the process. Knowledge was based solely upon experience and empirical evidence. Nevertheless, brewers knew quality was tied to temperature control and degree of fermentation. What they lacked was a means of measurement.

Thermometers were not introduced until the mid-1700s. First credited for using one in a brewery goes to Michael

Combrune, who outlined his application of temperature measurement in a book titled *The Theory and Practice of Brewing,* which he published in 1762.

Prior to the invention of the thermometer, brewers relied on practical experience, often passed down from one to another. They obtained the desired results from mashing by temperature control based upon the mixing of grain and boiling water in an exact ratio. Decoction mashing was another technique. By knowing the amount removed from the mash, boiled, and returned and mixed with the remaining grain, an approximation was made for mash-in. However, variations in the ambient temperature of the brew house from summer to winter rendered the process imprecise at best. Instructions for performing the mash were to bring the grain "just hot enough to bite smartly on your finger" and to let it remain at that temperature "until the steam is so far evaporated that you can see your face in it."[8]

The process of cooling the wort was beset by similar inaccuracies. Veteran brewers advised that it "should in cold weather feel quite warm, in mild weather rather warmer than the hand or finger, and in very hot weather it can not be brought into the tub too cool."[9]

Combrune's book eliminated the guesswork associated with brewing by providing tables and charts of the exact effect on grain imparted by specific temperatures. Although his findings were accurate and proven, many brewers continued to resist such "newfangled" gadgets. One brewer, James Baverstock, defied the prevailing wisdom and became a pioneer in the use of instrumentation in the brew house.

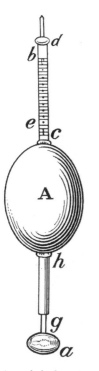

An early hydrometer.

Baverstock was born in Alton, Hampshire, England in 1741. In 1763 he accepted a position in his father's brewery and undertook an enthusiastic study of the brewing process. After reading Combrune's *Theory and Practice of Brewing,* he purchased a thermometer with the intention of perfecting the malting, mashing, and fermentation procedures in the brewery.[10]

Unfortunately, the elder Baverstock was a staunch traditionalist who saw no need to change things that seemed to work well. Proposals to use new equipment elicited particular ire; the father thought all the suggestions nothing more than useless novelties. In fact, Baverstock was forced to use his new thermometer in secret. Nevertheless, improvements in the brewery were gradually adopted throughout the industry.

In 1769 Baverstock added another device to his toolbox of scientific instruments: a hydrometer. Examining the principle that the level to which a floating object sinks into a liquid correlates directly to the density of the liquid, Baverstock understood the implications to brewers.

Purchasing a hydrometer from Benjamin Martin of Fleet Street, London, Baverstock worked constantly with the device for the next two years. At each new batch of beer he gathered data and studied the application of hydrometers in determining the density (specific gravity) of various strengths of beer wort. Using the device only when out of his father's sight, Baverstock slowly and carefully accumulated information and documented his findings.

Convinced he'd discovered a way to make brewing more precise, Baverstock made several attempts to demonstrate the usefulness of hydrometers to London's brewers. Only one was impressed, but that one was well placed. It was brewer, member of Parliament, and friend of Samuel Johnson, Mr. H. Thrale, of London's most noted brewing house. On completion of the study Baverstock compiled his data into a manuscript he titled "Hydrometrical Observations and Experiments in the Brewery," which he published in 1785.

Investigations conducted by Baverstock inspired, in part, the work of John Richardson. A brewer in Hull's brewery, Richardson published his own observations in 1784. Differing slightly from Baverstock, Richardson's work used a "saccharometer."[11] Measurement scales on hydrometers and saccharometers differed, but in each case the instruments measured the density of liquids. Saccharometers were specially built and graduated (scaled) to apply to the measurement of sugars derived from malt.

Baverstock was among those impressed, writing, "his last and former publications showed him to be more possessed of more knowledge of the brewery than any other person hitherto appears to have written on the subject."[12]

Richardson's other significant contribution was determining the relationship between temperature and the density of liquids. He stated that an accurate measure was attainable at only 62 degrees Fahrenheit and that to measure density at other temperatures required use of a correction factor.

Study, research, and data collection by Baverstock, Richardson, and others directly contributed to the density scale introduced in 1844 by Balling, which functions to this day as the standard method of calculating the amount of sugars, and thereby the strength, of beer. American brewers, like their English counterparts, were somewhat resistant to the new measuring devices, but by the start of the 1800s the instruments were gaining acceptance in U.S. breweries.

Of greatest concern to colonial brewers was the lack of bottles. Beer bottled in glass often stored better than many of the kegs in use, and it provided customers with a more convenient-sized selection.

Construction of glass factories began shortly after the colonies were founded. Jamestown had a glassworks operating at Glass House Point in 1608. New York started glass production in 1645, and in the early 1700s additional glassworks opened in New York, Massachusetts, and southern New Jersey. However, production of glass and availability of bottles remained severely limited.

Brewers suffered from critical shortages throughout the colonies, prompting brewers to plead continually for assistance from the consumers. John Mercer of Virginia was one of the many brewers driven to advertising for bottles. He placed an announcement in the *Virginia Gazette* on May 30, 1766: "Any person who sends bottles and casks may have them carefully filled and corked with beer and porter at 6s [shillings] or with ale at 4s the dozen. . . . I hope for, propose setting up a glass house for making bottles."[13]

Demand was equally high in the North, as illustrated by a classified ad in the *New York Gazette and Weekly Mercury* of December 25, 1769: "WANTED, any Quantity of QUART BOTTLES, for which a good price will be given by Jonathan NASH, at Mr. Anthony Rutger's Brewery in Maidenhead."[14]

Years passed, with little relief in the shortage, as indicated by another ad, dated May 23, 1774, that read: "Benjamin Williams . . . intends carrying on the business of bottling beer as usual. . . . Captains of vessels may be supplied with what quantity they please . . . if they return the bottles."[15]

Congress addressed the lack of glass in June 1790, when it recommended that the Treasury Department advance John F. Amelung of Maryland $8,000 dollars to help rebuild his glass factory. Specifically, the money was designated to increase the manufacture of beer bottles.

Bottling, precision measurement, steam power, and vessel construction were all advances introduced between the 1600s and 1800s that streamlined brewery operations and changed the shape of the industry. Quality improved with each addition, but none had the impact obtained through study of brewing's most enigmatic element.

Yeast was the great unknown in brewing. For years brewers simply called it "God is good," referring to what a great gift it represented, even if God was the only one who really knew how it worked. The first investigations of yeast began in the 1600s.

George Ernest Stahl, a German chemist, produced the first significant work devoted to yeast in the late 1600s. Close observation of fermentation inspired Stahl to write in his "Zymotechnica Fundamentalis," a description of the process: "the combining ties of the original components are torn assunder, the separated component parts, however, being reduced in size . . . form new and even stronger compounds."[16] Presented in rather general terms, this work was the first time biochemistry was discussed in relationship to yeast and the fermentation of beer. The work was often vague and details inaccurate, but the proposal was sound.

Shortly after Stahl's work was published, the Dutch physician Boerhaave identified three distinct phases in the fermentation process. He was followed in 1680 by Lowenhock. With the aid of magnification, Lowenhock correctly identified tiny particles: yeast cells. Unfortunately his work was largely ignored because it was not tied directly to the fermentation process.

The French scientist Lavoisier (1743–94) built upon the theories of Stahl, Boerhaave, and Lowenhock. Lavoisier was the first to demonstrate that fermentation was a process that broke sugar molecules into alcohol and carbon dioxide (CO_2).

In 1818 Erleben theorized that yeast was a living organism. The next significant research was that of Desmazieres, who in 1825 used a microscope to classify different types of yeast. In 1837 Caguard de Latour described yeast as an organism. This in turn inspired the team of Knetzing and Turpin, and their proposal that yeast caused fermentation as it passed through its life cycle. Knetzing and Turpin's work remained the definitive source on yeast until the exhaustive studies by Pasteur in 1857.

As these discoveries were made, brewers were putting all the new-found knowledge to practical use.

From the earliest days brewers spoke of two phases of fermentation: "principal fermentation" (i.e., primary fermentation), which was the process of converting saccharine to alcohol and carbon dioxide, and "secondary fermentation," which described the ripening of beers, during which the impurities were removed. Primary fermentation of ale took 48 hours, as compared to porter, which took somewhat less, and scotch beers,

266

which took 11 to 18 days or more.[17] Aging and its effect on beer seemed mystical.

In the early nineteenth century, Gabriel Sedylmayer of Munich and Anton Dreher of Vienna believed that refinement of techniques, recording of measurements, and collection of data resulted in cleaner and better beer. They visited the breweries of England to gather all knowledge possible. Credited with introducing modern methods to the German states, they were pioneers in refining the process of lagering. Sedylmayer was instrumental in persuading the Kaiser to establish a brewing school in 1836, and by 1840 he and Dreher were Europe's best lager brewers. When Dreher supplied Emil Hanson of the Carlsberg brewery with a sample of the yeast used in lagering, it was an act of generosity that turned the world of beer upside down. Hanson isolated the strain of yeast known as lager, which within a few short years would alter the world's taste for beer.

Lager's arrival in America followed shortly after the successful isolation of the yeast. The exact date and location of lager's arrival is a matter of debate. Most beer histories credit John Wagner of Philadelphia with producing the first lager in 1840, but this may not be correct.

U.S. beer history recounts that soon after clipper ships cut the time required to cross the Atlantic, Wagner secured a supply of German lager yeast. Before clipper ships, which, with their unique arrangement of sails, could sail nearly into the wind, most vessels had to take a southerly transit across the Atlantic. Sailing south along the African coast brought them to the current of east to west winds known as the "trades." Crossings were typically measured in months. Lager yeast, even when stored in nearly ice-cold water, could remain viable for only about 30 days. Clippers, with their streamlined hulls and favorable sail rigging, cut the sailing time to only a couple of weeks. Thus, development of the clipper arrived just in time for the introduction of lager yeast to America.

Wagner was one of the first Americans to receive the new yeast, and with a supply in hand he began brewing. Wagner had a small operation in the back of his house on Philadelphia's St. John Street, near Poplar. Limited to a space the size of a large kitchen, his production was close to that of a modern home-brewer. From the size involved and the state of brewing technology at the time, his output would have been barely sufficient to supply his German friends.

Even by generous descriptions, Wagner's facility was far short of a viable commercial brewery, so how did Wagner get credit for making the first lager beer in America? It began with an essay by Charles C. Wolf in *100 Years of Brewing,* a series of brewery profiles amassed in 1903. Almost every history of U.S. beer tells the same story of lager's introduction, but all of these histories spring from one source: Wolf's essay. When read more closely, Wolf's essay is ambiguous, implying a dismissal of Wagner while at the same time building a case that credits Wolf's business as spinning off the first lager, and Wolf himself as one of the first commercial lager brewers.

Charles Wolf was a sugar refiner. One of his employees, George Manger, was a friend of Wagner the lager brewer, and received a supply of lager yeast from him. (Manger would later establish a brewery at New and Second Streets that was the forerunner of C. Schmidt's Brewing.)

In 1844, another Wolf employee, Charles Engel, from Bavaria, began brewing with Wolf at the sugar refinery. Shortly

268

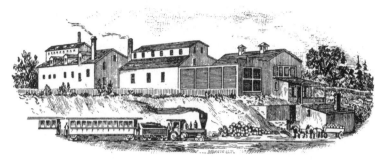

Engel and Wolf's brewery.

thereafter Wolf gave up his sugar business and opened a brewery with Engel at 352-354 Dillwyn Street. Eventually the brewery of Engel and Wolf became one of the best in the city. After 1870 it was known as Bergner and Engel, and continued to produce one of Philadelphia's favorite beers.

According to Wolf, the brewery was "for many years the resort of the Germans of Philadelphia, who more than once drank the brewery dry."[18] Wolf's account extols the virtues of both the beer and brewery. Thus, with two of his employees brewing from Wagner's original batch of lager yeast, a heavily biased Wolf spun a subtle tale he hoped would secure him credit as the first "significant" commercial lager brewery in America.

From a historical perspective, several problems surface in Wolf's account. First, he was writing more than 60 years after the events transpired, and stories do tend to get better with age. Furthermore, the relationships of those involved are questionable: Wolf's employees, Wagner, the yeast, and Wolf's brewery were all closely intertwined. Was the story accurate? Or was he clearing a place for himself in American lager brewing history?

Wolf both credited Wagner with being the first lager brewer and hinted that Wagner's brewery was of no consequence. Was his intent to manipulate history in order to lay claim to being the first commercial lager brewer in the country? Unfortunately Wolf was too close to the story and had too much to gain for historians to accept his essay as a reliable single source.

If Wagner wasn't the first commercial lager brewer, is it indeed Wolf who should get credit? Even if Wolf's story was true, he didn't establish his facility until 1844. Someone else was brewing lager earlier than that, in St. Louis. In 1840, Adam Lemp constructed what would become the first truly national brewery. At first he brewed only ale, but according to a variety of accounts, he began producing lager by 1842.[19]

So was the first American lager brewer Wagner, Wolf, or Lemp? We may never know for sure, but indications are that it wasn't Wolf. Wagner has a right to a small "claim to fame." Lemp's is the only verifiable claim to early brewing of lager on a commercial scale.

Regardless of the debate over who was the first lager brewer in America, the new style was destined for introduction in the early 1840s. Lager's popularity as a crisp, clean drinking beer had swept through Europe. In that same time period, Germany was experiencing a period of political upheaval. Germans, displaced by the resulting political, social, and economic pressures of a country in turmoil, headed for sanctuary in America. By the early 1840s some midwestern cities, such as Cincinnati, had Germans making up to one-quarter of their population.

Lager beer wasn't fashionable only among the Germans. Its traits seemed well fitted to the American climate and character. A cold lager was perfectly matched to the heat of American summers, and it further complemented the American practice of over-consumption. A person could more easily down a great quantity of lager than ale. It was one of the several external factors that were silently shaping the future of American beer.

Technological changes introduced in the late 1830s and early 1840s did not immediately alter the fabric of the American beer industry. Old methods of brewing and drinking would continue for another 30 years.

Industrial advances, first seen in the early nineteenth century, started an evolutionary process that inevitably altered the methods by which business was conducted. Other technologies also affected breweries, most important being the infant American railroad system. Within a few short years, brewers had an opportunity to increase their distribution areas vastly. Those with an eye to such affairs would gather riches equaling those of other great businessmen.

Swift and efficient transportation combined with progress in metallurgy, industrialization, and communication to open endless opportunities. Constant adaptation and modernization marked the road to ever-increasing profits. Some local brewers would become economic giants and captains of industry. Expansion may have been only a glimmer in far-sighted brewers' eyes in 1840, but it was waiting, nearly within their grasp.

Appendix

Colonial Beer Timeline

1500s

1584 *Virginia*—Earliest known date of brewing in the colony. Corn was used as an adjunct to supplement a shortage of malt.

1600s

1607 *Virginia*—Shipments of beer arrive from England to ease the colony's shortage.

1609 *Virginia*—In response to a continuing short beer supply, the colony advertises in England for the services of a brewer.

1612 *New York*—Adrian Block and Hans Christiansen open New Amsterdam's first brewery on Manhattan Island.

Most historians recognize it as the first brewery established in North America.

1614 *New York*—Pressed into service as a delivery room, Block and Christiansen's Manhattan brew house records the first offspring born to a white European colonist.

1620 *Massachusetts*—Pilgrims land at Plymouth. The crew's concern with maintaining a sufficient supply of beer for their return trip to England causes them to force the Pilgrims ashore. One of the first structures the new settlers build is a brew house.

1620 *Virginia*—Settlers learn to make beer out of maize.

1626 *New York*—Officials in New Amsterdam determine America can produce all of the raw materials to make beer.

1629 *Massachusetts*—Colony receives first recorded shipment of beer.

1630 *Boston*—The city's first brewery opens in Charleston.

1632 *New York*—The West India Company completes a brewery on a street that comes to be known as Brouwers (Brewers) Alley, in lower Manhattan. In less than a year it is followed by the brewery of Jean Vigne, who was born in the brewery of Block and Christiansen in 1614.

1633 *Massachusetts*—Emmanuel Dowling establishes a brewery that features a "new" English kettle.

1633 *New York*—In what was then known as Fort Orange, Albany's Rutger Hendrickson Van Soest opens one of the earliest of the city's many breweries. In the same year, Peter Minuit establishes a brew house farther down the Hudson River, in Manhattan.

1634 *Connecticut*—Homebrewing begins in the colony. Commercial brewing would not appear until the early 1800s.

1634 *Massachusetts*—City officials grant Boston's first brewery license to Samuel Cole.

1635 *Massachusetts*—Captain Robert Sedgwick is granted a brewers license.

1637 *New York*—Kiliaen van Rensselaer constructs a brewery near what will become Albany.

1637 *Massachusetts*—The colony awards its first brewery license to Captain Sedgwick.

1639 *Rhode Island*—The first brewery opens in Providence, operated by Sergeant Baulston.

1639 *Massachusetts*—Nathaniel Eaton is dismissed as president of Harvard when he fails to maintain the students' beer supply.

1641 *Massachusetts*—John Appleton constructs a small brewery in Watertown.

1643 *New York*—Manhattan opens the Stadt Harberg (City Tavern). Ten years later it becomes the first City Hall.

1645 *New York*—Peter Anderson establishes another in a growing number of breweries on New Amsterdam's Brouwers Alley. Later that year other breweries are opened by Albert Rittenhouse, Peter Gardner, Jaxsen Calder, Albert Amack, Issac Deforeest, and W. C. Eversten.

1647 *New York*—Jean LaBattie, first licensed brewer in Albany, brews his first batch of beer.

1648 *New Jersey*—Hoboken welcomes beer from the brew house of Aert Teunison.

1649 *New York*—The famous Rutgers brewing family receives a license to brew in Albany.

1650 *New York*—Hendrick Andriessen brews his first batch of beer in New York City. Later that same year Frans Barentse Pastoor opens his brewery as the population, and demand for beer, both grow.

1652 *Virginia*—George Fletcher is licensed to operate a brewery.

1655 *New Jersey*—Andreas Hudde constructs a brewery at Fort Nassau.

1657 *New York*—As brewers continue to gather along New Amsterdam's Brouwers Alley, the water discharged from brewing turns the street into a quagmire. The worsening condition prompts the city to pave it with cobblestones. On completion of the project they rename it Stone Street, in recognition of the colony's first paved street.

1658 *New York*—Jacob Kip enters the brewing business. He becomes a leading brewer and merchant in New York. The area known as Kip's Bay is named after him.

1660 *Delaware*—In New Amstel (New Castle), Hendrik Kip establishes a brewery.

1662 *Connecticut*—Governor John Winthrop is invited to present a paper to the Royal Society in London on the use of maize in brewing.

1664 *New York*—The Duke of York issues a proclamation that restricts commercial brewing to professionals.

1667 *Massachusetts*—Administrators institute beer quality regulations.

1667 *New York*—In Kingston, a Hudson River town that briefly served as New York's capital, Reynier Reynertsen Vandercoley opens one of the region's first breweries.

1670 *New Hampshire*—New Hampshire awards its first brewery license to Samuel Wentworth of Portsmouth.

1677 *Massachusetts*—Boston's licensed taverns reach a total of 27 in operation.

1680 *Massachusetts*—The first keg of beer is tapped in Boston's Green Dragon Tavern. Meeting place for the Sons of Liberty, it operated for nearly 120 years.

1683 *Pennsylvania*—William Penn has a brewery constructed at his colony at Pennsbury, near the Delaware River at Bristol. That same year Philadelphia's first brewery is opened on Front Street between Walnut and Spruce Streets (on Dock Street Creek) by owner William Frampton.

1687 *Pennsylvania*—Anthony Morris begins brewing on Front Street below Walnut Street. After its opening day the brewery operated continuously for the next 182 years until it was finally closed by then-owner William Massey.

1695 *New York*—The poor water supply, coupled with a rapidly growing population, encourages the partnership of Ben C. Corlaerand and Albert Ryckmann to open a brewery in Manhattan.

1700s

1703 *Maryland*—Benjamin Fordham opens a brewery in Annapolis.

1711 *Massachusetts*—Boston panics over a shortage of barley and forbids any export of malt.

1717 *Pennsylvania*—Joseph Taylor opens another of Philadelphia's growing number of breweries. He chose Second Street for the location between Walnut and Spruce Streets.

1720 *Pennsylvania*—George Campion establishes a small brewery on the west side of Front Street.

1728 *Pennsylvania*—In Bristol, Richard Mountain opens a brew house that supplies the town with beer for the next five years.

1734 *Pennsylvania*—May Lisle of Philadelphia assumes ownership of her family's Edinburgh brew house. She was known as the first brewster (woman brewer) in the colonies. It remained in operation until 1751.

1738 *Georgia*—The first brewery in the deep south opens at Jekyll Island on what became Riverview Drive.

1747 *Pennsylvania*—Abraham Bennet opens his South Hampton township (Bucks County) Brewery.

1751 *Pennsylvania*—The London Brewery opens on Walnut Street.

1754 *Pennsylvania*—While on militia duty in the western part of the state, Lt. Colonel George Washington records his beer recipe and brewing procedure in his notebook.

1756 *Massachusetts*—Boston's total of licensed operating taverns reaches 156.

1762 *England*—Thermometers are adapted to brewery use by Michael Combrune, as explained in *The Theory and Practice of Brewing.*

1763 *Pennsylvania*—Henry Eckert opens his brewery in Reading.

1765 *Pennsylvania*—The British establish a brewery in Pittsburgh at Fort Pitt. In the same year Illinois opens the first commercial brewery outside the original 13 colonies, in Kaskaskia.

1766 *Virginia*—Bottle shortages continue to plague brewers; John Mercer advertises in the newspaper in a desperate attempt to find bottles.

1771 *Virginia*—Andrew Wales opens one of Alexandria's first breweries at the foot of Duke Street.

1774 *Pennsylvania*—Robert Smith, one of Philadelphia's most famous brewers, establishes his brewery at St. John and Noble Streets. Through various forms, locations, and mergers it provided Philadelphians with beer for the next 212 years.

1774 *North Carolina*—On Old Shallowford Road, near Winston-Salem, the Single Brothers Brewery and Distillery opens for business.

1775 *Pennsylvania*—After convening in Philadelphia, the Continental Congress, in one of its first acts, authorizes the army to issue troops a ration of one quart of beer per day.

1780 *Connecticut*—General Israel Putnam constructs a brewery in the town of Brooklyn.

1784 *Pennsylvania*—The Brewery of Dawson and Spowden makes its debut on Philadelphia's Bywater Street. In 1854 it was acquired by William Massey. He eventually built it into one of the country's largest breweries, but it went out of business shortly after his death in 1894.

1785 *England*—James Baverstock publishes a manuscript titled "Hydrometrical Observations and Experiments in the Brewery." It outlines the application and benefit of using a hydrometer in the brew house.

1787 *Pennsylvania*—On September 17, following the final day of deliberations at the Constitutional Convention in Philadelphia, George Washington records in his diary: "The business being closed the members adjourned to the City Tavern."[1]

1789 Again George Washington stands by his beer, this time in support of American business. Washington declares he will only buy beer brewed in the United States. That same year, Massachusetts follows Washington's example by passing legislation designed to encourage local production of beer.

1792 *New Hampshire*—New Hampshire waives taxes imposed on brewing properties in an attempt to stimulate the construction of local breweries.

1796 *Washington, D.C.*—Dr. Cornelius Cunningham and James Greenleaf open the Washington Brewery at Twenty-first, Twenty-second, and B Streets only five years after the site was selected as the country's capital city, but four years before the government will convene there.,

1800s

1808 *New York*—Saratoga hosts one of the country's first temperance meetings.

1809 *Missouri*—John Coons establishes the first successful commercial brewery in St. Louis. It remained in operation for two years.

1810 *Missouri*—Jacques Delass opens a brewery in Belle Fontaine.

1810 In its first census of breweries, the United States lists a total of 132 operating brew houses producing 185,000 barrels of beer. Among the states with the largest number were Pennsylvania, with 48, New York, with 42, and Ohio, with 13.

1811 *Ohio*—Cincinnati's first brewery, operated by Davis Embree, opens at 75 Water Street.

1814 *Maryland*—Francis Scott Key writes the "Star Spangled Banner" in the Fountain Inn to the British drinking tune "Anacreon in Heaven."

1818 *Vermont*—William Warder opens a brewery in Burlington.

1818 *Pittsburgh*—Joseph Wainwright opens a brewery that will run until it is closed by Prohibition.

1819 *Philadelphia*—The first steam engine used to power a brewery is installed in Frances Perot's brew house at Second and Cherry Streets.

1819 *New York*—In Rochester, Nathan Lyman establishes the city's first brewery.

1826 *Massachusetts*—Boston witnesses the formation of the American Society for the Promotion of Temperance. Over the next three years it will attain a membership of more than 100,000. It is considered the country's first significant temperance group.

1828 *New York*—Steam power is used to heat and operate mash equipment at the John Beveridge brewery in Newburgh.

1828 *Kentucky*—Maysville: Samuel McOrkelle and Yancey Chambers open the Maysville Brewery.

1829 *Pennsylvania*—David S. Yuengling establishes what would become America's oldest continuously operating brewery.

1829 *Illinois*—Commercial brewing is begun in Bellville, Illinois, by F. Fleishbien.

1830 *New York*—Buffalo's first true commercial brewery is opened by Jacob Roos on Broadway between Church and York Streets.

1832 On a bleak day for the military, the issuance of daily rations of beer for servicemen is terminated by Secretary of War Lewis Cass.

1833 *Illinois*—Chicago's first successful brewery, built by William Lill, opens.

1835 *Missouri*—Jacob Fleisbien opens a commercial brewery in St. Louis.

1836 *New York*—Saratoga hosts the national American Temperance Union meeting. During the meeting the concept of "total" abstinence is first proposed. Prior to that time the definition of abstinence did not include not drinking beer.

1837 *Indiana*—Under the name of "Old Brewery," the partnership of Rice and Kroener establishes the first brewery in Evansville.

1840 *Pennsylvania*—John Wagner begins brewing lager beer in Philadelphia (credited with being as the first American to produce lager beer).

1840 *Missouri*—Adam Lemp starts brewing lager beer in St. Louis.

1844 *Wisconsin*—Jacob Best establishes a brewery at 917 Chestnut Street (Juneau Avenue). The brewery later changed its name to Pabst.

1844 *Iowa*—The state's first brewery is opened in Fort Madison by Garvasius Santo.

1845 *Michigan*—The state's first successful commercial brewery is opened by Elisha S. Avery on First Street in Detroit.

1846 *Massachusetts*—Boston's John Roessle establishes himself as the city's first lager brewer.

1846 *Maine*—In their first victory of note, the forces of temperance succeed in bringing prohibition to a state.

1847 *Illinois*—John Huck and John Schneider begin operation of the first lager brewery in Chicago.

1848 *Minnesota*—St. Paul witnesses the opening of the state's first brewery when Anthony Yoerg begins production of beer in his brew house on South Washington Street between Chestnut and Eagle Streets.

1848 *Germany*—Political unrest in Germany, which escalated throughout the 1840s, hits new heights and sends waves of German beer lovers to America.

1849 *California*—The state's first brewery is established by A. Schuppert on San Francisco's Stockton and Jackson Streets, as the Forty-niner's pour in during the gold rush.

1849 *Wisconsin*—The Milwaukee brewery, which would come to be known as Schlitz and grow to be the largest in the world by the 1960s, is constructed by August Krug.

1850 *Texas*—Both Julius Rennert and John Schneider open breweries in New Braunfels.

1850 National census statistics report a total of 421 breweries operating in the United States.

1850 *Arkansas*—The first successful commercial brewery producing beer is opened in Fort Smith. For the next 31 years the Knoble Brewery will conduct business at 442 N. Third Street.

1851 *Louisiana*—Jacob Zoelly establishes the City Brewery on Camp and Delford Streets in New Orleans.

1851 *Maine*—Portland's John Walker releases the first batch of beer brewed in Portland. His small brewery operated out of the basement of the Depot Hotel on State and Commerce Streets.

1852 *Missouri*—George Schneider establishes a brewery on Carondelet Avenue. Eight years later, in 1860, Eberhard Anheuser gains a controlling interest in the facility. It went on to become the cornerstone of the Anheuser-Busch brewing empire.

1852 *Oregon*—Henry Saxer begins producing beer in Portland from a brew house on First and Davis Streets.

1852 Prohibition is enacted in Vermont, Massachusetts, Rhode Island, and Minnesota.

1852 *Maine*—Portland's second brewery is established when Tristram Walker begins making beer at what was 46 Portland Street, a location now situated between Mechanic and Green Streets.

1853 *Michigan*—Michigan legislates prohibition.

1854 *Kansas*—The opening of the state's first brewery is celebrated. Constructed by owner John Grund, it produces beer from its location at 533 Delaware Street in Kansas City.

1854 *Connecticut*—Connecticut establishes statewide prohibition.

1855 Following a national trend, New York, New Hampshire, Delaware, Indiana, Iowa, and Nebraska adopt prohibition legislation.

1858 *Nevada*—Thirsty silver miners applaud the opening of the state's first brewery in Carson City (exact date of opening undocumented).

1858 *Nebraska*—Pioneer brewer Fredrick Beyschlag begins producing beer in Nebraska City.

1859 *Colorado*—Denver welcomes F. Z. Solomon's and Charles Tascher's Rocky Mountain Brewery, the first in Colorado. It was located at Seventh Street and the Platte River.

1859 *Tennesee*—J. Stiefel Company begins brewing operations. The facility changed hands several times but remained in business until 1954, when it was known as the William Gerst Brewing Company.

Notes

Introduction

1. *100 Years of Brewing* (New York and Chicago: H. S. Rich & Co., 1903).

Chapter 1

1. Quoted in *100 Years of Brewing*, 179.
2. Quoted in *100 Years of Brewing*, 179.
3. Quoted in *100 Years of Brewing*, 179.
4. Quoted in *100 Years of Brewing*, 179.
5. William Wood, *New England Prospects* (Boston, Mass.: n.p., 1635), 55.
6. William Bradford, *History of Plymouth Plantation*, ed. by Samuel Eliot Morison (New York, N.Y.: n.p., 1952), 78.
7. Bradford, *History of Plymouth Plantation*, 78.
8. Page Smith, *A New Age Now Begins* (New York, N.Y.: McGraw-Hill Book Company, 1976), 17.
9. Stanley Baron, *Brewed in America* (Boston, Mass.: Little, Brown & Company, 1962), 17.
10. *100 Years of Brewing*, 121.
11. *100 Years of Brewing*, 157.
12. Jack's Restaurant, Albany, New York (poster).
13. Woodrow Wilson, *History of the American People* (New York, N.Y.: Wm. H. Wise & Co., 1901).

14. Baron, *Brewed in America*, 44.
15. Samuel Elliot Morison, *The Oxford History of the American People* (New York, N.Y.: Oxford University Press, 1965), 114.
16. Thomas Paschall, "Papers and Account" (Historical Society of Pennsylvania:1705–1711, 1713–1728).
17. "Letters from Virginia in 1623," *Virginia Magazine of History and Biography,* vol. 6.
18. Baron, *Brewed in America*, 48.
19. William Nelson, "Documents Related to the Colonial History of the State of New Jersey," *New Jersey Archives Series,* 208.

Chapter 2

1. *100 Years of Brewing,*179.
2. *100 Years of Brewing,*174.
3. Albert Cook Myers, *Narrative of Early Pennsylvania, West New Jersey and Delaware,* vol. 19 (New York, N.Y.: n.p., 1912), 208.
4. *100 Years of Brewing,* 157.
5. Issac Newton Phelps Stokes, *The Iconography of Manhattan Island 1498–1909* (New York, N.Y.: n.p., 1935), 148.
6. Stokes, *The Iconography of Manhattan Island 1498–1909,* 153.
7. *100 Years of Brewing,* 166.
8. *100 Years of Brewing,* 167.
9. Thomas Hariot, *Narrative of the First English Plantation in Virginia* (London, England: n.p., 1893), 27.
10. Joel Munsel, *Annals of Albany* (Albany, N.Y.: n.p., 1871), 48.
11. William Penn, "A Further Account," *Pennsylvania Magazine of History and Biography,* vol. 9: 72–73.
12. Penn, "A Further Account," 72–73.
13. Smith, *A New Age Now Begins,* 64.
14. Kym S. Rice, *Early American Taverns: For the Entertainment of Friends and Strangers* (Chicago, Ill.: Regnery Gateway, 1983), 17.
15. Rice, *Early American Taverns,* 51.

16. Baron, *Brewed in America,* 36.
17. *100 Years of Brewing,* 164.
18. Quoted in *100 Years of Brewing,* 164.
19. Rice, *Early American Taverns.*
20. Baron, *Brewed in America,* 48.
21. Mary Edward Lender and James Kirby Martin, *Drinking in America: A History* (New York, N.Y.: The Free Press, 1982), 11.
22. Baron, *Brewed in America,* 37.
23. Colonial Society of Massachusetts Publications, vol. 15 (Boston, Mass.: State of Massachusetts, 1869–1922), 204.
24. Massachusetts, *The Acts of Resolves of the Province of the Massachusetts Bay* (Boston, Mass.: State of Massachusetts, 1869–1922), 259.
25. Alice Morse Earle, *Stage Coach and Tavern Days* (New York, N.Y.: The Macmillan Company, 1900), 128.
26. Susanna Barrows and Robin Room, *Drinking, Behavior and Belief in Modern History* (Berkley, Calif.: University of California Press, n.d.), 41.

Chapter 3

1. Peter Fanuel, "Letter Book" (Baker Library at Harvard, n.d.).
2. Baron, *Brewed in America,* 71.
3. Carl Van Doren, *Benjamin Franklin* (New York, N.Y.: The Viking Press, 1938), 147.
4. Van Doren, *Benjamin Franklin,* 148.
5. Charles Jones, *History of Georgia* (Boston, Mass.: n.p., 1886), 229.
6. William Stephens, "Journal of Wm. Stephens" (Athens, Ga.: n.p., 1958), 86.
7. Robert Beverly, *The History and Present State of Virginia* (Chapel Hill, N.C.: n.p., 1947), 266.
8. Baron, *Brewed in America,* 49.
9. Francis Louis Michel, *Journey of Francis Louis Michel,* 136.

10. Elise Lathrop, *Early American Inns and Taverns* (New York, N.Y.: Arno Press, 1977), 115.
11. *Boston Newsletter,* November 28, 1728.
12. Baron, *Brewed in America,* 71.
13. Van Doren, *Benjamin Franklin,* 54.
14. Lathrop, *Early American Inns and Taverns,* 96.
15. Alice Morse Earle, *Customs and Fashions in Old New England* (Williamstown, Mass.: Corner House Publishers, 1983), 341.
    Earle wondered why practitioners of this remedy went through all the bother. She thought it would have been much easier to rely solely upon the four gallons of strong ale.
16. Rice, *Early American Taverns,* 98.
17. Lathrop, *Early American Inns and Taverns,* 71.
18. Lathrop, *Early American Inns and Taverns,* 63.
19. Lathrop, *Early American Inns and Taverns,* 63.
20. Catherine Drinker Bowen, *John Adams and the American Revolution* (Boston, Mass.: Little, Brown & Company, 1950), 466.
21. Baron, *Brewed in America,* 98.
22. Baron, *Brewed in America,* 71.

Chapter 4

1. *Virginia Gazette,* May 30, 1766.
2. *New York Gazette,* November 22, 1764.
3. Smith, *A New Age Now Begins,* 282–84.
4. *Virginia Gazette,* December 14, 1769.
5. Baron, *Brewed in America,* 91.
6. Baron, *Brewed in America,* 91.
7. Morison, *Oxford History of the American People,* 204.
8. Morison, *Oxford History of the American People,* 206.
9. Smith, *A New Age Now Begins,* 392.
10. *Virginia Gazette,* June 28, 1770.
11. Smith, *A New Age Now Begins,* 420.

12. Smith, *A New Age Now Begins,* 436.
13. Smith, *A New Age Now Begins,* 436.
14. *Boston Evening Post,* September 10, 1750.
15. *Virginia Gazette,* April 1, 1775.

Chapter 5

1. Albert Bushnell Hart, *Commonwealth History of Massachusetts,* vol. 2 (New York, N.Y.: n.p., 1927–1930), 449.
2. *Journal of the Continental Congress 1774–1789* (Washington, D.C., 1904–1937), vol. 3, 322.
3. Harry Emerson Wildes, *Valley Forge*, 169, 172–73.
4. "Memorial of John Lowry, to the Governor and Council Calendar of Virginia State Papers," vol. 3, 268.
5. Paymasters Account, "Lingerwood Collections of Hessian Papers," May 31, 1777.
6. "A Scrap of Troop History: Memoranda of Thomas Peters, made in his copy of By-Laws of the First Troop Philadelphia City Cavalry," *Pennsylvania Magazine of History and Biography,* vol. 15: 227.
7. "A Scrap of Troop History," 227.
8. Marvin Kitman, *George Washigton's Expense Account* (New York, N.Y.: Simon & Schuster, 1970), 195.
9. Kitman, *George Washigton's Expense Account,* 195.

Chapter 6

1. Earle, *Customs and Fashions in Old New England,* 172.
2. Henry McNulty, *Drinking in Vogue* (New York, N.Y.: The Vendome Press, 1978), 135.
3. McNulty, *Drinking in Vogue,* 135.
4. Charles L. Mee, *The Genius of the People* (New York, N.Y.: Harper & Row Publishers, 1987), 18.
5. Mee, *The Genius of the People,* 91.

6. Mee, *The Genius of the People,* 201.
7. Catherine Drinker Bowen, *Miracle at Philadelphia* (New York, N.Y.: Book of the Month Club, 1986), 264.
8. Earle, *Customs and Fashions in Old New England,* 183.
9. John C. Fitzpatrick, ed., *The Writings of George Washington,* vol. 30 (Washington, D.C., 1931–1944), 187.
10. Fitzpatrick, *The Writings of George Washington,* vol. 31, 187.
11. James Grant Wilson, ed., *Memorial History of the City of New York* (New York, N.Y.: n.p., 1892).
12. Charles Theodore Greve, *Centennial History of Cincinnati and Representative Citizens* (Chicago, Ill.: n.p., 1904), 431.
13. Daniel Drake, *Natural and Statistical View, or Picture of Cincinnati* (Cincinnati, Ohio: n.p., 1815), 147.

Chapter 7

1. Louis Phillipe, *Diary of My Travels in America* (New York, N.Y.: Delacorte Press, 1976), 110.
2. Jefferson to Yancey, January 6, 1816 (Library of Congress).
3. Jack McLaughlin, *Jefferson and Monticello* (New York, N.Y.: Henry Holt & Co., 1977), 98.
4. Baron, *Brewed in America,* 147.
5. Coppinger to Madison, December 16, 1810 (Library of Congress).
6. Coppinger to Madison, December 16, 1810 (Library of Congress).
7. Coppinger to Madison, December 20, 1810 (Library of Congress).
8. Jefferson to Coppinger, April 25, 1815 (Library of Congress).
9. Baron, *Brewed in America,* 151.
10. *Poughkeepsie Journal,* June 10, 1812.
11. Morison, *Oxford History of the American People,* 501.

Chapter 8

1. Fitzpatrick, *The Writings of George Washington,* vol. 30, 20.
2. Baron, *Brewed in America,* 116.

Chapter 9

1. *100 Years of Brewing,* 159.
2. *100 Years of Brewing,* 162–63.
3. *100 Years of Brewing,* 160.
4. *100 Years of Brewing,* 163.
5. *100 Years of Brewing,* 163.
6. Massachusetts, *The Acts and Resolves of the Province of the Massachusetts Bay* (Boston, Mass.: n.p., 1869–1922), 502.
7. Baron, *Brewed in America,* 103.

Chapter 10

1. John Hull Brown, *Early American Beverages* (New York, N.Y.: Bonanza Books, 1966), 129.
2. Brown, *Early American Beverages,* 129.
3. Brown, *Early American Beverages,* 130.
4. Brown, *Early American Beverages,* 151–52.
5. Smith, *A New Age Now Begins,* 243.
6. Brown, *Early American Beverages,* 130.
7. Barrows and Room, *Drinking, Behavior and Belief in Modern History,* 29.
8. Brown, *Early American Beverages,* 138.

Chapter 11

1. John Bickerdyke, *The Curiosities of Ale & Beer* (reprint, London, England: Spring Books Westbook House, 1965), 388.
2. Earle, *Stagecoach and Tavern Days,* 112.
3. Earle, *Stagecoach and Tavern Days,* 108.
4. Earle, *Stagecoach and Tavern Days,* 108–9.
5. Earle, *Stagecoach and Tavern Days,* 113.
6. Earle, *Stagecoach and Tavern Days,* 132–33.
7. Bickerdyke, *Curiosities of Ale & Beer,* 388.
8. Bickerdyke, *Curiosities of Ale & Beer,* 386.

9. Bickerdyke, *Curiosities of Ale & Beer,* 384.
10. Bickerdyke, *Curiosities of Ale & Beer,* 384.
11. Quoted in W. T. Marchant, *In Praise of Ale* (London, England: George Redway, 1888), 273.
12. Quoted in Bickerdyke, *Curiosities of Ale & Beer,* 410.
13. Bickerdyke, *Curiosities of Ale & Beer,* 413.
14. Bickerdyke, *Curiosities of Ale & Beer,* 391.
15. Bickerdyke, *Curiosities of Ale & Beer,* 409–11.
16. Bickerdyke, *Curiosities of Ale & Beer,* 382.

Chapter 12

1. Brown, *Early American Beverages,* 29.
2. Baron, *Brewed in America,* 95.
3. *100 Years of Brewing,* 82.
4. *100 Years of Brewing,* 82.
5. Baron, *Brewed in America,* 96.
6. Baron, *Brewed in America,* 86.
7. Johann Martin Bolzius, "Johann Martin Bolzius Answers a Questionnaire on Carolina & Georgia," *William & Mary Quarterly* 15: 246–47.
8. Baron, *Brewed in America,* 97.
9. Stephens, *Journal of Proceedings in Georgia in the Colonial Record of the State of Georgia,* vol. 4, 86.
10. "An Impartial Enquiry into the State and Unity of the Province of Georgia" (London, England: n.p., 1741).
11. Baron, *Brewed in America,* 96.
12. Baron, *Brewed in America,* 99–100.

Chapter 13

1. Bill Severn, *The End of the Roaring Twenties* (New York, N.Y.: J. Messnez, 1969), 18.
2. Severn, *The End of the Roaring Twenties,* 26–27.

Chapter 14

1. Victor S. Clark, *History of Manufacturers in the United States,* 3 vols. (New York, N.Y.: n.p., 1929).
2. William Waller Hening, *Statutes at Large,* vol. 1 (New York, N.Y.: n.p., 1823), 374.
3. Baron, *Brewed in America,* 10.
4. Stokes, *The Iconography of Manhattan Island 1498–1909,* vol. 4, 78.
5. *100 Years of Brewing,* 88.
6. Greville Bathe and Dorothy Bathe, *Oliver Evans, A Chronicle of Early American Engineering* (Philadelphia, Pa.: Historical Society of Pennsylvania, 1935), 79–80.
7. *100 Years of Brewing,* 172.
8. *100 Years of Brewing,* 47.
9. *100 Years of Brewing,* 47.
10. *100 Years of Brewing,* 48.
11. *100 Years of Brewing,* 48–49.
12. *100 Years of Brewing,* 48.
13. Baron, *Brewed in America,* 62.
14. Baron, *Brewed in America,* 61.
15. Baron, *Brewed in America,* 61–62.
16. *100 Years of Brewing,* 45.
17. *100 Years of Brewing,* 99.
18. *100 Years of Brewing,* 207.
19. *100 Years of Brewing,* 212.

Appendix

1. Bowen, *Miracle in Philadelphia,* 264.

Bibliography

Abel, Bob. *The Beer Book*. London, England: Music Sales Limited, 1981.

Ade, George. *The Old-Time Saloon*. New York, N.Y.: Old Town Books, 1993.

Anderson, Will. *The Beer Book*. Princeton, N.J.: The Pyne Press, 1973.

———. *From Beer to Eternity*. Lexington, Mass.: The Stephan Greene Press, 1987.

Barbor, Thomas. *The Encyclopedia of Psychoactive Drugs*. New York, N.Y.: Chelsea House Publishers, 1986.

Barnard, Alfred. *Bass & Co. Limited*. Burton-on-Trent, England: n.p., 1889.

Baron, Stanley. *Brewed in America: A History of Beer and Ale in the United States*. Boston, Mass.: Little, Brown & Company, 1962.

Barrows, Susanna, and Robin Room. *Drinking, Behavior and Belief in Modern History*. Berkley, Calif.: University of California Press, n.d.

Bathe, Greville, and Dorothy Bathe. *Oliver Evans, A Chronicle of Early American Engineering*. Philadelphia, Pa.: Historical Society of Pennsylvania, 1935.

Batterberry, Michael, and Ariane Batterberry. *On the Town in Old New York*. New York, N.Y.: Charles Scribner's Sons, 1973.

Bayles, W. Harrison. *Old Taverns of New York*. New York, N.Y.: Frank Allaben Genealogical Co., 1915.

Berkin, Carol A., and Leonard Wood. *Land of Promise: A History of the United States*. Glenview, Ill.: Scott, Foresman & Company, 1987.

Beverly, Robert. *The History and Present State of Virginia*. Chapel Hill, N.C.: n.p., 1947.

Bickerdyke, John. *The Curiosities of Ale & Beer*. 1889. Reprint, London, England: Spring Books Westbook House, 1965.

Bolzius, Johann Martin. "Johann Martin Answers a Questionnaire on Carolina & Georgia," *William & Mary Quarterly* 15 (n.d.): 246–247.

Bowen, Catherine Drinker. *John Adams and the American Revolution*. Boston, Mass.: Little, Brown & Company, 1950.

————. *Miracle at Philadelphia*. New York, N.Y.: Book of the Month Club, 1986.

Bradford, William. *History of Plymouth Plantation*. Ed. by Samuel Eliot Morison. New York, N.Y.: n.p., 1952.

Brown, John Hull. *Early American Beverages*. New York, N.Y.: Bonanza Books, 1966.

Butcher, Alan D. *Ale & Beer: A Curious History*. Toronto, Ont.: McClelland & Stewart Inc., 1989.

Clark, Peter. *The English Alehouse: A Social History 1200–1830*. New York, N.Y.: Longman, n.d.

Colonial Society of Massachusetts Publications. Vol. 15. Boston, Mass.: State of Massachusetts, 1869–1922.

Dallas, John, and Charles McMaster. *The Beer Drinker's Companion*. Edinburgh, Scotland: The Edinburgh Publishing Company, 1993.

Dedman, Emmett. *Fabulous Chicago*. New York, N.Y.: Atheneum, 1981.

Digby, Joan, and John Digby. *Inspired by Drink*. New York, N.Y.: William Morrow & Company, Inc., 1988.

Downard, William L. *Dictionary of the History of the American Brewing and Distilling Industries*. Westport, Conn.: Greenwood Press, 1980.

Doxat, John. *The Book of Drinking*. London, England: Triune Books, 1973.

Drake, Daniel. *Natural and Statistical View, or Picture of Cincinnati*. Cincinnati, Ohio: n.p., 1815.

Earle, Alice Morse. *Customs and Fashions in Old New England*. Williamstown, Mass.: Corner House Publishers, 1983.

————. *Stage Coach and Tavern Days*. New York, N.Y.: The Macmillan Company, 1900.

Erikson, Jack. *Brewed in California*. Reston, Va.: RedBrick Press, 1993.

————. *Star Spangled Beer*. Reston, Va.: RedBrick Press, 1987.

Farb, Peter, and George Armelagos. *Consuming Passions: The Anthropology of Eating*. Boston, Mass.: Houghton Mifflin Company, 1980.

Fanuel, Peter. *Letter Book*. Baker Library at Harvard, n.d.

Fennelly, Catherine. *Life in an Old New England Village*. New York, N.Y.: Thomas Y. Crowell Co., 1969.

Fitzpatrick, John C., ed. *The Writings of George Washington*. 39 vols. Washington, D.C.: n.p., 1931–1944.

Fleming, Alice. *Alcohol, the Delightful Poison*. New York, N.Y.: Delacorte Press, n.d.

Forget, Carl. *Dictionary of Beer and Brewing.* Boulder, Colo.: Brewers
    Publications, 1988.

Foster, Terry. *Pale Ale.* Boulder, Colo.: Brewers Publications, 1990.

————. *Porter.* Boulder, Colo.: Brewers Publications, 1992.

Gayre, G. R. *Wassail in Mazers of Mead.* London, England: Phillimore &
    Co., 1948.

Gies, Joseph, and Frances Gies. *Cathedral, Forge, and Waterwheel
    Technology and Invention in the Middle Ages.* New York, N.Y.: Harper
    Collins Publishers, 1994.

Greve, Charles Theodore. *Centennial History of Cincinnati and
    Representative Citizens.* Chicago, Ill.: n.p., 1904.

Grossman, Harold J. *Grossman's Guide to Wines, Spirits, and Beers.* New
    York, N.Y.: Charles Scribner's Sons, 1955.

Grun, Bernard. *The Timetables of History.* New York, N.Y.: Simon &
    Schuster, 1975.

Haiber, William Paul, and Robert Haiber. *A Short, but Foamy, History of
    Beer.* La Grangeville, N.Y.: Info Devel Press, 1993.

Hariot, Thomas. *Narrative of the First English Plantation in Virginia.*
    London, England: n.p., 1893.

Hart, Albert Bushnell. *Commonwealth History of Massachusetts.* 5 vols.
    New York, N.Y.: n.p., 1927–1930.

Hening, William Waller. *Statutes at Large.* 13 vols. New York, N.Y.:
    1823.

"An Impartial Enquiry into the State and Unity of the Province of
    Georgia." London, England: n.p., 1741.

Jackson, Michael. *The New World Guide to Beer.* Philadelphia, Pa.:
    Running Press, 1988; reprinted 1989.

————. *The Pocket Guide to Beer.* New York, N.Y.: Simon &
    Schuster, 1991.

————. *Michael Jackson's Beer Companion.* Philadelphia, Pa.: Running
    Press, 1993.

Jones, Charles. *History of Georgia.* 2 vols. Boston, Mass.: n.p., 1886.

Journal of the Continental Congress 1774–1789. 34 vols. Washington,
    D.C., 1904–1937.

Kitman, Marvin. *George Washington's Expense Account.* New York, N.Y.:
    Simon & Schuster, 1970.

Kochan, James. "A Personal Index of Military Records." Morristown,
    N.J.: Curator National Historical Park, n.d.

Lathrop, Elise. *Early American Inns and Taverns.* New York, N.Y.: Arno Press, 1977.

Lender, Mary Edward, and James Kirby Martin. *Drinking in America: A History.* New York, N.Y.: The Free Press, 1982.

Levin, Phyllis Lee. *Abigail Adams.* New York, N.Y.: St. Martin's Press, 1987.

Lewis, Michael J. *Stout.* Boulder, Colo.: Brewers Publications, 1995.

Lowry, John. *Memorial of John Lowry, to the Governor and Council Calendar of Virginia—State Paper,* n.d.

Marchant, W.T. *In Praise of Ale.* London, England: George Redway, 1888.

Massachusetts, *The Acts and Resolves of the Province of the Massachusetts Bay.* 21 vols. Boston, Mass.: n.p., 1869–1922.

McLaughlin, Jack. *Jefferson and Monticello.* New York, N.Y.: Henry Holt & Co., 1977.

McNulty, Henry. *Drinking in Vogue.* New York, N.Y.: The Vendome Press, 1978.

Mee, Charles L. *The Genius of the People.* New York, N.Y.: Harper & Row Publishers, 1987.

"Memorial of John Lowry, to the Governor and Council Calendar of Virginia State Papers." Vol. 3.

Mendelsohn, Oscar. *The Dictionary of Drink and Drinking.* New York, N.Y.: Hawthorn Books Inc., 1965.

Michel, Francis Louis. *Journey of Francis Louis Michel.*

Miller, Dave. *Continental Pilsner.* Boulder, Colo.: Brewers Publications, 1989.

Morini, John. *America Eats Out.* New York, N.Y.: William Morrow & Co., 1991.

Morison, Samuel Elliot. *The Oxford History of the American People.* New York, N.Y.: Oxford University Press, 1965.

Munsel, Joel. *Annals of Albany.* Albany, N.Y.: n.p., 1871.

Muscatine, Doris. *Old San Francisco.* New York, N.Y.: G. P. Putnam's Sons, 1975.

Myers, Albert Cook. *Narrative of Early Pennsylvania, West New Jersey and Delaware.* New York, N.Y.: n.p., 1912.

Nelson, William. "Documents Related to the Colonial History of the State of New Jersey." New Jersey Archive Series, 1898.

New York Gazette, 1770–1789.

302

One Hundred Years of Brewing. (Supplement to the *Western Brewer.*) New York and Chicago: H.S. Rich & Co., 1903.

Paschall, Thomas. "Papers and Account." Historical Society of Pennsylvania, 1705–1711, 1713–1728.

Paymasters Account. "Lingerwood Collection of Hessian Papers."

Phillippe, Louis. *Diary of My Travels in America.* Translated by Stephen Braker. New York, N.Y.: Delacorte Press, 1976.

Pierce, Bessie Louise. *A History of Chicago:* New York, N.Y.: Alfred A. Knopf, 1957.

Prial, Frank J. "The Man Who Rescued a Brewery." *New York Times,* July 11, 1984.

Protz, Roger. *The European Beer Almanac.* Moffat, Scotland: Lochar Publishing, 1991.

————. *The Real Ale Drinker's Almanac.* Moffat, Scotland: Lochar Publishing, 1991.

Rae, Simon, ed. *The Faber Book of Drink, Drinkers, and Drinking.* London, England: Faber & Faber Limited, 1991.

Randel, William Pierce. *Centennial: American Life in 1876.* New York, N.Y.: Chilton, 1969.

Rice, Kym S. *Early American Taverns: For the Entertainment of Friends and Strangers.* Chicago, Ill.: Regnery Gateway, 1983.

Robertson, James D. *The Great American Beer Book.* New York, N.Y.: Warner Books, 1978.

St. James Gate Brewery. Dublin, Ireland: Arthur Guinness, Son & Co., 1931.

Schulter, Herman. *Brewery Workers Movement in America.* Cincinnati, Ohio: IUUBWA, 1910.

"A Scrap of Troop History; Memoranda of Thomas Peters, made in his copy of By-Laws of the First Troop Philadelphia City Cavalry." *Pennsylvania Magazine of History and Biography.* Vol. 15.

Severn, Bill. *The End of the Roaring Twenties.* New York, N.Y.: J. Messnez, 1969.

Smith, Gregg. *Beer: A History.* New York, N.Y.: Avon, 1995.

————. *The Beer Enthusiast's Guide.* Pownal, Vt.: Storey Communications, 1994.

Smith, Gregg, and Carrie Getty. *The Beer Drinkers Bible.* Boulder, Colo.: Brewers Publications, 1997.

Smith, Page. *The Nation Comes of Age.* New York, N.Y.: McGraw-Hill
    Book Company, 1981.
————. *A New Age Now Begins.* New York, N.Y.: McGraw-Hill Book
    Company, 1976.
————. *The Shaping of America.* New York, N.Y.: McGraw-Hill Book
    Company, 1980.
Stephens, William. *Journal of Proceedings in Georgia in the Colonial
    Record of the State of Georgia.* Vol. 4: 86.
Stephens, William. *The Journal of William Stephens.* 2 vols. Athens, Ga.:
    n.p., 1958.
Stokes, Issac Newton Phelps. *The Iconography of Manhattan Island
    1498–1909.* New York, N.Y.: n.p., 1935.
Tousey, Thomas G. *Military History of Carlisle and Carlisle Barracks.*
    Richmond, Va.: Dietz Press, 1939.
Tunis, Edward. *Colonial Living.* Toronto, Ont.: Fitz Henry & Whiteside
    Limited, 1957.
————. *Frontier Living.* New York, N.Y.: Thomas Crowell Co., 1961.
Van Doren, Carl. *Benjamin Franklin.* New York, N.Y.: The Viking
    Press, 1938.
Van Wieren, Dale P. *American Breweries II.* West Point, Pa.: Eastern
    Coast Breweriana Association, 1995.
Virginia Gazette, 1736–1774.
Wagner, Rich. "Brewing in the 17th Century." *Zymurgy* 15, 40–43.
Wheeler, Graham, and Roger Protz. *Brew Your Own Real Ale at Home.*
    St. Albans, England: CAMRA, 1993.
Wigely, Russel E. *History of the United States Army.* New York, N.Y.:
    Macmillan, 1967.
Wildes, Harry Emerson. *Valley Forge.*
Wilford, John Noble. "Trade or Colonialism? Ruins May Give Answer."
    New York Times, May 25, 1993.
Wilson, James Grant, ed. *Memorial History of the City of New York.* 4
    vols. New York, N.Y.: n.p., 1892.
Wilson, Woodrow. *History of the American People.* 5 vols. New York,
    N.Y.: Wm. H. Wise & Co., 1901.
Wood, William. *New England Prospects.* Boston, Mass.: n.p., 1635.
Yenne, Bill. "America's First Brewmaster General." *All About Beer
    Magazine* (April/May 1992).

Index

Abbott, George, 44
abstinence, 247, 248. *See also* prohibition; temperance
Adams, Abigail, 60–61, 114
Adams, Charles Francis, 114
Adams, John, 60–61, 65, 79
  on beer drinks, 212
  cider consumption, 114
  endorsement of Washington, 100–101
  friendship with Jefferson, 129
  as lawyer, 97, 206–7
  taverns and, 86–87, 200, 206
  as vice president, 123
Adams, Joseph, 78
Adams, Samuel, 77, 78–79, 84
  as revolutionary, 85, 207
  support of local brewing, 88–89
advertising
  for bottles, 264
  of land, 19–20
  of private breweries, 22
aging, 253, 266–67
aging rooms, 174
alcohol, 238–41, 244. *See also* drunkenness; prohibition; temperance
alcohol content, 15, 133
alcoholism, 239. *See also* drunkenness
ale houses. *See* taverns
ale stakes, 195
aleberry, 216–17
ales, 141, 172–73
  breweries, 176–77
  buttered, 216
  fermenting, 266
  milk, 216
  mumm, 215
Allen, Ethan, 102
Alrichs, Jacob, 28
alt beers, 131, 141
Amelung, John F., 265
American Philosophical Society, 68, 231
American Revolution

causes and precedent problems, 74–85, 87–91
war, 90, 97–110
American Society for Prohibition, 246
American Temperance Union, 246
Amherst, Jeffrey, 230
Anhueser-Busch, 178
apples, 113–14, 223. *See also* cider
Articles of Confederation, 117

Bailey's Blue Anchor, 39
bar spoons, 196, 211
Barentz, Daniel, 57
barley, 15, 20, 60–61
  in Boston, 59–60
  growing, 21, 26, 29, 90, 138, 227
  types of, 113, 199
barm, 226
barrels, 254
bars. *See* taverns
baseball, 154
Baverstock, James, 261–63
Beadleston, Ebenezer, 156, 157
Beadleston, William, 157
Beadleston and Woerz Brewing, 155–58
Beecher, Lyman, 245
Beekman, William, 190
beer
  appearance, 15
  buying, 60, 76, 235
  as college staple, 44–46, 56–57
  commercial production, 235. *See also* commercial breweries and brewing
  corruption of, 26–28
  cultural importance of, 2, 23, 59, 109–10, 239
  demand for, 49, 61, 70, 139, 167–68, 199. *See also* beer consumption
  education and, 134
  as food, 9–10, 13, 15, 23, 103, 127
  healthfulness of, 11, 53, 63–64, 65, 102, 103, 108, 109, 127, 135, 245

as medicine, 210, 219–21
for military recruitment/reward, 94,
    97–98, 205–6, 207
as necessity, 54, 63, 192
in southern colonies, 55–56
preservability of, 12, 25, 56, 197, 264
shortages, 226
sour, 214
spiced. *See* beer drinks
as spirits alternative, 132, 135, 242, 243
styles of, 15, 20, 51, 131, 141
warm. *See* beer drinks
work rations of, 47, 62–63
beer consumption, 40, 56, 68, 130
    excessive, 47–48, 64–66, 271. *See also*
        drunkenness
    limiting, 187–88, 191
    military, 100, 102
    as social activity, 127
beer cups, 217–18, 219–20
beer drinks, 116, 196, 209–24
beer importing, 11, 21, 28, 43
    abstention from, 88–89
    in Boston, 51, 55
    cost, 193
    dependence on, 61, 69–71, 81
    by southern colonies, 56–57, 116, 127
    taxation of, 77
    wartime, 107
beer ingredients, 59–60
    corn. *See* corn, use in beer
    hops, 216
    lack of, 199, 227
    molasses, 232
    production of, 29
    during Prohibition, 211
    pumpkin, 68–69
    spruce, 27, 104, 230–31
    substitutes, 26–27, 35, 104, 132, 217,
        227, 229
beer production, 40, 64, 70–71. *See also*
    breweries; commercial breweries and
    brewing
    during American Revolution, 103
    distribution, 156, 170, 175, 258, 271
    local, 81, 88, 193
    meeting demand, 167–68

supply sources, 122
beer substitutes, 14–15, 62
beer supplies, 26, 36, 69
Belcher, Andrew, 60
Belcher, Joseph, 55
Bellowstop, 213
Bergner, C. W., 169
Bergner, Gustavus, 168–69
Bergner and Engel Brewing, 166–70, 269
Betz Brewery, 163
Beverly, Robert, 57, 227
Beverwyck Brewery (Albany), 160–61
birch, 27
Black, William, 66
Block, Adrian, 17
Blue Anchor (Philadelphia), 43–44
blue laws, 240
Boardley, I. E., 234
Boerhaave, 266
bogus, 215
Bolzius, Johann Martin, 229
bootlegging, 238
Boston, 83, 85
    breweries and brewers, 54–55, 148–51
    taverns in, 38–39, 194
Boston Massacre, 97, 206–7
Boston Port Act, 83, 84–85, 88
Boston Tea Party, 82, 207
bottles and bottling, 133, 226, 264–65
Boyd, John, 96
Bradford, William, 9, 11–12
brand names, 40, 150
bread, in beer drinks, 214, 219
brew houses, 12, 19, 226, 253. *See also*
    breweries
brew kettles, 255–56
breweries
    commercial. *See* commercial breweries
        and brewing
    construction of, 253
    English versus German design, 255–56
    growth, 258
    in New York (New Amsterdam), 17, 34,
        41–43, 107
    in New Jersey, 44
    payment for, 32
    in Philadelphia, 21, 43

production during American
  Revolution, 103
public, 34, 226
Rensselaer's, 31
sales territories, 70
as settlers' priority, 2, 4, 8, 11, 12, 22
ship stocking, 29–30
taverns and, 33–34, 41
troop supply by, 105
brewers, 121
  availability of, 21
  importing, 132
  liability of, 29–30
  training, 132
brewing, 25–26, 44
  climate for, 51, 56, 176
  as community effort, 2
  cooling, 258–60, 261
  equipment and methods, 176–77,
    252–64
  German immigrants and, 140–41,
    143–45
  instructions for, 228–29, 234
  knowledge of, 252, 260
  measuring devices, 253, 260–62
  in New Amsterdam, 34, 43
  in New England, 13–14, 22
  regulation of, 27, 29–31
  in southern colonies, 89
  for supplemental income, 47
  yeast and. *See* yeast
brewing industry. *See* commercial breweries and brewing
brewing permits, 47, 254
brewing season, 139, 144–45, 176
Brewster, William, 8
Briggs, Richard, 63
Bromfield, Edward, 203
Brouwers Street, 17, 41–42
brown Betty, 214
Bunker Hill Brewery, 148–51
Burke, Edmund, 83
Burr, Aaron, 141
buttered ale, 216

calibogus, 215
Cambridge (Massachusetts), 194

Campion, George, 58
Carey, John, 54
Carney, James, 175
Carter, London, 227
caves, 176
celebrations, 120–21
cellar temperature, 197
Chicago, 126, 173–75
chicken in cider, 115
Child, Samuel, 228
Christiansen, Hans, 17
Christmas, 223
churches, 194–95, 239–40
cider (hard), 64, 113–16, 121–22, 245
Cincinnati, 125–26, 270
circuit riders, 37, 199, 200
Clap, Roger, 11
Clark, Victor, 253
Clark, William, 245
Clarke, George, 50
Clarke, Joseph, 232
clipper ships, 144, 267–68
cloudiness, 15
cold, 144, 176, 197. *See also* temperature
Combrune, Michael, 260–61, 262
commercial breweries and brewing, 31,
    35, 36, 48
  alternative production, 160, 171
  Beadleston and Woerz Brewing, 155–58
  Bergner and Engel Brewing, 166–70
  Boston, 54–55, 148–51
  Bunker Hill Brewery, 148–51
  Chicago, 173–75
  dependence on, 60
  effect of embargoes, 81–82, 85, 89
  Jacob Ruppert Brewery, 151–55
  lager, 177, 268–71
  Lauer Brewing, 163–66
  Maryland, 57
  mergers and acquisitions of, 160–61, 170
  Milwaukee, 176–77
  modernization, 155, 160, 161, 170, 178
  national, 153, 155, 161, 177
  national funding for, 135, 136–37
  New York, 40, 50–51, 62, 126–27,
    151–61
  Philadelphia, 49–50, 51, 53–54, 161–73

regional, 161, 169
Robert Hare Brewing, 161–63
Robert Smith Brewing, 171–73
Schaefer, 158–61
sponsorship by, 153
technology, 253, 271
troop supply by, 105, 107
Vassar's, 138–39
William J. Lemp Brewing, 177–79
Yuengling Brewery, 170–71
Connecticut, 229
Connecticut Society for the Reformation of
  Morals, 245
Constitution, 119–20
Constitutional Convention, 117–18
Continental Congresses, 85–87, 90, 100
cool ships, 259
cool tankard, 217
Cooper, John, 148
coppers, 255
Coppinger, Joseph, 134–36
corn, use in beer, 14–15, 20, 22, 26, 134,
  227–28, 229–30
courthouses, 139. *See also* taverns
crime, 238
currency, 60, 198
  availability of, 32, 36, 112, 193, 226

Dais, Caleb, 106
Davis, John, 176
de Latour, Caguard, 266
de Sille, Nicasius, 29
defenses, 204–5
density, 262–64
Desmazieres, 266
disease, 109
Diversey, Michael, 174, 175
diversity, 49–50
Doling, Emmanuel, 255
Drake, Daniel, 126
Dreher, Anton, 267
drunkenness, 22–23, 43. *See also* prohibition; temperance
  avoiding, 121–22
  curbing, 192, 247
  government concern with, 47, 64–66,
    131, 201–4

of soldiers, 97, 103
from spirits, 68, 242
taxing, 192
Duke's Laws, 29–30
Dunway, Wayland F., 198
Dutch colonies, 16–18

Earle, Alice Morse, 42
Eaton, Nathaniel, 44
ebulum (ebulam), 215–16
economics, 35–36
Edwards, Justin, 246
egg hot, 214–15
egg posset, 215
eggs, 210–13, 214–15
Embree, Davis, 125–26
Engel, Charles, 167–69, 268–69
England, 73–75, 77, 80
Erleben, 266
Europe, 3, 9
Evans, Oliver, 257

Faneuil, Peter, 50–51, 53
Faris, William, 67
farming, 35–36
Fenner, Thomas, 229
Fenwick, John, 22, 44
fermentation, 176, 252, 253, 260, 266–67
  study of, 265–66
Fisher, Miers, 87
Fletcher, George, 254
flip, 109, 212–14
flip-dog, 213
food, 87, 117–18
Fort Nassau (Camden, New Jersey), 18
Fort Orange (Albany, New York), 18
Fortescue, John, 3
Frampton, William, 20–21, 43
Franklin, Benjamin, 51–53, 63, 68, 81,
  114, 230
Franklin, William, 81
Fraunces, Phoebe, 108
Fraunces, Samuel, 108, 124
Fraunces Tavern, 108, 109, 110
Fredenburgh, William, 58
Freemason's cup, 222–23

games, 240
Gauch, Jacob, 175
Gauch and Brahm Brewery, 175
Georgia, 22–23, 58, 229, 242–43
Gibbs, Caleb, 109
Gillig, George, 152
gin, 36, 108
Girritsen, Philip, 41
glass and glassmaking, 133, 144, 264
Gould, Thomas, 148
grace cup, 217–18
grain growing, 29. *See also* barley
Green Dragon Tavern (Boston), 38, 207
grog shops. *See* taverns
Gunther Brewery (Baltimore), 161

Haas, William, 174
Haines, Rueben, 121
ham baked in cider, 115
Hamm, Theodore, 161
Hancock, John, 54, 78–80, 100
    cider consumption, 114–15
    wartime beer supply, 105–6
Hancock, Thomas, 54
Hanson, Emil, 267
Hare, Robert, 161–63
Hare, Robert, Jr., 163
Hariot, Thomas, 227
Harvard, John, 44
Harvard College, 44–46
health, 2–3, 29
    beer and, 11, 53, 63–64, 65, 102, 103,
        108, 109, 127, 135, 245
    beer drinks and, 210
    water and, 29, 39, 210, 239, 245
Henry, Patrick, 84, 88
Hewitt, Nathaniel, 246
Holloway, Thomas, 258
homebrewing, 27, 30, 31, 225–35
    equipment, 234
    as household chore, 226
    instructions for, 59, 228–29, 234
    Jefferson and, 129, 132–33
    need for, 60
    in New England, 40, 43, 229
    quality, 131, 226
    recipes, 104, 227–33

Stamp Act and, 76
    tax exemptions for, 191
    temperature, 225
Hone, Philip, 143
hops, 15
    alternatives, 230–31. *See also* spruce
        beer
    availability of, 59, 61–62, 104, 199
    Dutch use of, 17
    extract, 257
    growing, 90, 174
    importing, 26
    prices, 133
    wild, 29, 225
Hosier, Giles, 55
hottle, 213
Hudson, Henry, 16
Hudson River, 106–7
Hull, John, 39
hum, 211
Huston, "Cap," 154
hydrometers, 262–63

immigrants, 14, 18–19. *See also* Plymouth
        Colony
    beer's importance to, 2, 23, 59,
        109–10, 239
    German, 125, 130–31, 140–41, 143,
        270–71
    priorities of, 25
    westward expansion by, 124–25
immigration, reasons for, 2, 50, 130, 143
imports. *See also* beer importing
    agreements against, 76, 80, 81, 85, 88
    avoiding, 122
    taxation of, 77
Indian Queen tavern, 117, 118, 119
inns, 37. *See also* taverns
Intolerable Acts, 83

Jacobus (Dutch brewer), 43
Jamestown (Virginia), 21
Jefferson, Martha, 132–33
Jefferson, Thomas, 84, 129–30, 131
    brewing and, 132–34, 135–36, 258
Jervis, John B., 142
jingle, 223

Johnson, Ben, 219
Johonot, Andrew, 106
Jones, Christopher, 10, 12

Kerr, William, 257
Key, Francis Scott, 136
Knetzing, 266
Koch, Peter, 41
Krieft, Wilhelm (William), 40, 184–87

La Battie, Joan, 31–32
lager beers, 143, 144, 152, 267–71
    breweries, 177, 268–71
    brewers, 159, 164
    kettles for, 256
    popularity of, 159, 166, 173, 270
lagering, 131, 267
Lake Brewery (Milwaukee), 177
lambswool, 223
Lance, John, 55
land grants, 16
Lauer, Frank P., 166
Lauer, Fredrick, 163–66
Lauer, George F., 166
Lauer Brewing, 163–66
Lavoisier, 266
laws. *See also* licensing
    disregard of, 201–4
    effectiveness of, 48, 63, 188, 191, 243
    national, 246–47
    prohibition, 238–39, 246–47, 250
    ship supply, 29–30
    temperance, 63, 131, 201, 242–43
Lear, Tobias, 123, 163
Lee, Richard Henry, 84, 88, 120
legal process, 37–38, 199
Lemp, Adam, 177, 270
licensing
    of brewers/breweries, 31–32, 36, 47
    of taverns, 36–37, 65, 67
Lill, William, 173, 174, 175
Lill and Diversey, 174–75
liquor, hard. *See* spirits
Lispenard, Leonard, 50
loggerheads, 211, 212
Lowell, James, 213
Lowenhock, 266

Lowry, John, 103
Lunn, Thomas, 67

Madison, James, 117, 120, 122, 133, 134–35
maize. *See* corn, use in beer
malt, 21
    alternatives, 231. *See also* corn, use
        in beer
    availability of, 28–29, 59, 114,
        199, 227
    importing, 26, 80–81
    prices, 28
    quality, 27
    required amount, 30
    suppliers, 40
    supplies, 138
malting, 157, 253
maltsters, 53, 78
Manger, George, 268
Manhattan Island, 18
market development, 169
Marshall, John, 120
Marston, John, 68
Martin, Benjamin, 262
Maryland, 57, 66, 229
mash tuns, 234
mashing, 261
Mason, George, 84
Massachusetts, 26, 54, 77–80, 82
    beer quality laws, 27
    beer taxes, 191
    homebrewing, 229
Mather, Cotton, 38, 45
Mather, Increase, 45–47
Mee, Charles, 118
Mercer, John, 264
Michel, Francis Louis, 58
military supplies, 100, 109–10. *See also*
    soldiers
militias, 93, 94–95, 97–98, 204–6
milk ale, 216
Miller, Samuel, 174
Miller Brewing, 177
Milwaukee, 126, 140, 176–77
Milwaukee Brewery, 176–77
Minuit, Peter, 18, 34
Mitchell, William, 249

molasses, 27, 232, 241, 243
Monck, George, 200
Monck's Tavern (Boston), 38, 200
money, 32. *See also* currency
moonshining, 241
Morison, Samuel Elliot, 140
Morris, Anthony, 43, 53
Morris, Luke, 121
Morris's brewery, 44
Mueller, Adoph, 173
mullers, 196
mullet, 196–97
mumm, 215

Nash, Abraham, 156
New Amsterdam (Manhattan, New York),
    16, 17, 34
  beer taxes, 183–90
  defenses, 188, 190–91
New England, 113–14, 239–40
New Jersey, 81
New Sareden, 28
New Sweden, 19
New York, 18
  beer taxes, 191
  breweries and brewing, 107, 123, 141,
    143–44
  commercial breweries, 40, 50–51, 62,
    126–27, 151–61
  hop production in, 62
  water supply, 34–35, 55, 127, 141–43
Newport, 55
Nichols, Robert Carter, 88
Nicholson's brewery, 44
North, Lord (British Prime Minister), 83

oak, 225
oats, 20
October beer, 53, 88
Ogden, William, 174
Ogelthorpe, James, 22–23, 56, 242
Oliver, Nathaniel, 55
Otis, James, 77, 79, 97
Owens, Richard, 176–77

Pabst Brewing, 177
Pallet, William, 176

parlor, 198
parting cup, 218–19
Paschall, Thomas, 20–21, 53–54
Paschall, Thomas, Jr., 53
Pasteur, Louis, 266
Patroon system, 16
Penn, William, 18, 19–20, 35, 49–50
Pepper, David, 172
Pepper, George, 172
Perot, Frances, 258
Perry, Seth, 39
Peters, Thomas, 104–5
Philadelphia, 18–19, 80–81, 85, 87
  beer drinking in, 68
  breweries and brewing in, 35, 43,
    122, 141
  commercial breweries, 49–50, 51,
    53–54, 161–73
  German population, 167, 168
Phillipe, Louis, 131
Pilgrims, 8–10
pitching, 258
Pittsburgh, 124–25
Plymouth Colony, 8–14
porters, 131, 141, 162, 228–29, 266
  Washington and, 123, 124, 162
posset, 217
Potts, Joseph, 171–72
Powell and Pritchard, 177
Pownall (Governor), 38
Price, W. W., 157
prices, 28, 36
Printz, Jonathan, 28
prisoners' beer rations, 103–4
prohibition, 15, 238. *See also* temperance
  brewery closures from, 151, 155, 158,
    160, 169–70, 173, 178
  in Georgia, 242–43
  laws, 238–39, 246–47, 250
  movements, 116
  national, 248
public houses, 13. *See also* taverns
public works, 198
pumpkin ale, 231–32
purity laws, 27–28
purl, 223–24
Putnam (American general), 109

quality, 74, 126, 131, 224, 226, 260
quality laws, 29–30

Randolph, Edmund, 120
Randolph, Peyton, 88
recipes
    beer drinks, 210, 212–19
    beer medicines, 219–23
    for homebrews, 104, 227–33
    porter, 228–29
Red Lion Brewery, 40
refrigeration, 153, 176
religion, temperance and, 245
religious freedom, 20, 50, 239
Revenue Act (of 1764), 74
Revolutionary War, 97–110
    supply disruptions, 96, 100, 103, 105
Rhode Island, 13, 55, 229
Richardson, John, 263
roads, 69–70
Robert Hare Brewing, 161–63
Robert Smith Brewing, 171–73
Robinson, Jacob, 152
Rome, George, 55
rum, 23, 36, 68, 241–42
    in beer drinks, 210, 212, 213, 215
    outlawing, 242–43
Ruppert, Franz, 151, 152
Ruppert, Jacob, 152
Ruppert, Jacob, Jr., 153–54
Ruppert Brewery, 151–55
Rush, Benjamin, 108, 121, 244–45
Rutgers, Anthony, 50
Rutgers family, 32, 50
Ruth, George Herman (Babe), 154
Rutledge, John, 118
rye, 20

Sabree, Daniel, 55
saccharometers, 263
sailors, 39, 58, 80
Saint-Mery, Moreau de, 117
Salem (New Jersey), 22
Salter, Sampson, 54
Samoset, 14
sassafras, 15, 27
scantlings, 197

Schaefer, Frederick, 158–59
Schaefer, Maximilian, 159
Schaefer, Rudolph, 160
Schaefer Brewing Company, 158–61
Schlitz Brewing, 177
Schmidt, Christian, 173
scotch beer, 266–67
search and seizure, 77
Sedgwick, Robert, 36
Sedylmayer, Gabriel, 267
Segersz, Cornelis, 30, 31
settlers, 20. *See also* immigrants
Sewall, Samuel, 37–38, 200, 202–3
Shakespeare, William, 44
Shannon, Richard, 256
Shepard, Thomas, 44
Sherman, Roger, 118, 119
shipping, 70, 79–80, 82, 106, 125
ships, clipper, 144, 267–68
ships, supplying, 29–30, 39–40, 54–55
Shiras, Peter, 124, 134
Sickel, Fredrick, 172
signage, 195–96
slave trade, 241–42
slop shops. *See* taverns
small beers, 133, 167, 227, 232
Smith, Jacob, 163
Smith, Matthew, 248
Smith, Page, 36, 130
Smith, Robert, 172–73
smuggling, 241, 247
soda waters, 211, 219
soldiers
    beer rations, 93–96, 99–100, 107
    drunkenness and, 97, 103
    provisioning, 103, 109, 185, 190
    rum ration, 243
    training, 94
Sommers, Sebastian, 158
Sons of Liberty, 76, 79, 80, 82
speakeasies, 241
specific gravity, 262–64
spirits, 23, 65. *See also* whiskey
    bans on, 121
    beer as alternative to, 132, 135, 242, 243
    military consumption of, 102–3,
        243–44

spruce beer, 27, 104, 230–31
St. Louis, 177–79
Stadt Harberg, 40–41
Stadt Huys, 41, 42
Stahl, George Ernest, 265, 266
Stamp Act (of 1765), 69, 75, 192
Standard Brewing Company (Cleveland), 161
steam, 256–57
steam engines, 257–58, 259
stirrup cup, 218
Stone Street, 42
streets, 42
Strettell, Amos, 80
Stroh, 161
Stuyvesant, Peter, 183, 187–90
sugar, 27
Sunday drinking laws, 195, 240
supply and demand, 48
suttlers, 102, 108
Symmes, John Cleves, 125

taproom, 198
Tarrytown, 29
taverns, 24, 32–34, 52–53, 196
    breweries and, 33–34, 41
    Continental Congress and, 86–87
    court business in, 66–67, 139, 199, 200
    dockside, 58
    equipment, 196–97, 211
    income from, 67–68
    licensing of, 36–37
    local business, 38, 204
    location, 193–94
    as military headquarters, 98–99, 206, 207
    in New Amsterdam, 40–42
    as news center, 207
    number of, 38
    personnel, 197–98
    political gatherings in, 68, 77–78, 84, 116–19, 203, 206, 207
    religious functions in, 194–95
    signs, 195–96
    sleeping accommodations, 195, 198
    as social centers, 64, 66, 193, 199–200, 207
    in southern colonies, 66–67

    taxation of, 76
    trade and, 32–33, 37, 66, 203
taxation
    beer, 122, 165, 183–92
    by British, 74–84, 191–92
    illegal production and, 241
    tea, 82
technology, 253
teetotalers, 247–48
temperance, 23, 47. *See also* prohibition
    laws, 63, 131, 201, 242–43
    movements, 240–41, 245–50
    pledges, 247–48, 249
temperature, 260–61. *See also* cold
thermometers, 260–61, 262
Thomas, David, 126
Thomas, Edward, 67
Thompson, John, 44
Thorpe, George, 14–15
Thrale, H., 263
timeline, 273–88
tippling houses. *See* taverns
toasts, 201–3
tobacco, 57, 240
Townsend Acts, 69, 77, 82
trade
    inter-colony, 51, 56, 58, 70
    strategies, 76
    taverns and, 32–33, 37, 66, 203
    taxation and, 75–76, 185
    technology, 253
    transportation and, 69–70
trademarks, 150–51
trading posts, 18
transportation, 25, 69–70, 106, 125
trees and timber, 9
triangle trade, 241–42
Tryon, William, 62
tuns, 234, 254, 255
Turner, John, 200
Turpin, 266

Union Temperance Society of Moreau and Northumberland, 245
United States, 118–19, 130, 131, 178
United States Brewers Association, 165, 166

van Courtland, Oloff Stevenson, 43
van Couwenhoven, Jacob, 186
van Couwenhoven, Peter, 190
Van Nostrand, A. G., 149, 150
Van Nostrand, William T., 149
van Rensselaer, Kiliaen, 31, 184, 255
Van Twiller, Wouteer, 184
Vassar, Matthew, 137–39, 153, 155–56, 170
Vassar College, 140
Verplank, Gulian, 51
Vigne, Jean, 17
Virginia, 14–15, 21–22, 58
Virginia Assembly, 84–85

Wagner, John, 167, 267, 268, 269, 270
Wall Street, 191
Wallis, John, 202
Wallis Tavern (Boston), 38
Wampanoag tribe, 14
War of 1812, 136
Ward, Edward, 48
Warren, John, 162, 163
Warren, Joseph, 79
wars, 73, 97–110, 136, 165
Washington, George, 84, 88, 120
  beer recipe, 232
  as commander of American forces, 100–102, 106–8
  import use, 122
  porter and, 123, 124, 162
  as president, 123
Washington, Martha, 162
Washingtonians, 248–49
waste disposal, 42
water
  boiling, 2–3, 13
  for brewing, 170
  disfavor of, 3, 11–12, 21, 39, 127
  New York (New Amsterdam) supply, 34–35, 55, 127, 141–43
  pollution, 2–3, 135
  potable, 51

storing, 10–11, 39, 58
  unhealthfulness of, 29, 39, 210, 239, 245
Webster, Daniel, 207
Weems, Locke, 246
weiss beers, 141
Wentworth, Elijah, 174
West, Benjamin, 196
West India Company, 184
westward migration, 124–25
Whately, Robert, 54
wheat, 29
whiskey, 68, 102–3, 108, 131–32, 243
Whiskey Rebellion, 124
whistle (whip)-belly-vengeance, 214
white ebulum, 216
Whyte, William, 47
Wildes, Harry, 102
William and Mary College, 56
William J. Lemp Brewing Company, 177–79
Williams, Roger, 13
wine, 15, 37, 88, 224
Winthrop, John (Massachusetts governor), 26, 97, 194, 201
Winthrop, John Jr., 26
Woerz, E. G., 157
Wolf, Charles C., 167–69, 268–71
Wood, William, 11
wooden tools, 253–55
work, drinking at, 47, 62–63
wort cooling, 258–60, 261
Wright, John, 55
Wyatt, Francis, 21

Yale College, 74
Yankee Stadium, 154
yard of flannel, 213
yeast, 144, 167, 226, 265–66
  lager, 267–68
Young, Anthony, 55
Yuengling, David, 170–71
Yuengling, Fredrick G., 170
Yuengling Brewery, 157, 170–71

About the Author

Gregg Smith is an award-winning author and speaker on beer and brewing. He has been a featured lecturer at the Smithsonian Institution and at the prestigious Culinary Institute of America. Frequently appearing as a beer expert on national and international radio and television programs, he is a sought-after speaker who has hosted beer dinners at upscale restaurants across the United States. Other speaking engagements have included the Great American Beer Festival, historical societies, Beer Camp, and beer appreciation clubs around the country.

He has served as co-chair of the North American Guild of Beer Writers, and as both a member of the board and Associate Director of the Beer Judge Certification Program. He holds the rank of Master Beer Judge and has judged for four consecutive years at the Great American Beer Festival, and at the World Beer Cup.

Gregg is the managing editor of the *Beer & Tavern Chronicle,* a national monthly beer periodical, field editor of the *Brew Review,* and guest editor in *Yankee Brew News.* His articles have appeared in numerous publications throughout the United States.

In 1997 Gregg was named Beer Writer of the Year by the North American Guild of Beer Writers.